THE WINDOWS OF HOLLY

TRACI VANDERBUSH

THE WINDOWS OF HOLLY

Copyright © 2018 by Traci Vanderbush.

All rights reserved. No part of this publication may be reproduced, distributed, or transmitted in any form or by any means, including photocopying, recording, or other electronic or mechanical methods, without the prior written permission of the publisher, except in the case of brief quotations embodied in critical reviews and certain other noncommercial uses permitted by copyright law. For permission requests, write to the author, addressed "Attention: Permissions," at the e-mail address : tracivanderbush@gmail.com

Special discounts are available on quantity purchases by corporations, associations, and others. Orders by US trade bookstores and wholesalers. For details, contact the author at the e-mail address above.

This book is a work of fiction. Names, characters, places, and incidents are the product of the author's imagination or are used fictitiously. Any resemblance to actual events, locales, or persons, living or dead, is entirely coincidental.

Typesetting by Sally Hanan of Inksnatcher.com
Cover art and design by Bill Vanderbush
Photography by Bill and Traci Vanderbush
Cover models: Annie Knapp and Britain Vanderbush

The Windows of Holly. First Edition: September 2018
ISBN : 978-1979504737

To Bill, Britain, and Sara, with all my love.

CONTENTS

PREVIOUSLY 1

CHAPTER ONE 3

CHAPTER TWO 11

CHAPTER THREE 21

CHAPTER FOUR 35

CHAPTER FIVE 49

CHAPTER SIX 59

CHAPTER SEVEN 67

CHAPTER EIGHT 79

CHAPTER NINE 95

CHAPTER TEN 109

CHAPTER ELEVEN 121

CHAPTER TWELVE 133

CHAPTER THIRTEEN 151

CHAPTER FOURTEEN 161

CHAPTER FIFTEEN 175

CHAPTER SIXTEEN 199

CHAPTER SEVENTEEN 211

CHAPTER EIGHTEEN 231

CHAPTER NINETEEN 245

CHAPTER TWENTY 263

CHAPTER TWENTY-ONE 287

EPILOGUE 315

ABOUT THE AUTHOR 325

OTHER BOOKS BY TRACI 327

ACKNOWLEDGMENTS 331

"And sometimes the purest of hearts are birthed in the darkest places. This is one of the mysteries of grace. This is the mysterious way of love. And love lives in the people of Holly." ~ Dylan Vanberg

Previously

O N A PEACEFUL DECEMBER EVENING, Dylan strung Christmas lights across the front porch while Lynette watched him through their old bay window, rocking her newborn, Asa. She was in awe of who Dylan had become. The reality of his unending, unconditional love toward her penetrated her entire being. Lynette observed every movement he made and noted each intricate detail: the lines of his muscles beneath his shirt, striking eyes of compassion, and his tender hands that she had abandoned. She turned her attention to the painting above the fireplace, admiring the diamonds in the bride's veil and the brushstrokes of Dylan's hand that caused light to come from within. *Let the Spirit and the bride say come.* Tears filled her eyes. She was captivated by the man who had chosen her, not just once, but twice.

Across the street, Jackson and Lucy Sawyer snuggled together for an afternoon nap. Jackson wrapped his arm around his wife's small, pregnant belly, staring out the window at the house where his friend, Dylan, worked hard to wrap Christmas lights around his porch railing. *Finally, after five long years, life is coming back to the Vanberg home.* He smiled. Jackson basked in awe of the miracle that he and Lucy had witnessed on that front porch: Lynette's return to Dylan.

In Marshall City, Preston and Kat embraced each other by the

THE WINDOWS OF HOLLY

fireplace while their children decorated the Christmas tree. "O Holy Night" echoed through their home as the teakettle whistled. The couple's eyes remained locked in a gaze of pure wonder at the fact that their family was intact, resurrected from the ash heap of betrayal.

With long-held secrets unveiled, several residents of Holly gathered at Annie's Café to share their stories of hope and restoration. Secrets no more. Eyes wide open, yet the winds eerily moved through Holly with an objection to their newfound freedom. Many found themselves fallen into the saving arms of grace, but would it be enough to carry them through the storms to come? Though the frost of past failures attempted to harden hearts, an unseen, luminous presence would relentlessly descend and pass through the windows of Holly.

Chapter One

As LYNETTE ROCKED NEWBORN ASA in the home of her ex-husband, Dylan, both immense joy and enormous pain flooded her heart. She wondered how it was possible that she had cheated on her best friend, Dylan, and with a trusted deacon at that. Dylan had helped his friend, Owen, through some of his darkest moments in life. Lynette wondered how Owen, knowing the pain of divorce, chose to bring that same pain to his faithful, trustworthy friend. *How blind we are. How crazy is this thing called life?* An image of herself with Owen engulfed her mind. *And to think I married that man.* The thought caused her stomach to twist with nausea. What once seemed so right now presented itself as a dark hole of regret. *Shake it off, Lynette. Think of the baby.*

Studying Asa's tiny mouth and nose, tears of sadness washed over her soul and fell from her eyes. *How can a man walk away from his own child?* Lynette had always wanted children, but she never dreamed she would have a child whose life would begin with rejection. *Dylan never would have walked out on his child. Owen's a monster.* She peered out the window once more at Dylan as he wrapped a strand of lights around the porch railing. Dylan had found the lights underneath the guest bed as he fumbled about, creating a spot for himself to sleep that night. He relentlessly insisted on having Lynette stay and use his bed. Lynette watched

THE WINDOWS OF HOLLY

her ex-husband through the window, in awe of his kindness and acceptance of her. *How can he love me after all I've done? After all these years, he never gave up on me.*

Lynette replayed the events of the morning in her mind. Today was a day she would never forget. She woke up to divorce papers and a note from Owen informing her that she had two months to find a place to live. Owen had accepted a job as a ranger in the mountains of Oregon, a dream he desired even if it meant casting his wife and child aside. Months ago, Lynette expressed to him that living at a 5,000-foot elevation in the middle of nowhere was no place to raise a baby. He reluctantly agreed to drop the idea. She was blindsided that he took the job after all. *I can't believe he pursued the job behind my back.* Owen arranged to sell the Blakely-Smith Ranch, their home, without her knowledge. He planned to give her twenty percent of the profit. *I don't even want a dime from that man. And what's twenty percent? He's so manipulative, trying to push me out without giving his fair share. His lawyer is as dirty as he is.*

Lynette recalled how she nervously approached her former home that morning, Dylan's home, after she received the news that Owen was throwing her and his child away. The depth of rejection and utter abandonment pressed her to desperation. That desperation drove her to her knees, weeping and begging God to do something. As she knelt on the decrepit, mauve carpet that Owen had promised to replace, her tears bled into the old stains, reflecting the ugliness of what she felt she had become. As a guttural cry escaped her lungs, she heard gentle words in her ear, "Step into Me, Lynette. Remember the Dream Door."

The Dream Door was Dylan and Lynette's special spot, a hidden opening with a beautifully decorated door they had found on the side of their porch when they purchased their dream home in Holly. In it, they found letters containing a love story of someone who lived in the house decades earlier. Dylan and Lynette decided to fill that space with significant items that spoke of their own love story and their dreams for the future. After Lynette left Dylan, he frequently wrote letters and journal entries to Lynette, words that he longed to tell her, and he placed them behind the Dream Door. *Lynette, please, please remember our Dream Door.* She remembered his tearful plea not to forget as she walked out of their house for the last time.

This morning, after waking up to find the divorce papers and a letter from Owen, she dared to return to the Dream Door, hoping to find something to hold onto. To her surprise, she found numerous letters from Dylan expressing his regrets, his faithful love for her, and his hopes for her happiness. She sat on the porch swing, reading and weeping through each letter as Dylan slept inside.

The thing that brought Lynette to her knees for a second time this morning was the painting that Dylan had neatly wrapped and placed inside the Dream Door. Leaning just inside the door was a beautiful canvas filled with puffy white clouds in a bright-blue sky. The clouds spelled the name *Asa.* Seeing the name pierced her heart. *How is this possible?* There she knelt on Dylan's porch, with her baby, Asa, strapped to herself in a sling. Dylan always liked that name for a future son, but he wasn't ready to be a father when Lynette wanted children so badly. Now, the woman that he loved was on his front porch with a baby boy named Asa, but it wasn't Dylan's son. The thought nearly ripped Lynette in two.

It was at that moment that Dylan stirred from a dream in which he encountered Jesus. "Step into Me, Dylan." Dylan didn't understand the words that rang in his spirit. He wondered if he might die. He pondered the fact that he wasn't afraid to die. *What do I have to lose? To die is gain.* In the hazy dream, he lifted his foot and stepped forward, melting into Jesus as they became one.

THE WINDOWS OF HOLLY

He was in Him. As he melted into the heart of God, his eyes were opened to an awareness and knowledge he had never experienced. His heart was filled with a love so immense and deep, he was sure it would consume him. Overwhelming love infused him with peace and he knew he would live. He looked down at the spinning world below him. Compassion poured from his soul like a waterfall upon the turning globe. *The earth.* He wondered about humanity and the weight they carried in such a large universe, but from his new perspective, every problem vanished into nothingness. All he could see was love.

Upon waking from the dream, he pondered the vivid images as he brushed his teeth. As he stared into the mirror, an internal voice suddenly prompted him, "Go now!" Dylan rinsed his mouth and quickly ran to the front door, flinging it open. There, Lynette knelt weeping over the canvas. Dylan's eyes focused as he convinced himself that it was really her. Falling to his knees, speechless, he wrapped his arms around his ex-wife.

Lynette's recollection of all that had taken place earlier that morning was abruptly interrupted by the slam of the front door.

"Hey, Lynnie. Are you hungry?" Dylan came back inside from hanging the lights. She smiled at him.

"Dylan, you amaze me."

He grinned. "Oh yeah? How's that?"

She tilted her head inquisitively. "How is it possible that we're here now, together, after all these years? And with everything that's going on, you decide to hang Christmas lights?"

Dylan smiled. "Well, I know how much you love Christmas. I happened to find these lights in the guest room and figured we might as well do something cheery, being that you had a crappy morning. I threw out all of our Christmas decorations a long time ago. I honestly didn't know those lights were still here. When I saw them, I kinda figured it was a divine gift, of sorts." He winked.

Lynette turned her gaze downward, guilt flooding her heart. "Dylan?"

"Yes?"

"If this is too much trouble," she hesitated, "I can go back to the ranch tonight. Everything is happening so quickly, I don't know what I'm doing. I can't expect you to have me and Asa intrude and turn your life upside down."

Dylan knelt in front of her, placing his hand on her knee. His touch sent a wave of electricity through her body. *God, I've missed his touch.* She took a deep breath, capturing the feeling.

Dylan spoke gently. "Lynette, I don't want you to leave. I really want you to stay."

She felt the need to help him understand the reality of having a baby in the house. "What about the baby waking you up throughout the night? We're up a lot and…"

Dylan interrupted. "I seriously don't mind. I've been alone for a really long time. I need some noise in my life." He grinned. Dylan looked at Asa. "And I don't think you have any business being at the ranch alone." Dylan's face tightened over the fact that Owen abandoned her and the baby. "How can a man abandon his wife and child like that?"

"I keep asking myself that same question," she replied. They sat silent for a moment. She shifted. "If…I mean, if you're…" Lynette couldn't seem to get the words out.

Dylan lifted her chin with his finger, focusing his eyes on hers. "You don't have to be afraid to talk to me. You can say whatever you want. There's no need to fear here. Consider this a safe place."

Her chin trembled. Five years of living with Owen was five years of walking on eggshells. It seemed she could never quite say the right thing, and if she said the right thing, it was usually misunderstood.

7

THE WINDOWS OF HOLLY

Dylan held her gaze. "I'm telling you the truth, Lynette. You're free with me. No secrets. No fear of expressing your thoughts." Dylan knew Owen well enough to know that Lynette spent the last five years in a prison of a marriage with a very selfish man.

Dylan's words became a rush of life that blew through her soul. She crumbled into tears. Leaning over Asa in her lap, she reached one arm around Dylan's neck and drew him into an embrace. Hot tears flowed down his neck as she wept, "I'm sorry, Dylan. I am so sorry for all I've done. You didn't deserve this kind of pain." Her voice shook. She whispered, "I wish I'd never left you." Deep regret caused her eyes to squeeze tight. "Why did I leave?"

Her words released an unexpected torrent of emotion from Dylan's soul. Lynette heard him groan: the sound of mourning for what was lost. Asa was fast asleep in her lap. She gently moved Dylan aside while she put Asa in his car seat so she could offer her full embrace to the man she'd betrayed. Lynette turned toward Dylan again, wrapping both arms around him.

They sat on the floor, pressed together, letting the pain flow. The smell of Dylan's neck prompted memories of intimate moments with him. The realization of time lost with him nearly crushed her heart. Lost time threatened to trample her soul. "Oh, Dylan," she breathed in a long whisper.

Her warm breath sent waves throughout his body that he couldn't comprehend. Years of hoping, praying, and letting go collided.

A dam of pain and regret erupted from the couple, but waves of life pulsed through them, washing away the debris of their brutal separation. Heartache and torment mixed with relief and gratitude. Cheek to cheek, their tears mixed. Lynette longed to kiss him, but she knew she didn't deserve that privilege, not to mention she was still married to Owen. *But Dylan is my first and only love.* Still, Lynette knew she had made enough wrong decisions, and she didn't want to ruin this moment with a kiss.

Dylan leaned back, giving enough space to allow himself to study her countenance. Every muscle in his face moved in an effort to prevent more tears from falling. He cupped her face in his hands.

Lynette was overwhelmed by the love in Dylan's eyes which expressed five years' worth of yearnings. He touched the back of her head, lightly drawing her closer as he leaned in. Lynette surrendered herself wholly. *I've taken so much away from him. Not anymore.* She closed her eyes as their lips touched. She tasted the salt of endless tears. *Oh God.* Her body released all tension as she melted into him.

He spoke between kisses. "Lynette. I never stopped loving you."

His words flowed through her like a cleansing waterfall. The debris of bitterness, anger, and regret lifted from her heart like a weightless vapor. What threatened to kill her existed no more. In this moment, she was complete. In this moment, she had what she always desired.

Lynette wished she could pull Dylan inside herself. "Dylan, if I could take away all of the pain, if I could somehow go back and do it all over," her voice broke, "...if I could go back." She sobbed.

Dylan held her face again, "I know. Me too."

Across the street, Jackson and Lucy awakened from their afternoon nap. Lucy stretched as she peered at the clock. "Oh my gosh! We slept so long. It's seven o'clock! It's nearly time to go to bed again." She stretched. "I don't like this feeling. It's weird to fall asleep during the day and wake up to the dark. Meh," she muttered.

"That's gonna knock me off-kilter," Jackson yawned, "but

THE WINDOWS OF HOLLY

what a great nap."

Lucy quickly leapt out of bed and peered out the window. "Do you suppose Lynette is still over there?" She wore a smile like a little girl on Christmas morning. "I still can't believe she came back. What a miracle!"

Jackson inquired, "Do you see anything happening over there?"

She shook her head. "Nope. Should you go check on Dylan? I mean, in case she left and he's sitting there all alone?"

Jackson thought for a moment. "I have a feeling she's still there. I'm pretty certain I would have gotten a call from him if she'd left."

Lucy cupped her face in her hands. "Oh, Jackson, I can hardly stand it! I want to know what's going on. Can you imagine? After five years of being apart, she shows up on his front porch. Gah!" She squealed joyfully. "The whole town thought Dylan was crazy for holding out hope. Maybe he wasn't wrong after all." She beamed. "She may be married to Owen, but look where she is right now. Definitely redemption at its finest."

Chapter Two

MIKE AND CURT SAT IN ANNIE'S CAFÉ waiting for the special of the night: roast beef and vegetables. Though Mike's heart slightly softened over the last couple of years, his brash, distasteful, loud mouth was still widely known around the town of Holly. It seemed the entire population of 3,000 could identify Mike's voice in a crowd. Most of the townspeople considered him to be the local foghorn. They were thankful that his raucous commentaries on peoples' failures had become less common. During Dylan and Lynette's fallout, Mike enjoyed broadcasting sarcastic comments about their situation, but over time, he learned to have a bit of compassion, thanks to people like the outspoken waitress, Lucy. Curt, however, always played right along like a mindless comrade, enjoying the attention of listeners.

Mike let out a belch.

Curt crinkled his nose. "Dang it, Mike! I don't wanna hear that, and I sure as heck don't wanna smell it."

Mike grabbed his big belly and chuckled. "Don't worry, Curt. A little gas ain't gonna harm you. You're already full of it anyway."

Curt glared. "Speak for yourself. All I had for lunch was a cup of soup. You, on the other hand, ate enough to feed a whole circus.

THE WINDOWS OF HOLLY

I don't know why we're here anyway. We were just here three hours ago. How can you be hungry again?"

"It's my incredibly high metabolism kickin' in," Mike heckled, slapping his beer belly. "And to answer your question, we're here again because the food is good and we have nowhere else to be."

Ellie interrupted. "Here ya go. Roast beef and vegetables with cornbread. I'll come back with refills on that sweet tea."

The two men dove into their second meal at Annie's Café that day. There was something about this place. Its red-checkered tablecloths, the familiar smell, and the nostalgic items that spent decades on the shelves; it was all a warm invitation to "come home." The voices of wisdom, the stories of the weak, the trials and tragedies of Holly's citizens, their triumphs and shared laughter were forever etched into the walls. Even the voices of its most gruff citizens found acceptance somehow. The atmosphere carried a lingering, indescribable grace that endured gossip and the challenges of living; it was lying in wait to capture hearts, much like the prayers of a grandparent whose love is unconditional. That's what drew the town into the café. Home.

"Curt, when are you gonna find yourself a woman?" Mike enjoyed prodding Curt on that issue.

Curt wiped tea from his mouth. "Look who's talkin.' Where's your two-ton ball 'n chain? I don't see one around anywhere."

Like two boys who never outgrew second grade, their picking and bickering kept each other company, reminding them that they were on a level playing field. A twisted sort of camaraderie momentarily erased their loneliness.

Mike piped up, "I dunno. After watching all the married-people drama, I'm not sure I'd really want that. Heck, even Dylan and Lynette couldn't keep their marriage together, and they were pastors. One would think a pastor would have the best chance at survivin', you know?"

"Yeah. But don't you think it's better than bein' alone?"

Mike huffed. "That makes no sense, Curt. Dylan is alone. Just cuz you get married doesn't mean you'll stay married. A marriage certificate doesn't eliminate the possibility of loneliness."

"I guess so. Don't you wonder if Lynette and Owen will last? I mean, they got a baby now, and all."

Mike shook his head. "Owen's always been a stud. Before Cybil, he made his rounds with the women. After she divorced him, it didn't take long before he bedded the pastor's wife. I'd be surprised if he keeps her around."

Curt shrugged. "Even so, Mike, I don't like to think bout growing old alone. Maybe the risk is worth it."

Mike raised an eyebrow. "Maybe."

Curt wasn't one to focus on a serious subject for too long. He shifted his attention back to his food. "Dang, this roast beef is good. Sure hits the spot."

They enjoyed the rest of their meal in silence until Mike felt the need to break it.

"Hey, Curt. I just had a brilliant idea."

"Yeah?"

"You should pursue Beverly." Mike smiled cleverly.

Curt nearly spat out his tea. "You've got to be kiddin!"

"Nope, I'm not kidding. Didn't you see the way she looked at you when we all had lunch together today?"

"Mike! That's ridiculous. Bev is nice to everybody. She looks at everyone like that."

Mike showed his haggard, untamed smile. "Nah. I think she might want a piece of the Curt-man." He wasn't so great at keeping his beard trimmed, and he certainly didn't know how to prune his twisted ideas. Mike continued his heckling. "Bev's been single for years, and I'd bet she's a bit on the desperate side. You should give her a whirl." Mike winked.

The chime on the door stole their attention. Upon seeing Beverly, Mike kicked Curt under the table. "Well, I'll be. Look who's here."

Beverly noticed the two men immediately. Her sunny smile radiated. "Hey. What are you guys doing here again? Can't get enough jelly in your belly?"

Mike replied, "A man's gotta have dinner, ya know? Lunch isn't enough. What brings you in here again?"

Beverly replied with an amused tone, "Oh, you know how carried away I get when I'm with old Emma. We got to laughing so hard with you guys, I think I left my change purse in the booth." She peered into their booth. "If you don't mind, I need to check your seats, sirs." She flashed a silly grin.

Curt motioned to his friend. "Mike, lift your big carcass outta the way. Is it under there? If it is, Bev's gonna have to sanitize her coin purse."

Beverly laughed. "Oh, Curt. It probably fell on the floor." She knelt down to peek under the table.

Curt tapped her back. "Bev, I'd highly recommend you don't put your nose down yonder. Mike here has been cuttin' the cheese ever since we arrived. You know, all that food he eats doesn't set too well."

Beverly stood up, chuckling. She could laugh with the best and worst of them. She had plenty of experience working on farms with all kinds of men and animals. Nothing could phase Beverly. She learned that laughter, forgiveness, and grace truly were the best of medicines, and she knew all of humanity needed a regular dose. Curt and Mike were no different.

She shook her head with a smile. "You two. Always a show. Always a show."

"Here it is," said Curt, setting the little red coin purse on the table.

14

Beverly was relieved. "Oh, thank goodness. Thanks, Curt."

Mike grinned. "Well, look at that. Bev, I think you owe Curt a reward. Maybe a lunch date?"

Curt kicked Mike and eyed him with a look of warning. "She don't owe me anything."

Beverly opened her coin purse, dumping it on the table. "I'd be glad to take you to lunch, Curt, but it looks like all I can buy you is a packet of ketchup." She giggled.

Curt smiled. "You're one funny lady."

The light of the fireplace glowed from the windows of David and Marcy's home. The couple snuggled together on the sofa, sipping hot cocoa. The cool December air always put them in the mood for a good fire and cocoa, no matter the time of day or night. Marcy leaned her head into David's chest, reminiscing. They sat silently as she thought of his transformation from being a harsh, heavy-handed, legalistic disciplinarian. Now he was a gentle soul. She closed her eyes, relishing the goodness of God in their lives.

Watching her husband face his own demons, disappointments, anger, and attempt to control everything and everyone around him had taught her more about the grace she frequently spoke of. His gentleness moved him from persecuting Dylan for "failing the church" to embracing him with humility and kindness.

Marcy recalled the day that she spotted Lynette's car on the side of the road. There she witnessed Lynette weeping as she knelt in the grass, overwhelmed by the love of God. Marcy had reassured her that she was loved and forgiven, worthy of hearing the voice of God, even after destroying her marriage to Dylan. Something about Marcy's relentless kindness gave her the opportunity to witness the most beautiful transformations. Tonight, she breathed deeply, making sure to engrave those moments in her heart and mind.

THE WINDOWS OF HOLLY

The phone rang, bringing her back to the present moment. "David, would you mind answering that?" He stood to retrieve the phone.

He cleared his throat. "Hello?"

Marcy picked up her needlepoint to pass the time while David was on the call. She listened to his voice.

"What? Oh my goodness. Oh my goodness!" David exclaimed.

His words and tone prompted Marcy to run to his side. She tried to hear the other end of the conversation, curious to know what was happening. "That is astonishing. Yes, I'm praying. Wow. Thank you so much for calling."

David excitedly turned to Marcy, eyes wide with joy. "You are not going to believe this. That was Lucy. She said that Lynette was on Dylan's porch this morning. She said something about letters that Dylan left for her. Apparently Lynette was reading them and Dylan came outside and they hugged. They went inside together and Lucy is pretty sure she is still there with Dylan!"

Marcy clasped her hands together on her chest and smiled. "Oh my! This is good news. Can you imagine how good this is for Dylan?"

David's eyes moistened with hope. "It'd be miraculous if those two got back together. I know that might seem impossible, but, Marcy," he spoke in a hushed tone, "I hope that's what happens."

Marcy nodded in agreement, eyes shining with joy.

David's excitement turned to concern. "Dylan waited for her for years. I thought he was out of his mind. Now she has a brand-new baby with Owen." He shook his head. "It's all too complicated."

Marcy, being the endless optimist, chimed in, "But it's sometimes the most complicated, horrible situations that turn out to be the most beautiful."

David wiggled his head. "What are we doing, Marcy? We're

talking about things that we probably shouldn't. I mean, Lynette is a married woman. Besides, maybe she and Dylan are just talking things out, clearing the air, and then they'll move on with their separate lives." The thought pained his face.

"Well, dear, we'll see. I'm just happy she found Dylan's letters and they're communicating. This will bring much-needed healing."

Forty miles away, in Marshall City, Preston and Kat Richland tucked their children into bed for the night. As Preston read a bedtime story to their daughter, Kat studied his face. *How can someone do something so awful, yet be so wonderful?* She hated those moments when the past interrupted her peace.

Too often, during the best of times, bad memories invaded the moment and thoughts of Fay consumed her mind. *God, I still don't understand. She was my friend. And how he could fall for her...ugh. Please help me forget. Please help me forget.* She examined his current state of being and tried to fix her heart on the truth of the present moment.

As Kat walked down their long, azure-blue hallway, images flashed across the screen of her mind: the photographs from the private investigator, the night of confrontation, Preston throwing up on the church steps when he realized that Kat knew the truth, drops of Fay's blood from her suicide attempt in the airport bathroom. "Ugh. Fay." The woman who betrayed her by stealing her husband's affections; Kat knew that Fay was a wounded soul.

She daily chose to forgive her, despite momentary rage over the woman's selfish pursuit of Preston. The images caused Kat to groan quietly to herself. She closed her eyes tightly, attempting to squeeze out and erase the thoughts that threatened to crush her. *Why is this still so hard?*

She fluffed the pillows on their bed and turned down the

comforter, begging God to fix her brain. *If there was a pill that could erase these memories, I'd take it.* Ironically, there were times when she nearly found herself grateful for the painful memories because they served to highlight who she and Preston were now, giving testimony to how far they had come. *Daddy used to say the stars shined the brightest on the darkest nights. Why be afraid of the darkness? It is no threat.* Kat frequently replayed his advice in her head, forcing it to arrest the thoughts that crippled her ability to love.

"Hey, love," Preston called to Kat. She turned to look at him, responding with a smile. He cloaked her in his arms. Kat closed her eyes in wonder at how affectionate Preston had become over the last couple of years. The way he held her brought security and a sense of safety. Her mind would try to convince her otherwise, but she knew what was true. His heart was true. He was finally true to himself and to her. It was evident in the way he lived and loved. Kat relaxed and embraced him more tightly. "I love you, Preston."

He smiled. "I love you too, Kat. More than I can begin to describe."

They stood in a long embrace, something they'd never done until their marriage nearly ended. Kat pondered the mysterious way that darkness only served to destroy itself and cause their love to grow. Darkness raged against them, but love won, and the darkness was swallowed by perseverance and grace.

Forgiveness feels good. She pressed her cheek harder into his neck. *What if he hadn't changed his mind?* She couldn't bear the thought.

Sometimes Preston and Kat felt guilty that their marriage survived while someone as wonderful as Dylan felt the sting of divorce. Dylan, while suffering his own pain and disappointment, did everything he could to keep Preston and Kat together. Perhaps the misery and torment of his own condition pressed him to save others from knowing the anguish and desolation of disunion.

Preston and Kat fell asleep, hand in hand, face-to-face, breath to breath.

Chapter Three

THE NEXT MORNING, Lynette opened her eyes slowly. Allowing her eyes to adjust, the blurry room came into focus. *Oh my gosh.* She smiled. *I can't believe I'm waking up in our old bedroom.* It seemed like forever since she used to sleep here, yet it seemed like yesterday. *How ironic.* Dylan's paintings surrounded her and she marveled over them. The brilliant, vivid colors; the realistic nature of the water; and the liquid gold and honey captivated her. The words of love that he carefully inscribed onto the canvasses, the detail of every line and curve, intrigued her. *He really loves me.*

Lynette wondered what might have happened had she waited faithfully for him to come around during the time he was caught up with the needs of the church. She wondered if things would have changed or if she'd have always felt like an afterthought. *What if he never put me first? Could I have stayed and been faithful?* The questions were too difficult to answer. One thing was evident now. Dylan loved her more than anything or anyone else.

As she ran her fingers over the soft cotton comforter, she wondered about the nights that Dylan spent in their bed feeling abandoned and alone. She contemplated how he must have felt. *He lost everything. Not just me, but the church, his reputation, friends.* She clenched her eyes shut as the realization weighed on

THE WINDOWS OF HOLLY

her heart.

Poor Dylan. The revelation of the result of her selfish decisions caused her to feel like a murderer. Images of Dylan's face at the moment he realized she was a liar, deceiver, and betrayer stabbed at her heart.

Her mind began to wander. *Has he slept with anyone else?* Obviously, Dylan was still single after five years and she was not aware of him dating anyone else. She wondered why the thought of Dylan being with another woman pierced her heart. *I have no right to feel this way.* She mulled over the feeling of sadness at the thought that he may have given himself to another. She knew he was far too handsome to avoid being pursued.

Lynette peeked at Asa, who slept soundly in his carrier. She only had to feed him twice during the night, which was a welcomed accomplishment. She quietly stood and wrapped Dylan's robe around herself. *He's so kind to let me sleep in his shirt and use his robe.* She pressed her face into the softness of the fabric, breathing in the remnants of his cologne. Lynette hadn't packed any belongings yesterday when she came to Dylan's house. How could a woman think clearly after being stunned by the news of a pending divorce, the sale of her home, and her husband abandoning her? It was all surreal. And she never dreamed that Dylan would ask her to stay at his place.

She tiptoed down the hallway to the guest bedroom. The door was slightly cracked open. Dylan slept peacefully beneath the velvety purple blanket. She smiled at the sight. *He kept the bedding set that I picked. He hated that set.* She beamed, remembering their argument over her choice in color and style. Dylan told her it looked like it belonged in a brothel in an old Western. Lynette had laughed at him while he rolled his eyes and reluctantly let her have her way. Now, he was sleeping under the blanket he once despised.

After years of being apart from the man she always loved, she couldn't seem to pry herself away from staring at him. Dylan had gained a handful of grays that stood out in his beautiful dark hair. His eyes had a couple of wrinkle lines that she didn't remember seeing before. *He's so beautiful.*

She stared, trying to remember what it was like waking up in his arms. Lynette couldn't bear to walk away. His goodness overwhelmed her, and the safety she felt with him was something she never wanted to be without.

She walked toward him and gently sat on the edge of the bed, watching his face. She carefully leaned over and softly kissed his cheek.

Dylan opened his eyes, smiling. Without a word, he reached his arms around her neck for a hug. Lynette surrendered to gravity and his touch, falling into his embrace. She rolled over, snuggling her back against him in the golden light of morning. The ticking of the grandfather clock in the hallway echoed in the room.

"I can't believe you're here," he said.

"I know. I can't either."

They rested in the moment, listening to the sound of time passing. Dylan smiled. "I've always liked the ticking of that old clock."

"Me too," she replied with sincerity.

He thought for a moment. "I hated it for a while though. After you left, the ticking reminded me of every moment I was living without you. It reminded me of lost time, time that I wanted back so I could do things right. But now the sound speaks about redeemed time and time to come. And I like that," he said hopefully.

"Dylan, that's beautiful, but isn't it too early to be so philosophical?" She giggled.

"Not really." He squeezed her.

THE WINDOWS OF HOLLY

As they cherished the quiet, Lynette's peace was interrupted by details of things to come. The divorce. The house. She needed to move. There would be legal issues. *What about custody of Asa? Will it be shared?* The thought of shared custody horrified her. *I can't let Owen have Asa up in the mountains all by himself. What if something goes wrong? Owen didn't mention anything in his letter about wanting Asa.* That fact brought Lynette both peace and frustration. *How can he not care for his son?*

"Dylan?"

"Yes?"

She sighed. "I'm scared."

Tick-tock, tick tock. The clock echoed.

"Why are you scared?" Dylan caressed her arm to bring comfort.

She didn't know where to start. "There are so many unknowns. What about Asa? What if Owen wants shared custody? What will people think of me running back to you? No one will understand the situation. Honestly, I want to be with you more than anything, but I can't do this to you."

Dylan sat up, using his hand to guide her face toward his. "Listen to me. I don't care what anyone thinks. This is between me and you, and I want you. I've lost you once. Please don't let the judgments of others take you away from me." Desperation filled his eyes.

Lynette looked at him. "But, Dylan," she hesitated, "I have a child."

Dylan replied quickly, "I want him too."

Shocked, she asked, "How can you possibly want Owen's child? Won't Asa be a constant, painful reminder of him?"

Dylan sighed. "I didn't say it would be easy, but the fact is that Asa is part of you and he's an innocent party in this whole deal. I can't blame the baby for crappy circumstances. I know we can

24

make this work."

Lynette's chin quivered. *How can it be possible to cry so much without dying?* She traced Dylan's jawline with her finger, barricading her tears with all her might, but they found a way out. "I don't know what to say."

He assured her, "You don't have to say anything. Just don't leave me again. I know what I've always wanted and that hasn't changed and it won't change, no matter the circumstances." He smiled sincerely. "You're here and that's what matters the most."

Asa began to cry in the other room. Lynette hugged Dylan solidly, hoping that her wordless expression would convey everything in her heart. "Thank you," she whispered in his ear. "Thank you, Dylan. I love you so much."

Those were the words he only dreamed of hearing over the last few years. Now that they were spoken, he could hardly contain the satisfaction of his heart and soul. "I love you too."

"I'd better get Asa." She stood and left the room. Dylan watched through a foggy lens as her silhouette slipped through the doorway. "Like a ghost," he mumbled. He thought back over several hazy dreams in which he'd seen Lynette appear in their bedroom. Like a ghost, half visible, she had asked him, "What will you paint, Dylan?" It was a dream he never fully understood. Sometimes he was sure it was his conscience killing him for not attending painting classes with Lynette as she desired. Owen went to the classes. *If only I had gone with her.* On the other hand, he thought the dream to be supernatural, perhaps the voice of God telling him he had a choice of what he could paint for his life. Could the flick of his wrist save Lynette? In one of those dreams, she was engulfed in black liquid that formed a whirlpool in the floor. She was slipping away from him, desperately asking that question that echoed in his soul for months. *What will you paint, Dylan?*

THE WINDOWS OF HOLLY

Shaking off the memory of ghostly dreams, he pressed himself into now. He got up and prepared himself for the day. Looking in the mirror, he noticed a light in his eyes that he barely remembered possessing.

The light caused the edges of his mouth to turn up. A half smile. The image convinced him he was alive again. "I'm a dead man walking, but I'm still alive and I see light again," he spoke to himself quietly.

As he entered the kitchen, Lynette sat at the table, pouring two bowls of cereal with one hand while holding Asa to her breast with the other. Dylan couldn't believe her coordination skills. "Holy cow, Lynette!" The common phrase he often spoke brought a smile to her face. Dylan laughed. "Look at you! Feeding a baby and pouring cereal at the same time? You're like Wonder Woman."

She smirked. "I'm not so sure about that."

Dylan's attention was arrested by her as she nursed the little life in her arms. Seeing Lynette as a mom was fascinating to him. They sat together eating in silence. The sounds of crunching helped distract him from watching Lynette be a mother, yet he couldn't help himself. He had to watch. He thought it was puzzling how someone could walk out of his life one way and return as a whole other person, a stranger, somewhat. Yet the connection remained complete and perfect. Ironic.

Her voice broke his concentration. "Dylan?"

"Yeah?" He quickly stuffed a spoonful of cereal into his mouth, pretending he hadn't been staring at her. Lynette knew his eyes were set on her, but she didn't mind. It was comforting.

"I have to go back to the ranch today to get some things. I didn't bring clothes or enough diapers. Should I stay there for awhile? Maybe you need some space?" She was still afraid of imposing on him, but she hoped he would insist that she come

26

right back. Being alone at the ranch would be too depressing, and she loved Dylan's company. Still, she wanted to give him an out.

He wiped his mouth with a napkin. "You and the baby shouldn't be alone out there. This is still your home, Lynette." He smiled. "I don't mind going to help you pack." While Dylan meant what he offered, the thought of going to the ranch and seeing where she lived with Owen would be too much for him to handle. He was almost certain that being there would decimate his soul.

Lynette knew she needed an extra hand, but she loved Dylan too much to make him face such a nightmare. "That's kind of you, but I'd better go alone. I can pack enough for a few nights and make arrangements to get the rest later."

"Are you sure Owen won't be there?" Dylan felt troubled.

"Yes. He made sure he was gone before I ever woke up," she grimaced. "Long gone. Can you imagine? A man who's too chicken to throw me away face-to-face. That's the way he's always been. Running away from everything, pursuing what he wants. Absolutely selfish." Her jaw stiffened. "I suppose that's why I ended up with him. I was selfish too. So stupid." She shook her head.

"We're all selfish at some point," Dylan replied. "If I hadn't been selfish…," he lamented.

Lynette interrupted. "Stop, Dylan. Don't even go there. It wasn't your fault."

He sighed. "It was both of us, Lynette."

Dylan and Lynette walked down the street to her car. She had parked out of sight, not wanting the nosiest of neighbors to see her arrival at his house.

Despite her plan, Jackson and Lucy, and old lady Emma, knew she had returned. They watched, filled with pleasure. None of them dared to interrupt. Not one knock on the door. Not one phone

THE WINDOWS OF HOLLY

call. It seemed Dylan and Lynette were living in a private bubble in which no one risked disturbing the precious reunion.

Fastening Asa's car seat, Dylan interrogated Lynette. "Do you have your phone? Is it fully charged? Do you have your phone charger? How about gas? Do you need more gas?"

She appreciated his care. This was more than Owen ever expressed. "Yes, yes. I've got this," she answered confidently.

He kissed her cheek. "Call me if you need anything, and keep your phone handy. I might want to call and check in on you."

"Okay." She kissed him back. "I love you."

"I love you too." He smiled.

AT THE RANCH

Upon her arrival at the ranch, Lynette breathed deeply. *Father, help me.* Driving onto the Blakely-Smith Ranch never quite felt like home, despite her best efforts to build a new life there. The view was lovely. Being the highest elevation in the area, the vantage point offered solace, but her heart never felt the kind of peace that the scene displayed. Her eyes quickly surveyed the area. No cars in the driveway. "This is all unreal," she sighed. "How did I even end up here?"

She recalled the day she and Owen married on the ranch. She remembered her struggle with deep doubt and wondered why she went through with the wedding. As she questioned herself, she glanced in the backseat at Asa, reminding herself that he wouldn't exist if it wasn't for Owen. After a couple of miscarriages and years of trying to have a baby, Asa was an answer to her prayers, but she certainly never dreamed that his arrival would be under these circumstances.

Why did I keep trying when Owen and I had so many issues? Lynette realized her desperation for a baby was a desperation for love. Desperation for love had driven many people to do senseless things and, certainly, she was one of those held captive by the despair of being deprived of love.

Carrying Asa into the house, she stood in the doorway eyeing the empty place. "Lifeless. Completely lifeless," she mumbled under her breath. She wondered how she'd survived living a lie. *At least I tried to make it work.* She looked down at little Asa in her arms. "Well, buddy. It's a good thing you're too young to remember all of this. It's okay though. I'm going to make this right. I'm taking you home to your real daddy." The thought of Dylan enraptured her soul. In her eyes, Dylan was Asa's father. "You deserve a really good father."

Stepping into the nursery, she set the baby in his crib, feeling a rush of life at the thought of returning to happiness. "Here you go. Rest here while Mommy gets our things together." Asa fell asleep while Lynette rustled through her dresser and closet, determining which items were needed the most. She only planned to gather enough for a few days, but she desperately wanted to move everything at once.

The thought of making multiple trips to the ranch overwhelmed her. *I might as well pack as much as possible.* She packed a suitcase with enough clothing, diapers, and toiletries for several days, but it wasn't sufficient. Stopping now would delay the final exit. "The sooner I can get out, the better." She continued packing.

In the other room, Lynette's phone kept ringing. She was unaware of the incoming calls and texts due to the fact that she forgot to turn her ringer on after a long day and night. She became accustomed to keeping the volume down for the sake of Asa's napping, or rather for her own sake, finding rest between feedings and diaper changings.

Lynette went to the garage to gather two sets of luggage. She and Owen only used their luggage once: for their unflattering honeymoon in Owen's family's Minnesota cabin. She rolled her eyes at the memory of him whisking her away to the dilapidated, outdated, dusty cabin. Their honeymoon began with her fighting back tears of disappointment, and it was that night when she first encountered Owen's careless words that pricked her heart with total regret.

In her recollection, Owen's numerous promises of little getaways and a trip to Europe might have been a reason she held on. Always waiting for the magical moment, the turning point, the event that would change everything; but the trips never came and neither did the magical moment. *All those empty promises.* She sighed.

Lynette dragged the luggage back to her closet. Pulling items from the shelves, she was struck with the awareness of how little she actually owned. When she moved in with Owen, she left everything behind that held sentimental value in an attempt to erase every memory that would hold her back from a new future, a new life. The things that had mattered most to her remained in Dylan's home. *How appropriate. God must have known.* She hoped with all her heart that Dylan hadn't thrown her things out. *But why would he have kept them?*

Lynette stepped into the nursery to peek at little Asa, who was fast asleep. She studied every detail of the nursery that she worked on for years in preparation for her dream come true. White bead board lined the lower half of the walls, highlighting vivid colors of farm animals above. White wrought iron lettering above the crib spelled the baby's name. Lynette built a façade of stability in a home that lacked true love, but she was determined to build something real and lasting. *You'll never be fatherless, little guy.*

Lynette returned to her closet, eyeing the shelves once more. She began rustling through drawers filled with trinkets. She made note of the fact that most of Owen's clothes and shoes were gone. She pushed her hands through his old, neatly-hung jackets, feeling for his prized rifle behind them. It was gone. *Of course. He got what he cared about the most.* She rolled her eyes. "Had to have your gun, didn't you? You can leave your son behind, but God forbid you live without your stupid rifle," she muttered.

The sound of footsteps approached the closet. She gasped and turned, laying eyes on Owen's best friend, Will. She screamed. "Oh my God, Will! What are you doing here?"

Will was Owen's crony in seeking refuge from the demands of life. They often ventured out together on camping and fishing trips. Will never liked Lynette, yet he had applauded his friend for his ability to steal the pastor's wife. When Owen decided to marry Lynette, Will tried to convince him he'd be better off "enjoying the fling" instead of tying himself down with a wife. Years later, he was glad that Owen married Lynette because it kept Owen nearby. He didn't want his friend to leave Holly. Now, Will stood before Lynette as she was packing up her things. Drunkenness caused his resentment toward her to pour out like venom.

Will glared at Lynette as he gritted his teeth. "Well, there she is. The whore of Babylon!" He reached for her head, clutching a handful of hair.

Lynette screamed. "Stop it! Stop it, Will!"

He glared into her eyes. "Look at you! He's gone less than twenty-four hours and where do ya go? Back to your ex-husband! You just couldn't wait, could ya?" He slapped her across the cheek.

She gasped as she shielded her face, bracing herself for more. "Will, you don't understand."

He foamed at the mouth, slurring his speech. "No, I understand all right! I know what you are. A lying whore. That's what you are."

She breathed hard, holding her cheek. "Please, Will. Leave me alone."

31

THE WINDOWS OF HOLLY

Will jabbed his finger into her chest. "I told Owen he shoulda left you a long time ago."

Lynette's rage poured through tears. "He did leave me! He doesn't want me. Not even his own son!"

She smelled alcohol on Will's breath as he screamed in her face, "Whore!" He backhanded her, knocking her to the floor. Blood poured from Lynette's mouth. Asa's cry sent fear through her. *Oh, God. Please don't let him hurt the baby!* Will stood over her, seething, "Did you think I wouldn't have my friend's back?"

Trying to compose herself and keep his attention from turning to Asa, she grasped for words to distract. "Will, you knew Owen was planning to leave, didn't you?"

"What does that matter? Doesn't change the fact that you're a cheatin' whore!"

She corrected him. "I didn't cheat on Owen. I've been faithful to him," she heaved, trying to control her fear. Asa's cry grew louder, but she feared if she tried to get to him, Will would follow. *God, calm Asa. Please, God.*

Will leaned down, spitting in her face. "He left you because he knows what you are. And I'm gonna teach you a lesson." He reached down and grabbed her blouse, jerking her to her feet. Will shoved her into the wooden shelves. She whimpered as pain shot through her neck. Will drew back his fist. Lynette knew it was critical that she get herself and Asa out of the house.

The baby's cry strengthened her determination to defeat him. As Will threw his fist at her face, she ducked, ramming her fist into his crotch. Will bent over, grabbing himself. He groaned as she pushed past him and ran out of the closet.

Running down the hall toward the nursery, Lynette heard Dylan's voice, "Lynette! Lynette!"

"Dylan!" she screamed. Dylan rounded the corner. He was horrified at the sight of her. Blood ran from her mouth. Her cheeks were red and swollen. Her hair was tussled and her shirt torn.

Panic pierced Dylan's heart. "Oh my God! Lynette!" He reached for her, but she pushed past him toward the nursery.

"We have to get Asa," she commanded.

Dylan followed her to the nursery, trying to piece together what was happening. "Owen did this to you?" His face turned bright red.

As she lifted Asa from his crib to comfort him, she answered frantically. "No. It's Will. He's still here." She trembled. "We've gotta get out of here!" They turned to exit.

Will stumbled into the room after them. "Well, look at this. Isn't that sweet?" He snickered. "The ole pastor and his lil Jezebel."

Dylan lunged at Will, striking his nose with his fist. Will's head flung back against the doorframe and he fell, laid out cold on the floor. Dylan turned to Lynette. "Are you okay?" She nodded in shock. "Are you sure?" Again she nodded yes. Dylan pulled his phone from his pocket and dialed 9-1-1.

Chapter Four

ACKSON'S PHONE RANG. The screen display read, "Dylan Vanberg." Jackson was ecstatic, ready to hear about the reunion with Lynette. He hollered to Lucy, "Lucy! Dylan is calling."

"Finally," she exclaimed. Since they had seen Lynette on Dylan's front porch yesterday morning, the two could hardly wait to find out what was happening.

Jackson answered excitedly. "Hey, man."

"Hey, Jackson." Dylan didn't sound as enthusiastic as Jackson had hoped. "I need your help."

Worry crossed Jackson's face. "What's up?"

Dylan told Jackson about the events that had unfolded in the last twenty-four hours and how Will attacked Lynette.

Jackson was shocked. "Oh my God! Are you and Lynette okay?"

Dylan sighed. "I think so, but Lynette is roughed up a bit. She'll have some bruises and soreness for a few days, I'm sure. The hospital will release her in a few minutes. Would you and Lucy be able to pick up some groceries for us? I don't have any food at the house."

"Sure thing." Jackson was eager to help.

Dylan knew Lynette would need help with Asa. He wasn't confident in his own babysitting skills. "And would Lucy be

THE WINDOWS OF HOLLY

available to help with Asa if we need her?"

Jackson didn't hesitate. "Absolutely. I'm sure she'd love to help."

Dylan breathed deeply. "And one more thing. Lynette can't go back to the ranch. I'll need someone to go out there and get the rest of her things."

Jackson assured his friend, "No problem. We've got you covered."

Dylan was genuinely relieved. "Thank you, man. I can't thank you enough. Once again, you're my lifesaver."

Jackson considered it a privilege to be there for such a good man. "Dude, it's an honor. We love you guys. You know…" he paused for a few seconds, "I'm really happy that Lynette came home. I know the circumstances are terrible, but I hope she sticks around."

Dylan smiled. "Thanks, man. Me too. I'm glad to have her back in my life. We have a lot ahead of us, but I know we'll work through the details as they come. One thing I know for sure is that we have to get her out of that house. She needs to be here with me."

AT ANNIE'S CAFé A FEW DAYS LATER
Lucy clocked in for her shift at the café after two busy days of assisting the Vanbergs. The enjoyment of her job as a waitress was enhanced by the expectation of her own baby. Something about being a regular part of the lives of Holly's people fed her nurturing spirit and infused her with joyful expectation of things to come. Lynette's return to Dylan fueled her even more. *Anything is possible. Even in the worst of circumstances, good things can happen.* She had a passion to highlight hope for those who wrestled their demons and the fallout of faulty, human decision-making.

Lucy stood at the counter, neatly wrapping silverware in soft, white napkins, listening to the chatter around her. There were always a few drifters who wandered through Holly, stopping at the café for some old-fashioned sustenance, and it seemed there were always the regulars who prided themselves on their own rump prints in the booths and chairs.

Thankfully, most of the regulars knew how to share. They learned long ago that even though a table might be "theirs," it also belonged to "them," and ultimately, they were all just "us." Lucy's daily interactions with residents assisted in bringing that revelation of union. Lucy's spirit seemed to awaken the atmosphere to the possibility of graciousness and common courtesy.

As Lucy poured coffee, she overheard conversations. "No. No. That's not what I heard," a woman argued. "She was having an affair with her ex-husband. Her husband's best friend showed up to beat the crap out of him."

Another woman responded, shaking her head, "No. You've got it backwards. She was having an affair with her husband's best friend. Her ex-husband showed up and busted them. He went nuts on her because she'd done the same thing to him, so he beat her."

The woman insisted, "No! I'm positive she was seeing the ex-husband. He ended up fighting with the other guy who was trying to defend her husband." The redheaded woman rolled her eyes.

"Hmph. Whatever. I'm pretty sure I'm right though."

The redhead asked, "How do you know?" She gulped her drink.

Her exasperated friend responded, "My brother works for the police department. I should know."

Lucy wondered who the two women were talking about. She was afraid the victims of their gossip might be Dylan and Lynette. She continued to listen.

"And the ex-husband is that man who used to pastor the church

THE WINDOWS OF HOLLY

down the road from me."

Lucy's heart sank. Sure enough.

Smirking, the woman responded, "Well, that's no surprise. Isn't that always the story with church people? There's always a scandal behind the pulpit. 'Don't do this and don't do that,' they say. And then they do what they tell others not to do. It's a hypocritical circus."

Lucy had spent hours with Dylan and Lynette over the last few days. Knowing their story and listening to their doubts and fear, knowing what they went through and knowing what they faced, she couldn't bear the thought of them being misjudged.

Lucy approached the two women. "Ladies, how are we doing over here?"

"Good, thanks," one of the women replied.

Lucy lowered herself, squatting at the table to make eye contact with them. "Listen. I heard you talking about the couple: the guy who used to pastor the church?"

The redhead was obviously offended by her eavesdropping. "Yeah? What about it?"

Lucy sighed. "I know this couple very well. They've been friends of mine for years. I won't dishonor them by divulging their personal lives, but one thing you need to know for sure is that neither one of them was having an affair. No one in that situation was having an affair. Whoever's spreading that rumor is wrong."

The ladies stared at her for a moment. The vibrant redhead piped up, "Yeah, well of course you'd think they didn't do anything wrong. If they're your friends, you'll believe their side of the story."

Lucy tried hard to keep her cool. "Ma'am. There are many things you don't know. Things like, there are people who are hurting badly and they are trying to rebuild their lives in a right manner, yet they're facing unwarranted judgment, rumors, and embarrassment."

Lucy tilted her head, squinting her eyes questioningly. "Now, don't you think most everyone faces moments like that in their lives? What if it was you?"

The women sat silent.

Lucy continued, "I think the least we can do is shut down rumors by not creating and spreading them."

One woman glared. "You sure are preachy, aren't you? And you have no business eavesdropping on our conversation. You should mind your own business."

Lucy stood unapologetically. "And you should mind yours. Have a good day." She turned and walked away.

"Well, she has a lot of nerve."

The redhead shrugged. "You've gotta admire her. Feisty little thing."

Lynette sat quietly, deep in thought. She focused on the environment outside the bay window, watching a couple of squirrels scampering around the tree in a game of chase. December days in the south were unpredictable: sometimes iced over and sometimes warm enough to keep wildlife active, as if spring was already around the corner.

The ticking of the grandfather clock soothed her soul, reminding her she was home. Dylan's love for that old clock once annoyed her because they couldn't agree on where it should stand. Now its sound served as a tranquilizer, and she appreciated its existence. She'd felt numb the last few days. The clock, the house, Dylan and Asa reminded her that she was real, still breathing.

She speculated about her parents and Dylan's parents. *I wonder what they're saying about all of this.* She didn't have the strength to speak with anyone about the situation, so she left that to Dylan. He conveyed to them what took place. They were surprised yet

THE WINDOWS OF HOLLY

pleased that Dylan was caring for her and the baby.

Lynette's phone buzzed on the side table. She glanced over to see who was calling. *Owen.* The name nauseated her. The buzzing continued as she stared at the phone. "Lynnie, are you going to answer that?" Dylan questioned. No response. He was growing worried about her silence the last couple of days. He knew she was traumatized. In a twenty-four-hour period, she learned that her husband was divorcing her, selling their home, and she was attacked by a man. *That's a lot to swallow in one day.* Dylan approached her, knelt down, and peered into her eyes. "Lynnie?"

She explained, "I can't answer the phone, Dylan. It's Owen."

The phone stopped buzzing. In a minute, a voicemail notification appeared.

Dylan touched her arm gently. "Would you like me to listen to the message?"

She agreed hesitantly. "Yes please."

Taking the phone, Dylan left the room to give her peace. She continued peering at the scene through the window, taking note of everything beautiful, anything to give her hope and comfort. Anything to remind her of the purity and innocence of simply being. The childlike display of the squirrels diverted her attention away from the insanity that threatened to consume her mind.

She observed the moving branches. *The trees don't seem to mind the wind. It makes them stronger.* She glanced at the ground. *The roots don't mind the dirt. They need each other.* She moved her gaze upward, admiring the sunlight that pressed its rays through the clouds. *And no matter how dark the clouds, the sky above them remains blue. The light always gets its way eventually. Right?*

She managed a painful half smile. The clouds moved and a ray of light fell on her face. The warmth compelled her to close her eyes and relish the feeling. *Father, you're still with us, aren't You?*

40

The voice of compassion whispered clearly within her, "Yes. I am."

His presence led her to her knees. The soft, white robe that clothed her became a covering: a blanket of purity and safety. Lynette put her face to the floor in reverence and awe as waves of love washed through her.

A voice vibrated through her bones. "You stepped into Me. Now you will see in Me."

In response to the voice, she spoke out loud, "What do you mean?"

The sound responded, "See in Me. You will see as I see."

Dylan returned to the living room to deliver the details of Owen's voicemail, but he saw Lynette on her knees, bent over with her face toward the floor. He stood silently, not wanting to disturb her sacred space.

Her voice trembled with emotion. "Yes, please help me see as You see. If I can't see as You do," her voice faltered, "I don't know how I can survive the mess I've made. If I can't see the way You see, I won't be able to live with the pain I've caused." She held her position in silence for a minute, until a gentle song of gratitude for forgiveness flowed from her lips.

Dylan watched intently, overwhelmed by the beauty of a humble heart. The sight of his ex-wife bowing in his living room, praying and singing was surreal. He hated the circumstances but he stood in awe of the depth that their relationship had reached within a number of days. *How utterly ridiculous and grand.* Dylan marveled over the baffling way that hell produced Heaven in his living room.

But hell can't produce anything. He lingered in thought. He wondered how many times he lived his life as if the light wasn't powerful enough to obliterate darkness.

The light is so powerful that hell cannot remain hell. One day,

THE WINDOWS OF HOLLY

even hell itself will be obliterated. If this picture that I see now foretells anything, perhaps it's that because of God's grace and hell's weakness, even hell itself ends up revealing the redemptive nature of God, who is love. His eyes moistened with satisfaction.

He wasn't sure that what he was thinking was theologically sound, but he recalled the book of Revelation speaking of hell being cast into a lake of fire, so he figured it was possible. *God is an all-consuming fire. God is love. Hmm. Purified by fire.* These days, he was often surprised by the thoughts that entered his mind. Something about trauma, something about pain and redemption seemed to pry open the heart and mind to glorious possibilities.

Lynette sat up. Opening her eyes, she took a deep breath that made Dylan's hairs stand on end. The newness and rush of life that emanated from her pierced his heart. She turned to look at him. "Dylan?" She waited for him to respond.

"Yes?"

With the eyes of a child, she asked, "Do you think suffering is necessary?"

He shrugged. "It seems to be."

"I'm sorry that I've been the source of your suffering. I won't ever cause you pain again as long as I live."

He was struck by her sincerity. "Don't you think that's a pretty big promise to make? Isn't that impossible to keep?"

She shook her head no. "I think it's easier than we've believed it to be. I'm thinking a lot lately about love. What it is and what it isn't. I don't ever want to hurt your heart again."

Dylan wasn't sure how to respond. Sometimes he felt his heart was already dead. Moments of life would spring up and at times, he felt it beating strongly. Then there were days when he wondered if it really existed anymore. *Am I just a walking dead man? Will I ever be able to love again?* But his actions declared that he was fully alive and fully in Love Himself.

He locked eyes with Lynette. "I don't ever want to hurt your heart again either. But I think that love is willingness to suffer. Love opens the heart to suffering. Maybe it isn't always such a bad thing."

She stood to embrace him. "That's a beautiful thought. Willingness to suffer."

As they held each other, he marveled at the paradox of life. None of it made sense but he was enjoying the moment and looking forward to the day they would remarry.

Lynette dared to ask. "So," she paused, "what did Owen have to say?"

Her question prompted Dylan's memory back to Owen's voicemail. He stepped back and took Lynette by the hands. "Owen said he heard about what Will did. He wanted you to know he's angry with Will, that it was 'uncalled for,' and he's sorry about the trouble."

She waited for more information. "That's it?"

Dylan hesitated. "And he said there's paperwork coming. He got an offer on the ranch."

She was stunned. "That quickly? How in the world? That was fast."

Dylan continued, "And he said that if you don't have any objections to the divorce petition and decree, once you sign, his lawyer can have it all finished within three months or less."

She raised an eyebrow. "Well, he's in a hurry, isn't he?" Despite the punch to her gut, she giggled in an attempt to suppress the rejection. "I felt it coming, but I thought with a baby on the way, it would magically change everything. So stupid," she chided herself. "Dumb, dumb, dumb."

Dylan caressed her arm. "Don't talk about yourself that way." He could see the impact of Owen's treatment of Lynette.

Dylan was disturbed by the obvious signs of disempowerment

and control that she lived under, and he pondered the damage done.

"Well, it is what it is, isn't it?" She shrugged. "Are you sure you want to be with someone so dumb?"

"Lynette. Stop calling yourself names. You're not dumb and you're not stupid. You're human." He wanted so badly to draw her into now, into himself, wrap her up where she could never be taken from him again. "And I want to be with you. You're my wife, never his." Dylan's words caught her attention. "You were never truly his wife. I don't care what any marriage certificate or legal document says. Our divorce decree didn't even have the power to dissolve my commitment to you. In my heart, you've always been part of me."

Her face was stilled by the gravity of his declaration. She didn't know if his words were true or not. *Weren't those paper documents the final word?* She wanted him to be right. How she wished his words were true, but her body, soul, and mind carried the scars of a reality she couldn't deny. "I want that to be true, Dylan."

He assured her, "To me it's true, Lynette."

She laid her head on his chest, overcome by such daring faithfulness. She couldn't help but wonder if he'd been involved with other women over the last five years. There were many unknowns.

She couldn't resist asking, "Were you with anyone while we were apart?"

"No," he answered without hesitation.

She had a hard time believing that, but she knew Dylan to be a truth teller. "Didn't you date anyone?"

He was slightly embarrassed by the lack of excitement in his life after his divorce. "Only one girl. One date."

Lynette wondered. "Just one date? Did anything happen?"

He knew what Lynette was asking. "We kissed," he answered.

Her curiosity about his life as a single man pressed her to question him further. "Just one little kiss or what?"

He found it interesting that she'd care to know such things. "Why do you want to know?"

She sighed. "Because I do care, believe it or not. I don't have the right to care, but I do."

Dylan divulged, "It was our first date and she invited me to her place. At the time, I was in a really bad frame of mind and I didn't care what happened. I actually thought about throwing everything away, you know. Why have any standards? We made out for a few minutes and then something kinda struck me. I just couldn't do it. I mean, I kind of wanted to, but I told her I was sorry, and I left."

Lynette was impressed, unsure if she should believe his story, yet she knew he had no reason to lie. *Dylan's never been a liar.* "How could you be so strong? You're a man. I mean, how does a guy just quit like that?"

He replied without delay, "Because I thought about you."

His words melted her yet grieved her heart at the same time. Lynette shook her head at her own ignorance. "How foolish I was to throw you away. You're really incredible, Dylan." She squeezed her eyes closed, wincing at her utter idiocy.

"I'm not anything special," he replied. "I was blind."

She shook her head. "If anyone was blind, it was me."

"We may have been blind, but at least we're not deaf too." Dylan's attempt at humor made her smile. "Then we'd really have a problem."

Silence lingered.

"Dylan. I've wasted so much time being apart from you. I want every possible day that I have left in this life to make things right, to love you, laugh with you, and grow old together. I'd still love to have your babies," she said, smiling. "You know, like we used to talk about? You and me sitting on an old porch swing together, sipping tea and watching our grandbabies grow up?"

Dylan was elated. "I'm game."

Concern interrupted her hopeful happiness. "Do you think that me having Asa will be a problem for us? I mean, he is Owen's son." She feared that Asa's origins would be a constant thorn in Dylan's side, or rather, his heart.

He shrugged. "No. I can't say it'll never bother me that he's not mine, but I'll love him like he's mine. Besides, he looks more like you than Owen, thank God. That helps."

"Well, let's hope that remains the case." She picked at her fingernail. "Oh God. What if he grows up to look just like him, Dylan? How could you stand that?"

He looked at the floor for a moment. "Well, that could happen, I suppose. But we aren't really supposed to regard anyone according to the flesh. These physical costumes are not really who we are. It's a temporary shell, so if I can't look beyond that, I'm not much of a good human, I suppose. Besides, Asa had no choice in this. How can I judge him for his father's wrongs? He may carry Owen's DNA, but he's an innocent soul. He's worth loving."

Pleased with his response, she wondered about another detail. "What about staying in Holly? After all that's happened, how is that possible? We're kind of in a glass bubble here."

Dylan tried to imagine the ramifications. Most of the community knew them to some extent. He shrugged and managed to find a response. "The grace of God outlives and overpowers the judgments of man. I guess we'll just have to decide if Holly is still home for both of us. If we stay, people will eventually get over it and move on to other things. After all, I work for the newspaper. All I have to do is create news headlines that'll make them forget all about us. It's that simple. People are fickle."

"True." Thoughts about the rapid change of life and how things would play out danced in her head. "You know, Owen will see to it that the divorce is finalized quickly," she stated matter-of-factly.

Dylan waited for her to finish her thought. "And?"

She declared, "And I'm ready for that to happen."

He hoped she meant it. "Are you sure, Lynette?"

She nodded ferociously. "Absolutely! Are you kidding? I'm ready to move on with my life."

Dylan couldn't help but ask, "The same way you were ready to move on from me?" His words stung not only her, but himself. *Oh my God. I can't believe I just said that.*

He watched the shock overtake her face. Her chin began to quiver. "I deserved that."

Dylan backpedaled, appalled at the bitterness that had emerged from his soul. "I'm so sorry, Lynette. That wasn't right."

She shook her head. "You don't have to apologize for anything. It's a valid question. To answer you, no, it's not the same. When I left you, I had to force myself to do it. I convinced myself that I'd gone too far and there was no turning back. Even though I had reservations about Owen, I thought he understood me and wanted the same things I wanted. I thought being with him was the only possibility of returning to normalcy."

Dylan listened as she continued verbalizing the illusion that caused her to leave him. "The damage done was too deep to ever repair, so I forced myself to leave and make something new happen. You know, create a new life? That was the most foolish decision I've ever made. And I've paid for it with five long, hard years of spinning my wheels, waiting for the magical moment when things would be good again. And I've never felt at home." Tears filled her eyes. "I was in a strange land. This...me saying that I'm ready for the divorce...it's not me forcing myself to leave. It's me simply surrendering to what should have always been. It's me willingly coming back to the one I've always loved."

THE WINDOWS OF HOLLY

Dylan didn't know what to say. Her words chipped away at the doubt of her love for him. He grasped for words, trying to reciprocate her line of thought. "I want you to know that I'm willingly stepping back into relationship with you, Lynette. It's not out of need or trying to fix everything. It's out of desire: desire for you and to spend my life with you. You don't ever need to worry about me walking out on you. I'm not going anywhere."

Light filled her eyes and face. Dylan took note of that light. *The eyes are the windows to the soul. What brilliant light lives in her soul?* He pondered how darkness could exist within her windows, yet light was streaming through them now. *But darkness and light can't exist together. How is that possible? How can someone do such wrong, yet still contain goodness at the core of who they are?* He smiled at Lynette, hoping she couldn't read the questions in his mind. He wasn't afraid of the answer.

Chapter Five

T THREE O'CLOCK IN THE MORNING, Dylan was awakened by Lynette's voice softly calling from his bedroom. "Dylan?" He rubbed his eyes, trying to clear his foggy vision. He shuffled his feet along the wooden floors of the hallway, entering the master bedroom.

"Yeah?"

Lynette was sitting up in bed with her back supported by pillows, leaning against the headboard, holding Asa as he slept. A bedside lamp lit her face. "I keep dozing off and having bad dreams. Can you stay in here for a bit?"

Dylan sat on the edge of the bed. "Sure. Asa's asleep. Why don't you put him in his crib?"

She closed her eyes tightly, sighing. "I keep dreaming about Will and Owen showing up, taking the baby."

Dylan touched her arm and yawned, looking half drunk. "That's not going to happen. Will is in jail. Owen is in his own world. You don't have anything to worry about." He lay back, dipping his feet under the blanket.

Lynette needed more assurance. "How can you be so sure?"

Dylan quipped lightheartedly, "I can be sure because it's three o'clock in the morning and I'm too tired for an intrusion."

She jabbed her knuckle in his arm playfully. "Thanks for the

THE WINDOWS OF HOLLY

comfort."

He grinned. "You're welcome."

Lynette put Asa in his crib and nestled herself into bed. "Thanks for being here. I'm sorry to wake you up. I just didn't want to be alone."

He smiled. "Not a problem at all. I like it. Sweet dreams." Dylan drifted into a deep sleep within a few minutes. His subconscious mind took him into a gray world of hazy wisps of slow-moving clouds, his body lightly suspended above an unseen floor. Wind whispered in his ears with the slight sound of words. *See in Me.* He turned his head to the right. Lynette's lighted silhouette blurred in and out like a hologram trying to stay in focus. He couldn't see her clearly, but where her eyes would be, light broke out. The ghostly image turned toward him, rays of light beaming from the eyes into his heart. The light penetrated his chest. *In Me, you see clearly.* He squinted, attempting to focus his eyes on the light.

Dylan questioned the being. "Where were You when she sinned? Did you hide away?"

Winds rushed past him. *I've always been here.*

"No! That's impossible. Light cannot exist with darkness."

I overcome the darkness. Light will shine out of darkness.

"So you're even in the darkness?"

I AM.

"I don't understand."

Darkness is no threat to Me.

"I want to understand. Isn't that like prostituting Yourself? Polluting Yourself?"

Can We be tainted? Can We be defiled? Can darkness overcome the light?

Dylan thought for a moment. "You're not affected by the absence of light?"

50

I am the light. I am all and in all. There is no absence of light.

He threw his hands in the air, "But that's so offensive! You can't possibly be in all."

I am limitless. You do not comprehend because darkness cannot comprehend the light. See in Me and you will see clearly.

"What does that even mean?"

The wind swirled around Dylan. He watched as the silhouette of Lynette exploded with light. Like shattered glass, fragments of brightness shot through Dylan. Painless. His chest rose and fell rapidly, overwhelmed by the rush of life. Every cell of his body was alive and vibrating with power. *Now you will see.*

Dylan opened his eyes, heart racing. He wanted to jump up and write down what he'd seen and heard, but he didn't dare wake Asa. He reached over to the bedside table and felt for a pen in the dark. Got it! Unable to locate paper on the table, he began scribbling notes on his hand and arm. The moonlight barely gave him light to see the ink on his arm, but he knew it was there.

He rolled over, looking at the outline of Lynette's face as she slept peacefully. He wondered about covenant. He wondered about the power of the words he spoke when he promised himself to her. *People break promises all the time, yet we let it go. Forgiveness. Can forgiveness really restore the value lost? Can mercy restore the promise, or is the promise forever intact even if we break it? Is it really ever broken?*

He thought about people recorded in the book of Hebrews. God seemed to rewrite the history of many who had failed. *Abraham. Sarah. King David. God remembered them differently, apart from their failures and brokenness. Are our wrongs temporary illusions in His eyes? Maybe repentance makes that possible? If grace much more abounds when sin abounds, then surely sin's lifespan is short. The lifespan of grace is forever. His love endures forever.*

Dylan's mind was on overdrive as he mentally navigated his

way through Scriptures he used to teach. *If love covers a multitude of sins and God is love, and I am in Him and He is in me like John 14:20 says, then I am in Love Himself. And Love covers a multitude of sins. Oh my God. He covers a multitude of sins.* Dylan couldn't seem to shut his thoughts off and return to sleep. *I am literally in Love. I'm in Love. He is in me. If this is so, I can love Lynette despite the pain she's caused me.*

The thought brought tears to his eyes as he stared at his ex-wife. Dylan replayed their marriage in his mind. Once they became senior pastors at Hope Fellowship, he gave everything to the church. All of his time and attention was wrapped up in the daily needs of people and the demands of numerous programs and ministry departments. One idea for reaching the world always presented more needs that he felt obligated to meet. He recalled times when he cancelled his date night with Lynette in order to fulfill an obligation to the church. *I didn't love well. I forgot the most important one.*

For such a small community, Dylan had masterminded enough departments and ministries to give the whole population of Holly work to do, or so it seemed. *But for what purpose?*

The ticking of the grandfather clock echoed into the bedroom. Like a metronome, the sound guided the rhythm of his mind. Dylan moved his toes with the ticking, becoming conscious of his heartbeat. Words formed in his head. *Step in time. Step in time.* He grinned as lyrics from Mary Poppins presented themselves, but he began to form new ones.

Step in Me. Step in Me.

No matter the season, in Me you will see.

See in Me. See in Me.

No matter how hard, you will find the key.

Random rhyming at the most inappropriate times was one of Dylan's oddest quirks. He thought to himself, *Dylan, you're such a weirdo.*

⸙

Across the street, Jackson and Lucy slept peacefully, tucked into each other. A few doors down, old Emma Gray shuffled her feet across the rug for what she called her "3 a.m. piddle parade." Waking up in the early morning hours was a very lonely experience. The term "parade" helped to lighten her loneliness. She figured, after all, that the ghosts of her past might be following her, keeping her awake. Emma knew that 3 a.m. was often referred to as "the witching hour": the time when witches, demons or ghosts were thought to be most active. The secrets of her past that she carried for decades frequently robbed her of peace and sleep. She'd become a sucker for superstition. Guilt and shame caused her to believe that something dark was on her heels, waiting for the moment to unleash doom upon her.

When her daughter, whom she had given up for adoption during her college days, showed up out of the blue, a crushing weight had lifted off her. Joy flooded her soul that day when they reunited, yet she couldn't seem to escape the guilt of not telling her dearly departed husband about her secret.

Tonight, Emma's 3 a.m. piddle parade led her to stare out the living room window. It was too cold outside for a porch sitting. She used to sit on that old porch with her notebook, gathering details about her neighbors as she peered through windows and created stories in her head of what was hiding beneath the surface. Always the cynic, she found comfort in her pessimism and distrust. But now that she had her daughter in her life, her heart had softened a bit. Still, Emma was slightly wary of people and the life they presented to others. Old habits were hard to break.

She stared through the chilly glass at the porch swing that swayed in the night breeze. The chains creaked. The branches of her weeping willow swung like ropes on a pirate ship at sea.

THE WINDOWS OF HOLLY

"What is that?" she mumbled to herself. Bright headlights made their way slowly down the street. "Who would be out at this hour?" Emma watched as the car slowed in front of Dylan's house. She didn't recognize the dark sports car. Emma knew most of the vehicles that frequented the town of Holly.

A gust of wind slammed against the old, heavy window, rattling the glass. Wind whisked through the failed attempt at weather stripping. Emma gasped as a man stepped out of the car, camera in hand. A black hoodie concealed his face, but his muscles spoke for his masculinity. She watched as the man approached Dylan's front porch, squatting low to snap a picture of the house. "What does he think he's doing?" Emma reached for her phone to dial Dylan, but before she could press the buttons, the man dashed into his car and disappeared. *I guess it's not worth waking the baby.* She called the police instead.

While waiting for the officer to arrive, she pondered the eerie winds that infiltrated the night. "Stupid witching hour. Why does this happen to me at this time every night?" Long ago, Emma adopted the superstition to give reason for her inability to sleep with her deep, dark secrets. Now that her secret was out, she wondered why she was still bothered. *Horrid regret.* Here, alone, she paid the price for her regrets. The price was her peace. She frequently reminded herself of Beverly's words. *Perfect love casts out fear. There is no fear in love.* "Ain't no power in the witchin' hour," Emma giggled to herself, putting fear aside.

⸕

The sun cracked through the slit in the morning sky, casting gold across Holly's frosty terrain. The chill in the air convinced people the temperature had fallen below freezing, but it was only a misleading impression of reality. Something about December's southern, gray days brought a mixture of joyful anticipation of happy holidays and a lingering sadness of things lost. While most of Holly's children remained oblivious to the melancholy, a segment of the town's population shielded themselves from an onslaught of memories that threatened to steal their joy, yet the sunlight faithfully arrived each morning to remind them they were worth its return.

Light streamed through the window, falling on Dylan and Lynette. Peace. The warmth of brilliant beams lit their faces with the stillness of promised hope. The calm assured them of salvation as they were awakened by the touching of feet that reminded them that they were not alone. Lynette's toes were nestled into the crook of Dylan's ankles. Upon waking, the sensation caused her heart to leap. Not wanting to hinder the pleasure, not wanting to move away from the one she loved, Lynette studied his eyes with a smile. A look of delight permeated Dylan's face. They didn't dare to speak. After all, morning breath could ruin everything.

She kept a closed-mouth smile as her eyes consumed amazing grace. *Goodness and mercy followed me through the valley of the shadow of death.* The thought pushed tears to her eyes. *I don't deserve this.* Beneath her joyful gratitude, the sting of regret threatened her with doubt. *What if he changes his mind?*

Dylan's eyes lingered in thought, considering the loss of five years. He pondered what life would be like with a child infused with the DNA of his betrayer. He wondered how long it would bother him that his wife's body had been touched by another man, his own trusted deacon. *It hurts so badly, but she's here where I always hoped she'd be.*

The burn branded his heart. He counted it a miracle that the human heart could sustain such injury yet continue to grow in love. He caught himself nearly feeling thankful for the atrocities. *Darkness destroys itself. Darkness served to awaken me to love.* He grinned with satisfaction.

Their moment of quiet was interrupted by a thud on the front

THE WINDOWS OF HOLLY

door. Dylan patted Lynette's arm as he rolled over to investigate. "That sounded like a rock, didn't it?"

Lynette agreed. "Sure did. Maybe something fell?"

"Like what?" He slipped his feet into his house shoes.

She shrugged.

Dylan opened the front door and pushed the screen door wide. At his feet lay yellow paper wrapped around an object. He rolled his eyes, reaching down to inspect the suspicious item. As he held it in his hand, he muttered, "Well, isn't this original." *A rock wrapped in a mysterious note.* After Lynette abandoned him five years ago, someone left a message in the same fashion that read, "Fallen from grace. Just like the rest of them." He wondered what this note would say.

He removed the rubber bands and unwrapped the yellow paper from the rock. He read the words aloud:

Nemesis Reveals the Hypocrisy of Holly.
The Dispenser of Dues Awaits.
Divine Retribution Comes.
She Reveals What Lies Behind the Windows of Holly.
You Cannot Hide.

Dylan's shoulders sagged as his confidence and hope were rattled. *When will the drama ever end?* He wondered if life would ever be normal again. The circumstances taunted his mind. *Of course it won't, you idiot!*

"Dylan! Yoo-hoo," a voice called. He looked up to see old Emma Gray shuffling across his lawn in her puffy pink slippers, her plump body wrapped in a big, red robe. The sight made him grin. "Yoo-hoo," she called again.

Dylan responded, "Good morning, Miss Emma. How are you today?" He found the sight of her puffy, bouncing slippers to be comical.

Emma could see that he was analyzing her morning fashion sense and grinned. "Good mornin' to you, young man. Please excuse my appearance." She gripped onto her red robe, explaining, "It may be a robe to you, but I call it my smoking jacket." She chuckled. "I don't smoke, you know, but the name makes me feel classier than I actually am."

Dylan laughed. "Aw, you're plenty classy, Miss Emma. Even without a smoking jacket."

She puckered her lips with a look of suspicion. "I'm not that gullible, Mr. Vanberg. But you go right ahead and tell me I'm classy."

He joked, "Especially when you don that purple muumuu, Miss Emma. That's one piece of your wardrobe I can never forget." He winked.

She wagged her finger at him jokingly. "Now, now. Don't get sarcastic with me, young man."

Dylan was curious. "What brings you over this morning?"

I've got to tell you about something that happened last night." She proceeded to tell him all about the mysterious car and the man with the camera. "I filed a report with the police."

"Well, that must have something to do with this strange note that was thrown at my door this morning. I'll call the police and let them know."

Emma tilted her head inquisitively. "What does the note say?"

Dylan twitched his right shoulder, making a no-big-deal kind of face to cast off worry. "It's just some nonsense. Don't worry about it."

Emma tapped her foot on the ground. "Young man, I just ventured over here unkempt, risking my reputation in this neighborhood. The least you can do is tell me what the note says."

Dylan chuckled at her feisty attitude. "Oh, Miss Emma. It's really nothing of any interest. Thanks for stopping by though. I'd

THE WINDOWS OF HOLLY

better get back inside and take care of some business for the day."

Without hesitation, she chimed in, "Like taking care of that ex-wife of yours?" She winked.

Dylan wasn't sure if Emma was trying to be funny or attempting to pry details out of him. He figured he'd satisfy her meddling. After all, she was an old woman in desperate need of stories to tell. Dylan and Emma had become great friends since the day he witnessed the unfolding of her big secret. He gave her a brief summary of his current situation. "Lynette's been through a lot. Owen took a job in another state and left her and the baby behind. She came by yesterday and I asked her to stay." He smiled. "I'm glad she's here."

Emma played with the belt of her robe. "So I've heard. People are talking, and, of course they're speculating." She smiled. "But I'm sure glad she came home, Dylan. That's good news to me."

His countenance displayed pleasure. "Thanks, Emma." Shared gratitude seemed to multiply the experience of contentment.

She turned to leave. "Well, I'm off like a herd of turtles."

He quipped, "I don't know, Em. With a magnificent smoking jacket like that, you don't resemble anything like a herd of turtles. More like a flock of red birds sweeping across the landscape." He shook his head.

Emma flicked her hand at him as if she was swatting a fly. "Ha ha. Well, if only I could fly."

Chapter Six

YLAN SAT QUIETLY AT HIS DESK, peering at the mysterious note that was left at his door earlier that morning. His eyes pored over the typewritten note, endeavoring to decipher the cryptic words.

> Nemesis Reveals the Hypocrisy of Holly.
> The Dispenser of Dues Awaits.
> Divine Retribution Comes.
> She Reveals What Lies Behind the Windows of Holly.
> You Cannot Hide.

He promised himself he wouldn't mention the note to Lynette. She had enough to worry about. Dylan hoped it was just some bored local kid, but he couldn't help but believe it was more likely a twisted individual behind this fearmongering. He wracked his brain trying to figure out who would do such a thing. *It's most likely someone I know. Obviously, I'm the target, so they must know me. Why would anyone even care what's going on in my life? I have no secrets, so what do they mean by 'You can't hide?' I don't see why Owen would waste his time doing something like this. He's off to a new life, far away. Surely it can't be Will.*

Dylan sighed as he exhausted his brain. *It's been well over five years since I pastored the church.* Dylan thought back over his

THE WINDOWS OF HOLLY

time at Hope Fellowship. He couldn't recall making any enemies. Other than butting heads occasionally with a couple of board members about trivial issues, there was nothing. *It can't be church related. Not after all these years.*

Dylan packed up his computer and headed to the newspaper office. Thankfully, the small staff of the *Holly Herald* encouraged him to take a week off work after Lynette showed up with Asa. Everyone was kind and sensitive about the situation. His coworkers were unashamedly happy about Lynette's return.

Dylan was loved by everyone, it seemed. His habit of exuding kindness to every creature he encountered was evident in that he never attempted to demolish the man who stole his wife. His actions nudged souls toward goodness. Dylan gave of himself without really trying. His vulnerability and humility, his relentless bravery in living out his brokenness along the path to healing was something everyone admired.

As Dylan drove to the *Holly Herald* office, he pondered the note once more. *Was it something I wrote in the paper that upset somebody?* Surely his effort to write positive, uplifting articles for the community wouldn't have provoked such a response. He sighed. "God, who would want retribution?" Flipping through his memory bank, images of his journey over the last five years flashed before him. Most of it made his stomach turn. "Why does it still make me ill?" Speaking out loud reminded him that he was never really alone, and he hoped that one day, an all-knowing, audible voice would address his questions. "Help me focus on the good parts, the beautiful parts." Dylan learned the necessity of pulling the beauty from life's ash heaps. He knew he would have died from heartbreak long ago had he not made it a daily practice to focus on the good in life.

In an effort to force his mind toward goodness, he tensed his jaw and focused his eyes on the road ahead, giving himself a pep

60

talk. "C'mon, Dylan. Stay focused. Think of the mercy that's met you along the way. Friends. Dreams. Visions. Moments when God held your breaking heart."

With those words, the remembrance of the Presence that rescued him during those times when he felt crushed and utterly obliterated drew warmth to his eyes. Gratitude began to take over. "Goodness and mercy follow me."

Pulling into the parking lot, he centered his focus back to the present. The sight of the tiny, old newspaper office filled him with thankfulness. Dylan knew it was a gift to be able to write and edit for the town that captured his heart long ago. The newspaper gave him a voice. Having a voice in the pulpit once meant the world to him, but now he had the ability to communicate with those who wouldn't dare to pass through the doors of a church, and he considered that to be a greater privilege.

Stepping into the outdated office, that familiar smell of 1950's wood and ceiling tiles greeted him. The office had became a second home to Dylan. When being in his beloved home provoked painful memories on lonely days, he always had the office as a refuge. Something about the look, feel, and smell reminded him of his grandparents' home. In their home was comfort and perfect peace. Everything in the world could be going wrong, but going to his grandparents' place seemed to reset the entire universe to perfection. It was outdated and old, but perfect.

"Hey, Dylan!" Jackson's eyes were bright with joy at the sight of his best friend.

"Jackson! It's been too long, neighbor." The two embraced.

Jackson reminded him, "It's only been a week, but yeah, it does seem like forever." The two were used to seeing each other on a daily basis. Jackson explained the reason for his lack of communication over the last few days. "I haven't meant to ignore you. Lucy and I wanted to give you and Lynette some privacy. I

THE WINDOWS OF HOLLY

know you must have a lot to catch up on."

"Thanks, man. We sure appreciate your help. You're always my lifesaver." Dylan smiled.

Jackson resettled himself at his desk across from Dylan's. "I hope your time off has been okay despite the challenges."

"The time off was good for us. It's been interesting: good, hard, crazy, but happy all at the same time. All the feels, man." Dylan twirled a stray pen. "I did have something weird happen this morning though. I've gotta show you this."

Dylan reached into his pocket, pulling out the crumpled note. "It appears I've got an enemy."

Jackson read it, shaking his head. "What the heck? Who would do something like this?"

"That's what I've been asking myself all morning."

"Dylan, I'm so sorry. This is the last thing you deserve, especially after all you've been through."

Dylan shrugged. "I don't know, man. The rain falls on the just and the unjust alike, right? Guess it's just another round. We reap what we sow, you know? Kinda like the karma thing? But my karma seems a little broken right now." He grinned.

Jackson quipped, "If that's the case, then your sowing and reaping and karma principles are screwed up and malfunctioning."

Dylan crossed his eyes and puckered his lips comically. He shrugged. "Stuff just happens, I guess. Things that make no sense and don't seem to have a purpose. But I'm sure it'll turn out all right in the end. If you get any leads or have any clues to follow though, I'd like to know who wants 'divine retribution.' And why do they insinuate that I have something to hide?"

Jackson tapped his forehead with his pen. "Maybe the note was left for Lynette, not you."

Dylan raised an eyebrow. "Perhaps, but I've had a rock thrown at my place before. That happened right after Lynette left me."

He tapped his pen, thinking for a moment. "I'm sure it was meant for me, not her. I've wondered if it could be Owen trying to pull something? It can't be Will. He's in jail. I double-checked."

Jackson reminded him, "People in jail know people. Maybe Will is having someone mess with you. It sounds to me like Owen is too busy with Owen. I don't think he cares about anyone but himself."

"Good point."

Jackson rubbed his chin. "I think you should spend a few hours going back over every article you've recently published. Read through the highlights and see if there was possibly anything that might have offended someone. I don't see how that could be the case, but you never know."

"Sadly, it's hard to do life without rubbing somebody the wrong way, whether you mean to or not." Dylan sighed. "And I feel weird going back, reading everything I wrote."

"Why?" Jackson inquired.

Dylan stretched as he pondered Jackson's question. "It's uncomfortable reading my own thoughts. It's awkward. I tend to want to forget about the last several years, man. Especially with all the crap that's happened, it's like I can't stand looking back through my thought processes during that time. I think everything I write reflects where my heart is, so it's scary to look back, you know?"

Jackson shook his head. "You're overthinking it. I've read your articles. Trust me. You'll find them to be enlightening."

Dylan began poring over his files. Most of his writings were basic encouragements. Only a couple were more vulnerable and encompassing. He came across an article, one of his firsts, that moved him deeply, evoking memories of his momentary affliction.

SNAPSHOTS OF HOLLY. LOVE: ONE OF LIFE'S

THE WINDOWS OF HOLLY

GREAT MYSTERIES
by Dylan Vanberg

Love. All have desired it. Some have tasted, touched, and seen glimpses of authentic love while wading through the mire of self-discovery. Part of love's mystery is the way that it makes itself known in the midst of hatred, confusion, and all kinds of darkness. Often, we learn what love is by experiencing what love is not. Many have experienced the outer core of love, but how much of humanity will be able to touch the core of love and be immersed in its fullness?

Being immersed in the fullness of love requires vulnerability, nakedness of the heart and soul, and a life without secrets. I once heard someone say, "You are only as sick as your secrets." And he was right. "Therefore, confess your trespasses to one another, and pray for one another, that you may be healed" (James 5:16). We are not to confess for the purpose of receiving judgment, but rather to receive the prayers and support of others, which brings healing. We are not to hear confessions for the purpose of oppressing and ridiculing another, but rather to lift him up.

Confession to a heart of authentic love brings healing, because the hearer fervently prays for the freedom of one tormented by secrets, and the authentic lover will never treat one according to what he has done wrong, but according to his true identity as a whole person. Once a man has stripped his heart bare, his eyes become opened to see himself clearly in the mirror, and he is empowered to live a life of wholeness. This is what love does. And I believe that love lives in Holly.

The vulnerability and revealing of ourselves that brings the face of love into our vision, and takes us deep into the heart, is a risky, sometimes painful journey. But if one pushes past fear and embraces even the difficult parts of the quest, there will be no room for disappointment. Each of our journeys is different.

I have come to believe that no one's journey is easy. Along the pathway created by our choices and the choices of others, ultimately we will come to know that love is not a feeling or a philosophy, but love is a person. And He has been with us all along.

And sometimes the purest of hearts are birthed in the darkest places. This is one of the mysteries of grace. This is the mysterious way of love. And love lives in the people of Holly.

The "Snapshots of Holly" stood out to Dylan. *Snapshots*. He remembered Miss Emma mentioning that the man was taking pictures. Various words and phrases from the note and his article washed through his mind. He wondered if his phrase, "You are only as sick as your secrets," had anything to do with the threat, 'You cannot hide.'

Chapter Seven

AT ANNIE'S CAFE, Emma and Beverly anticipated the lunch special of the day. Emma scooted herself into the booth. "Well, Bev, it's my favorite lunch special today!"

"Oh yeah?" Beverly replied. "I thought every lunch special was your favorite. One day, it's chicken, the next it's meatloaf."

Emma rolled her eyes. "All right, you clown. I like a lot of them, but my favorite is the King Ranch chicken, and you know that, you old, ornery goose."

Beverly placed both hands on the table in front of her, palms down. With prim and proper posture, she spoke with a British accent. "Pardon me, Madame. You have referred to me as both a clown and a goose within the last ten seconds. Neither is glamorous or enticing. One lays eggs and one dons a fake nose. Neither do I lay eggs or have a fake nose. I have no feathers and I have no brightly colored garments such as yourself, dear Emma."

Emma grinned. She always enjoyed her time with Beverly. Having a friend who wasn't afraid to be her delightfully unique self was a true gift. Beverly helped Emma over the years to escape her dark perception of herself, others, and life in general. Bev faithfully chipped away at Emma's hardness, relentlessly, with love and laughter. Emma was grateful for a friend with whom she could be herself.

Emma raised her eyebrow. "So what are you having for lunch, goose? Eggs?" She snickered.

Continuing with her British accent, Beverly frolicked in speech. "Madame, I shall follow your lead despite the name-calling. I shall have the King Ranch chicken with a glorious spot of tea. I trust that your taste in food is not atrocious." She winked.

Emma declared, "Oh, I've got good taste all right!"

Beverly leaned down, peeking underneath the table. Clearing her throat, she huffed, "Uh hm. Please be aware that there are brown cows on your pants, Madame. Is this what you call 'good taste,' my lady?"

Emma rolled her eyes. "Dear, sweet Beverly. At my age, good taste is anything that brings enjoyment. You're not too far behind, so I'll be sure to leave my brown cow pants for you in my will. I'm telling you, there's a point in life when you just want all your britches to have elastic waistbands. You get to a point when you'll decorate yourself with anything that makes you feel young again. For me, it's flowers, cows, dogs, cats, and basically anything with fur that doesn't bite and gives unconditional love."

Beverly chimed in. "Oh! That explains your famous purple muumuu. How many years have you had that ancient piece hanging around? Since 1923?"

Emma bobbled her head. "Ha. Very funny. You know that dress means a lot to me. My husband bought it for me on our one and only trip to Hawaii. I thought those native ladies were so beautiful in their muumuus, so I wanted one for myself."

"I know," said Beverly. "I know how much you love that old dress, and your husband. It's beautiful, friend. I'm glad it makes you happy." Beverly patted Emma's hand.

Lucy rushed to their table, breathless. "I'm so sorry for the wait, ladies. What can I get you today?"

Emma reached for Lucy's hand. "Sweet girl. Slow yourself down and take a breath. You've gotta take it easy for that baby."

Lucy smiled. "I know. It's been a little crazy here today. Lunch rush, you know?"

Emma assured her, "We're in no rush. Bev and I have all day."

Beverly interjected, "Ha! More like all year!"

They giggled.

Lucy let out a deep breath. "Thank God! I'll take my time then," she joked.

Emma couldn't wait to hear about Lucy's interaction with Dylan and Lynette. She didn't hesitate to ask Lucy about the couple. "How are Dylan and Lynette doing?"

Lucy smiled at the way Emma said their names together. "They're hanging in there. Lynette's adjusting with the new baby, and, of course, her difficult situation. She's recovering from a really rough week." Lucy hesitated.

"Yes, I know, dear," said Emma. "I heard about what Will did. Any man that hits a woman is no man at all. I know he was under the influence, but that's no excuse."

Lucy agreed. "That's true. I suppose he's got his demons to overcome."

Emma inquired, "Did you or Jackson happen to see the man who drove up about three o'clock this morning? He got out of his car and took a picture of Dylan's house."

Lucy was shocked. "What? I didn't hear about that."

"Yes, and then someone threw a rock at Dylan's door."

Sadness crept over Lucy's face. "Why would anyone do that to him?" She sighed. "He's had to deal with so much. Gosh, just when redemption draws near, then come the obstacles. Poor Dylan. What kind of car, Emma? What did the man look like?"

Emma puckered her lips. "Oh goodness. I don't know. All cars look the same to me, especially in the dark, but I think it was a

THE WINDOWS OF HOLLY

sports car of some kind. The man had one of those things over his head. You know, a jacket with a head cover."

Lucy helped her. "A hoodie?"

Emma threw her hands in the air. "Yeah, I guess that's what they call those things. It was dark. Maybe black. Everything was dark!"

Lucy wondered, "And what were you doing up at that hour?"

Emma held her stomach. "You'll understand when you get older. Nature calls. Potty patrol happens around the witching hour."

Lucy giggled. "Emma, you're so funny."

Beverly dropped her fist on the table. "All right already. Enough with words. I want food! Two orders of King Ranch chicken and two sweet teas, please."

Lucy saluted. "Yes, ma'am. You've got it!" She marched off to duty.

THE VANBERG HOME

Lynette stood in front of the fireplace, studying the painting above the mantle. She was moved by Dylan's creations. She cherished every meaningful brushstroke, intrigued by the mystery of her union with Dylan and the dreams that spoke to both of them throughout their separation over the last few years. It was a cruel irony to her that the connection she believed was gone had remained all along. *We've always been connected. How could I be so blind?*

The relentless, ancient desire of humanity to turn back time nagged at her soul. *Is life a game we play blindfolded? We stumble around, thinking we know exactly what we're doing, until we find ourselves fighting to save our souls from the choices we've made.* "But God," she said aloud. *We think we lack something or someone.* Lynette pondered the course of her life and how often she strived to gain something she believed to be missing. *It's all a perception of lack. We create scenarios, thinking ourselves to be brilliant storywriters.* She shook her head. *I've really screwed up my story.* "But God," she said again, reminding herself of His kindness toward her.

The clock chimed, echoing through the house. With each chime, she envisioned the cleansing of her heart, cleansing of her soul, cleansing of her mind. *Make me clean.* At the last chime, she closed her eyes, allowing the vibration to move through her, pushing aside the debris of her choices. *God is not confined by time. Neither am I confined by what's taken place in time.* The thought surprised her. She was thankful for the author of time. *All things new.*

She peered through the cold window, longing to sit on the old porch swing. It was a place of peace and promise for her, and she wondered why she ever left it behind. Images of the journey of her last five years swirled through her mind. Fragments of time pierced her heart. Regret threatened to consume the hope she battled to keep.

She spoke to herself. "Take your eyes off the storm, Lynette. Look at now. Go to now." While she loathed the sound of her own voice, she understood the power of hearing and receiving. She knew she needed to get her head right and stay in a good place. Otherwise, she'd be destroyed. Turning toward the bridal painting once more, she breathed in deeply, anchoring her heart where it was always meant to be.

The sound of the doorbell broke her concentration. "Oh no. I'm a mess," she mumbled to herself as she peered through the window to observe the visitor. "Marcy!" She was delighted to see her friend. Lynette threw open the door and wrapped her arms around the one she knew as grace incarnate. "Oh, Marcy. I'm so happy to see you."

THE WINDOWS OF HOLLY

Marcy smiled warmly. "I hope you don't mind me dropping by unannounced, sweetheart. I was in the area and felt inclined to stop," Marcy apologized.

Lynette's eyes filled with light. "Not at all! Seeing your face is good for my soul. Come on in. Can I get you some tea?"

Marcy beamed with kindness. "Tea sounds lovely. You and I haven't had tea in ages. It'll be like old times." Marcy's eyes searched the living room, taking in the miraculous fact that Lynette was back in her old home. *This is where she belongs.*

Lynette adjusted her robe. "Please excuse my appearance. I haven't been getting out much lately. I didn't want people asking questions about the bruises."

"I don't blame you. And, my dear, I remember what it was like being a new mom. Believe me, I didn't get out for weeks. It's an accomplishment just waking up after sleepless nights, multiple feedings and diaper changes, but don't worry. They grow up way too quickly. What seems like forever now is really just a vapor. Enjoy him while you can, because the next thing you know, he'll be grown and married."

"I'm just glad he's sleeping right now so we can visit. Cute little guy."

Marcy studied the remaining bits of bruising left behind by Will. She knew Lynette was battered more deeply than her body revealed. *God, help her to heal, inside and out.*

Lynette poured tea into their glasses, taking note of the rays of sunlight igniting the amber liquid. "Gosh, isn't tea beautiful?"

Marcy smiled, glad that someone else understood her affection for the delightful beverage. "It sure is. That reminds me of a quote a friend sent me the other day. In fact, I have a picture of it." Marcy pulled her cell phone from her purse. "You'll appreciate this." She smiled as she scrolled through her photos. "Aha. Here it is. My friend sent this from the Prince of Wales Hotel somewhere in Canada."

She handed the phone to Lynette. "Take a look."

Tea is wealth itself, because there is nothing that cannot be lost, no problem that will not disappear, no burden that will not float away, between the first sip and the last.

~ The Minister of Leaves, The Republic of Tea

Lynette laughed. "I think I can agree. I suppose that's why teatime is such a part of life. God knows I've missed it. Owen never understood my tea obsession." With the mention of his name, her smile diminished as she turned to retrieve sugar from the pantry. She sighed. "I'm sorry I ever made a mess of things, Marcy."

Marcy nodded with understanding. "Sweetheart, I know you're sorry. I know your heart. I've watched you enough over the years to know who you truly are. We all make decisions at times that lead us down a bad path. But look where you are now! You're here, with Dylan. That man is a jewel. More importantly, he sees you as a jewel. I know things will never be the same for you two, but it can be better than before."

Lynette raised her eyebrows, taking a deep breath. "I hope so. It's hard to see how that's possible with the obstacles I've created. I don't mean that Asa is an obstacle, of course, but you know what I mean?"

"Yes. There will certainly be challenges along the way, but if you're both committed, you can make it work."

Lynette stared into the glass of glistening amber. Disjointed thoughts began to tumble from her mouth. "I didn't plan things this way. It's just that over the years, I'd remember Dylan asking me not to forget our Dream Door: the little door on the side of our porch. It was like our time capsule. The day I left him, he begged

73

me to remember. I was tempted so many times to see what was in there, especially on difficult days with Owen. After awhile, I assumed Dylan gave up and threw everything out." She looked at Marcy. "When Owen left me, I didn't know where to turn. Honestly, I wasn't surprised that he left. I could feel it coming, almost since the very beginning. But I never dreamed he would leave his own child. When he did, I became desperate for something to hold onto. The weight of what I've done, it's like it shredded me internally from the moment I left Dylan. Once Owen left, I needed something to keep me breathing." She paused, catching her breath. "I guess I needed to know if anyone loved me." Her chin quivered.

Marcy listened intently, allowing Lynette time to finish her thoughts.

Lynette swallowed, trying to keep her tears at bay. "This was the last place where I remembered feeling loved. Opening that door on the side of the house was one of the scariest moments of my life. What if it was empty?" Emotion captured her voice as tears erupted. "But you know what I found instead? It was full, full of loving notes and letters from a man I broke into a million pieces." Streams ran down her cheeks. "Even the notes that expressed his anger and pain, they still ended with love." She swallowed hard, shaking her head. "How is it even possible he could still love me through that?"

Marcy's countenance of genuine compassion showered Lynette with peace. "Oh, Lynnie. Dylan never stopped loving you. That was evident to all of us."

She wiped her eyes. "How could I have done something so evil?"

Marcy comforted her. "Listen, sweetie. You have to forgive yourself. Everyone is capable of doing horrible things. We all have vulnerabilities, and not one of us does everything perfectly."

Lynette rubbed her eyes with the sleeve of her robe. "I don't even understand how it all happened. It's like a fog."

That's the nature of deception," Marcy explained.

Lynette listened to Marcy's wisdom. "Deception always begins with a perception of lack. One of the greatest deceptions is to think we can find a deeper love outside of Love Himself, you know? We are made for love, and when we don't believe we're loved, we seek it out in any form. And my goodness, all of us married people hit points in our lives when we believe we've gone as deep as we can possibly go with our spouses. When you think you can't go any further, and when you feel uncertain about love, is usually when our decision-making gets skewed. Things get foggy."

"It seemed right at the time. I mean, I knew it wasn't right, of course, but there was a period of time when it didn't seem wrong. It's strange, Marcy. It's like I didn't even realize I was having an affair at first. When I acknowledged what it was, I made excuses, so much so that I didn't care if it was wrong."

"Well, honey, we try to justify our actions to soothe our conscience. I think, in God's mercy, we learn by deduction. Sometimes it's even by seduction that we learn. Oh, it brings great pain though. But if we're intent on walking that path, He still loves us enough to allow us to find out what true love is by letting us see what it is not. I think it's amazing how in the middle of our own destructive path, we slowly come to realize that what we thought might be love eventually reveals itself as something very contrary to love. Perhaps the true miracle in it all is that our conscience isn't completely demolished in the process. I think when we get desperate for grace, forgiveness, and restoration, our eyes become wide open to recognize love."

Lynette agreed. "I think I'm beginning to see."

Marcy continued, "The challenge for you will be to receive

grace and love, to forgive yourself. For Dylan, the challenge will be to give grace and love to those who've caused him pain. I'm not sure who has the more difficult part."

Lynette dabbed her eyes with a napkin. "Sometimes I feel I can't live with myself, but if Dylan will allow me to, I want to live a long life by his side and love him the way I should have."

Marcy smiled. "I'd love nothing more than to see that."

Lynette shook her head in wonder. "Marcy, he talks about marrying me again. Can you believe that?"

Marcy nodded with a smile that radiated joy. "Of course I can. That's the nature of love. Have you talked about when this marriage might take place?"

"Dylan says as soon as my divorce is finalized, which should only be a matter of weeks, according to Owen. That jerk pursued the divorce long before I even knew what was happening. He had the ball rolling, so there's not much to haggle over. I don't want anything from him. I'm ready to sign off and be done with that chapter of my life." She sighed, shaking her head. "I could never be with a man who'd abandon his child."

Marcy patted her hand with sincere compassion.

Lynette turned her eyes toward the scenery outside the window. She wondered, "Marcy, what do people out there think? What are they saying about us?"

Marcy cleared her throat. "Lynnie, I don't know, dear. They know better than to talk their hogwash with me and David. Besides, it doesn't matter what anyone thinks. This is a private matter between you and Dylan, and those in whom you choose to confide. The others don't know the whole story and they haven't walked in your shoes. If anyone thinks they're above walking through this kind of valley of the shadow of death, they're foolish."

Marcy's terminology grabbed Lynette's attention. Lynette

repeated, "The valley of the shadow of death. Yes, it is." She pondered her choices and where they had led her. "Death to ego. Death to confidence. Death to self-reliance, self-assurance, and death to character." Her eyes widened as she considered the ramifications. "Death to friendships and family relationships." She sighed. "And death to love." She pondered that thought for a moment. "Well, no. In my case, it didn't kill Dylan's love for me. Death has no power over love, does it?"

Marcy smiled joyfully. "No, it doesn't. I've seen evidence of that my entire life. My gosh, look at me and David! You know how he used to be. I watched love transform a rock-hard, stubborn old coot into a gentle, kind, and loving man. After decades of marriage, it feels like we're back in the honeymoon phase. It's amazing what love can do."

Lynette admired Marcy. "If it wasn't for your constant kindness and grace, David wouldn't be who he is now."

Marcy raised an eyebrow. "Well let me tell you, I didn't do it all right! There were times I wanted to smack that man so hard and knock him across the room. I had thoughts of walking out on several occasions, but I loved the stubborn goat so much, I couldn't imagine leaving. I fumed at times, stomped around and slammed doors, but eventually, that got old and I needed my home to be a place of peace. The older you get, the more you value peace. I figured I wouldn't have peace without him either. Somewhere along the way, things began to shift. Actually, it was the situation with you and Dylan that really began breaking down his walls. He was so angry and accusatory, but seeing Dylan's pain and relentless faith, and hearing what your friend, Jackson, had to say, affected him deeply."

Lynette was lost in thought as she processed Marcy's words. "Wow." She placed her hand over her heart. "That's unbelievable."

THE WINDOWS OF HOLLY

"What?" Marcy questioned.

"Marcy, do you really believe that somehow, some way, our situation impacted David positively?"

Marcy smiled. "I do. I've seen the darkest, ugliest things bring beauty from ashes in the most mysterious ways." Her eyes shined brightly, angelic like. "That's why I'm so in love with him."

"With David?"

Marcy lifted her hands upward. "With God. And with David."

Lynette smiled.

Chapter Eight

THE HAZE OF SUNDAY MORNING'S TWILIGHT pressed its cold breath into Holly's windows. A few souls were awake, preparing for a restful day. Pastor Dean of Hope Fellowship was fully alert, his thoughts consumed by the sermon he had rehashed in his mind a million times during the night. Others remained in a state of slumber, lost in another world with no obligations demanding their attention. The wintry air whistled through forgotten cracks in old dwellings.

Dylan stirred awake, recounting nightmares that taunted him throughout the early morning hours. His dreams consisted of Lynette walking out on him. Images of her with Owen and scenes of the day of discovery replayed in his mind. "Dang it," he muttered. Lynette heard him as she walked past the room with her morning tea. She stepped in the room to inquire.

"Dylan? Dang what?"

He sighed, rubbing his temples. "Oh. Stupid dreams."

She pressed, "About what?"

"Just old stuff." He wished he could forget.

Lynette was relentless when it came to details. "So tell me about it."

He sat up on the edge of his bed, eyes to the floor. "It's just unpleasant things I wish I could forget, and things you'd rather not

THE WINDOWS OF HOLLY

hear about."

"No," she quickly interjected. "I want to hear. We've spent enough time playing games, shutting down communication, and ignoring each other in the past. I want to hear it, Dylan. No more secrets. No more hiding. Whether it's good or bad, we have to live as open books and work through things together. We're a team now."

He appreciated her desire to listen and bear the weight of his struggles. "I suppose you're right. It's not pleasant though." He sighed, still gazing at the floor.

She sat next to him. "I can take it."

"Well," he hesitated, "I guess it comes down to..." He feared speaking the truth, afraid to hurt her. "You've stolen my trust."

His words didn't surprise her. "I know. And I hate myself for that. I'm sorry, Dylan."

"Lynette, it's been five years since I found out about you and Owen. Five years. People say time heals everything, but I don't agree. It's like, sometimes I think time just serves to remind us of things we'd rather forget. Since you've come back, I've struggled with a few nightmares that have to do with you leaving again. I see you and him in my dreams. I see you driving away. I see his watch in your purse...the watch I bought for him, ironically. It all haunts me."

Lynette wrestled the crushing weight of guilt and shame, trying to decipher whether or not her presence was healthy for Dylan. "Would you like me to leave?" she asked sheepishly, with sincerity, hoping his answer wouldn't be yes.

Dylan reacted strongly. "Good God! No, of course not!" The movement of his chest revealed the rise in his heart rate. "Do you know how many years I hoped and prayed you'd come home?" The fear in his eyes pierced her heart. His voice trembled. "I don't ever want you to leave again."

Relief flooded her heart. "I will never leave you again, Dylan. I promise." The word 'promise' caused her to grimace, knowing that Dylan had no reason to ever believe her promises.

Lynette's words were salve to his wounded soul, yet he fought the nagging voice of distrust. *She's broken promises before.* Dylan focused on her eyes as he searched for confirmation of authenticity. He knew Lynette meant what she spoke, but the nightmares threatened to plunder his assurance.

She put her hand on his knee. "Look, Dylan, I know you have no reason to believe a word I say, but I truly promise I'll never be unfaithful to you again. I've been given a second chance and there's no way I'm throwing it away. I hate that I caused you pain, and I hate that I was a fool. I hate that I broke my promises to you. I'll never go there again. I'd choose death over that."

Dylan placed his hand on top of hers. "Thank you." He needed to hear her passion.

She searched his eyes. "Please, Dylan, don't be afraid to tell me what's going on in your head. Do you have any more secrets?"

He thought for a moment. "No." He thought some more. "Oh yeah. Maybe. I lied to you the other day."

Struck with a surge of adrenaline, Lynette tried to hide her disappointment. "Oh? About what?"

"Do you remember the morning when we heard a thud at the front door?"

"Yes."

"Someone threw a rock at the door with a cryptic note wrapped around it. Jackson and I are trying to figure out what it means and where it came from." He sighed.

Lynette's stomach lurched. *What have I brought upon this man?* "What did it say?"

Dylan walked to the closet to retrieve the crumpled note. "Listen to this and see what you think."

THE WINDOWS OF HOLLY

Nemesis Reveals the Hypocrisy of Holly.
The Dispenser of Dues Awaits.
Divine Retribution Comes.
She Reveals What Lies Behind the Windows of Holly.
You Cannot Hide.

Lynette was alarmed. "What in the world is that supposed to mean? And who would do something like this?"

He rubbed his head. "That's what I'm trying to figure out. I've read over articles I've written for the *Herald* to see if I might have offended someone. I've mulled over possible enemies I've made, and I can't come up with anything. I thought of Will, but he's still in jail. I wondered about Owen, but would he actually take the time to mess around with us like that? He's the one who did the leaving."

She shook her head. "I doubt it's Owen. He got what he wanted and he doesn't care what's going on here. He talked as if he expected you and I would be back together, and he didn't seem bothered by that idea. In fact, I think that's what he hoped would happen so Asa and I would be a burden off of his back."

Dylan informed her, "Jackson did some research on some of the phrases and he thinks it's referring to Nemesis, the Greek goddess of retribution. I don't believe I've done anything to anyone that would warrant retribution though."

Lynette let out a deep breath. "It's because of me, Dylan. I'm the only one here that's deserving of this. We both know that."

Dylan was afraid of causing distress. *She has enough to deal with.* "Nah. I'm sure it's meant for me."

She tilted her head in wonder, knowing he was trying to protect her heart and mind. "Why are you so nice to me?"

"I'm just giving the facts." He smiled.

She nudged his arm playfully. "So that was your big lie? Hiding the note from me? Are there any other confessions, sir?"

He shook his head. "Well, let me think about it." He paused for a moment, thinking through embarrassing situations he'd pocketed in the back of his mind. "One time, when we pastored Hope Fellowship, I was in the middle of counseling a couple. You remember Jason and Alexa?"

She searched her mind. "I do."

He continued, "It was real serious. She was crying her eyes out and Jason seemed embarrassed to be there. I was having a hard time understanding what she was saying because of her crying. While she was going on and on, I leaned back in my chair and felt something crunch right under my butt cheeks! I mean, right by my crack."

Lynette crinkled her nose. "Eww. That's disgusting."

"It freaked me out and I was so distracted by it, I wasn't really listening to her. All I could think was *what the heck is in my pants?* I was eating peanut butter crackers earlier that day. While chowing down on them, I got a phone call." He laughed. "I was starving, so I couldn't wait to eat them. I just wanted the guy to get off the phone. I had to eat slowly so I wouldn't crunch in his ear. He kept going on and on. Then I needed to go to the bathroom so badly, I put a whole cracker in my mouth and ran to the toilet. I tried covering the phone so he couldn't hear me peeing. I guess, in the process, I dropped part of the cracker in my underwear."

Lynette was laughing. "Oh my gosh." Her face was red with laughter. "Dylan, I just have one question for you. Why didn't you hit the mute button?"

Dylan was dumbfounded. "Holy cow." He smacked himself in the head. "I feel like an idiot. I always forget about the mute button!"

Lynette nearly doubled over with giggles. "Why didn't you ever tell me about this?"

He shrugged. "I don't know. Anyway, Alexa was crying,

83

THE WINDOWS OF HOLLY

telling me about their serious issues, but I had no idea what she was saying." He giggled. "I totally zoned out on them because I was distracted by the crushed cracker in my underwear. I mean, how could I focus on anything else? Alexa asked me if I thought something was a good idea, but I didn't pay attention to what, so I just said, 'Yeah, that's a great idea.' Jason just stared at me and Alexa gave me the look of death, like I had just committed the unpardonable sin."

Lynette wondered, "What did she ask you?"

Dylan shook his head. "Oh, Lynette. It was awful. Apparently, she was complaining about Jason never taking her out on dates. She said he only takes her out once a year or something like that. Then she asked if I thought that was a good idea. I said it was a great idea!"

Lynette's mouth dropped open. "Dylan! That's terrible. How did you get out of that one?"

He caught his breath. "I didn't. When I saw the look on their faces," he chuckled, "I knew I'd done something wrong. I didn't know how to get out of it, so I told them, 'I'm so sorry, but I just realized I have peanut butter in my pants.' I excused myself and left. They never came back to church."

Lynette was amused. "I wondered why they left! Alexa told me that God told them to leave. She never even mentioned the counseling session."

Dylan laughed. "When people want to leave church, they almost always use God as their excuse. Honestly, I feel kind of bad about it now, but she needed to loosen up."

Lynette seemed concerned beneath her amusement. "Did you ever apologize or reach out to them?"

"Of course I did! I sincerely apologized, but Alexa wouldn't accept it. That's why I never mentioned it to you. It was embarrassing."

She grinned. "I suppose people just can't handle having a pastor that's so easily distracted by peanut butter up his crack. Can't win them all. Maybe they're the ones who want retribution, Dylan. You can't hide!" she jokingly jabbed.

His laugh brought peace to her heart. *If I could make him laugh forever, I would.* Lynette admired the childlike sparkle in his eye and the way his smile revealed youth hidden beneath the weight of adulthood. How quickly one could turn from pain and sadness to laughter. *Only a child. Gosh, if we could just go back to the beginning.*

Dylan switched gears in their silly conversation. "Seriously though. This Nemesis thing is bothering me more than I'd like to admit. Emma saw a man taking pictures of our house at three o'clock that morning. She called the police to file a report. I made a copy of the note and let the police know about it. I wanted to hang onto it, though, for clues. It might be some kid messing around, but I don't know."

She picked at her finger nervously. "I'm sorry if my being here is what brought this on."

"Don't worry about that. We'll figure it out. I ordered a couple of security cameras online yesterday."

She tried to hide her concern. "I'm sure everything will be fine, but why didn't you order the cameras right away?"

He shrugged. "I was trying to blow it off, but I can't seem to shake it. I need to know who it is and why they're doing this."

Lynette stared out the window in thought. "You don't have anything to hide, do you, Dylan?"

His eyes shifted toward her. "Nothing at all."

She sighed. "Then it has to be referring to me. Do you think we're in danger?"

He placed his hand on hers. "Absolutely not. Don't worry about it. I'm taking measures to make sure we're safe and secure.

THE WINDOWS OF HOLLY

It's most likely just a meaningless threat, Lynette. The game of intimidation is more satisfying than actually doing something."

"I hope you're right."

They sat together in silence for a minute.

Dylan tried to shift the atmosphere. "Hey, Lynnie. Let's get out and do something we used to love."

"Like what?"

"Let's go to Annie's Café, just like old times. We'll have some tea and good home cooking. The best part is we don't have to do the dishes." He smiled.

She was pleased with the idea. "On a cold day like this, that actually sounds really nice and cozy." A flicker of life flashed in her eyes. "I'll go put some makeup on to cover the remnants of the bruises. The last thing we need is to give people more reasons to speculate."

He agreed.

At Annie's Cafe

The little bell clanked against the glass door as Dylan and Lynette entered their beloved café. They pressed through, shrugging off feelings of inadequacy in the eyes of possible spectators who would dare to condemn or gossip. Dylan felt Lynette's hesitation as they stepped into their old hangout.

Touching her arm, he encouraged her to enjoy the place she once considered a second home. "Don't worry. They'll get used to seeing the three of us in here." His eyes smiled upon Asa in the baby carrier.

Old Emma threw her hands in the air, bouncing her body up and down in the booth. "Well, hallelujah, thine the glory! The Vanbergs!"

Dylan and Lynette felt the warmth of her acceptance. Unstoppable smiles crept across their faces, thankful for the approval of their reconciliation. Gratitude mixed with embarrassment at what others might think. After all, in walks the once-beloved pastor of Hope Fellowship whose wife cheated with a deacon. Their demise had grabbed the attention of the entire town and resulted in Dylan's rejection. One of the most-loved and well-regarded men in town became an instant leper to a society that once embraced him.

When Lynette married Owen shortly after the dramatic fall, Dylan was nearly destroyed. Her marriage to Owen meant no possibility of redemption, at least in the eyes of all who witnessed the fiasco. Now here they were, together. Not just the two of them, which was climactic enough. Now there were three. And the third was from another man: the betrayer.

As they embraced a handful of close friends and enjoyed their meal, Dylan couldn't help but notice an old, familiar face.

"Dylan, what do you keep looking at?" Lynette inquired.

He couldn't help but stare. "I thought I recognized a guy over there. I think he used to attend Hope Fellowship back in the day. Maybe you'd recognize him. Don't look yet, but when you can, check out the left corner, by the bar. He's wearing an orange jacket."

Dylan didn't want to tell her that the man stared their way with a sinister scowl. He wondered if he might be the person who left the threatening note. Dylan's eyes briefly locked with his. Dylan purposefully cast a smile his direction, but the man promptly looked away. *Who the heck are you? What is your problem?* He tried brushing away his concern.

Lynette stood, "I'll be right back. Gotta hit the restroom." She winked.

Asa began to wake up, stretching and puffing air through his little nose. As he tried to open his eyes, a quiet whimper arose. Dylan leaned over, unlatching the baby harness. "It's okay, buddy.

THE WINDOWS OF HOLLY

Shhh."

Lifting Asa into his arms, he gently wrapped the blanket around him. "Mommy will be right back." Dylan studied Asa's perfect features. His nose and lips were an exact copy of Lynette's. He traced the baby's fingers with his, marveling over the miniature human. While fully aware of the healing a new life could bring, he was also fully aware of the intense ache of it not being his own child. *The child of my betrayer.* The thought pierced his soul. *But it's not the baby's fault.*

Fighting back emotion, Dylan looked away from Asa's perfect face. His eyes captured the glare of the mysterious, familiar man in orange. Daggers seized Dylan's attention. He pulled the blanket up, shielding Asa from the man's anger.

Lynette returned to the table. "Dyl, what's wrong?"

Her interruption startled him. He shrugged his shoulders in an attempt to shake off the discomfort. "So did you get a look at him?"

"Yeah. I remember seeing him. I think he used to attend the church on occasion. I talked to him once, but I don't remember his name. Maybe we should say hello and break the ice."

Dylan glanced at the man. "I don't think so. He doesn't look friendly. In fact, he looks like he hates me."

She saw his concern. "Well, maybe that's all the more reason to break the ice. See what's up."

The Vanbergs were known for talking to everyone in town. Long ago, they were the life of Holly. Their home, the "Christmas House," was once a place of unity for even the outcasts. Lynette knew Dylan couldn't possibly pass up the opportunity to soften a hardened heart.

He relented. "I suppose." Dylan placed Asa in Lynette's arms. "Here goes."

Walking toward the man, he took a deep breath. A grin crossed his face as he considered that he might regret this moment. It was clear that the man was pretending not to see Dylan approaching. Eyes down, focused on his bowl of oatmeal, he fidgeted as Dylan drew near.

Dylan extended his hand. Before Dylan could say a word, the man looked up suddenly. "Yeah, I see you, Vanberg. Don't you offer me that dirty hand."

Dylan couldn't help but laugh nervously. "Dirty hand? Wow. I've never heard that before. I couldn't help but notice you looking my way. You look familiar."

The fifty-something, black-haired menace stared at Dylan smugly and wiped his mouth before responding. "That's because you saw my face at Hope Fellowship several years ago. I sat in some of your services, and not once did you say hello. Never shook my hand. Nothing."

Dylan relied on his sarcasm to carry him through the uncomfortable encounter. "Maybe that's because your face was radiating death vibes, perhaps?" After the trials and hardships that Dylan experienced over the last five years, there was a sliver of his compassion that gave way to sarcasm. His desire to be kind was occasionally challenged.

The man slammed his fist on the table. "You sorry, no good..."

Dylan quickly interrupted, holding his hands up in surrender.

"Look! I'm sorry I failed you so deeply. I'm sorry I hurt you in any way, but that's no reason to sit here, glaring at me and my family years later. And frankly, sir, I've been through hell too. Obviously, you've been through some hell yourself. I came over here to find out your name. Is that too much to ask? What's your name?"

The man was taken aback. He reluctantly replied, "I'm Mark. I came to your church because I needed help for my family. I was there just long enough to find out that you couldn't even manage your own family. Imagine that, preacher," he sneered bitterly.

Compassion washed over Dylan's anger. "I'm sorry to hear that, Mark. Believe me, I have many regrets. And yeah, I suppose I couldn't 'manage' my own family. But look," he motioned toward Lynette. "I think I've been given a second chance. I hope you'd give me one too."

The man shook his head. "I don't know. Looks to me like you've got a mess. That's Owen Smith's baby. And that's his wife."

His words seared Dylan's entire being. Anger threatened to envelop every cell of his body. *God, help me. I'm losing it.* He mustered up a controlled response. "That may be his child, but she's no longer his wife. And maybe the fact that he isn't man enough to be a father to his child negates his fatherhood. That's my wife and my child that you keep glaring at. If you're a friend of Owen's, you let him know that. And if that's you throwing rocks at my house and leaving threatening messages, you'd better stop before you end up in jail."

The man looked puzzled. "I'm not throwing rocks or leaving messages." Mark appeared half-delighted that he got under the preacher's skin. "And I don't know Owen."

Dylan questioned, "Then why did you mention his name?"

Mark cleared his throat. "He and I have a mutual friend. I know the story of that romance," he scoffed with a smirk on his face.

Dylan fought to maintain control of his anger. Being reminded of Owen and Lynette's "happy days" was more than he could handle. Dylan begged his body not to punch the man. Instead, he spoke firmly with control. "That was no romance. That was deception, the work of a womanizer."

Mark slightly admired Dylan's strength, but his own bitterness caused him to cut the preacher's soul as much as he could.

"Deception may be short-lived, but the rude awakening comes with circumstances that can never be changed, doesn't it?"

Dylan's jaw tightened. "You have a sick need to inflict pain. I'm done here."

He returned to Lynette who watched prayerfully, afraid to interfere due to Asa's presence.

Noting the struggle on his face, Lynette was worried. "Dylan, what the heck was that?"

He placed his elbows on the table, resting his forehead in his hands. He lamented, "It's amazing how you can unknowingly fail someone, and years later, the pain is still so fresh. I never knew the danger involved with being a pastor."

"What do you mean, Dylan?"

He sighed. "Apparently, all it takes is failure to shake someone's hand or say hello. If you miss doing that, you've destroyed someone's life. Thank God I'm out of the ministry!"

She reached for his hand. "Look, we came here to relive good times. Don't let anyone steal that away."

He shook his head with doubt. "Maybe I've ruined it all, Lynette. I failed you. I failed the church, a whole congregation, and an entire town. Five years later, there's still fallout."

She snapped her fingers in his face. "Snap out of it, Dylan Vanberg. I refuse to let you spiral down. We're going to have a nice dinner and we're going to enjoy every second of it."

He couldn't seem to resist the gravitational pull of fear. "Maybe we should leave Holly."

At that, Lynette promptly stood and walked over to Mark, pouring words out with the speed of a machine gun. "Hey. I'm Lynette Vanberg." She held out her hand. "And you're Mark? Well, Mark. I'm really sorry we offended you many years ago. Are you just going to stare at my hand or shake it?"

She grabbed his hand. "You'll be happy to know we no longer

work in the church, therefore we can't disappoint you again. More importantly, you've sorely disappointed me today. You see, Dylan and I have been living like hermits, trying to figure life out and deal with a ton of stress. All we wanted was a pleasant time in a place that used to bring us joy, but instead, we ran into you. My husband came over here to befriend you, and you treated him like a piece of crap. Now he can't seem to enjoy the meal we hoped for and you've caused him to question his entire existence. I'd appreciate an apology so we can move forward and eat because," she slammed her fist on the table, "I'm tired, I'm frustrated, and I'm starving!"

Mark stared at Lynette with amused respect. "Okay, okay. I surrender. I've got to give you credit, lady. I admire your militant pursuit of a good time."

Mark stood, marching his way toward Dylan with an apology. "Sir, I am truly sorry. Please, for the sake of this strong woman, enjoy your meal and forget about what I said."

Dylan shook his hand, still trying to release himself from the grip of regret. "I'm sorry too, Mark."

The stranger that carried himself like a villain ready for revenge quickly transformed into a kinder individual. His face relaxed. "By the way, you mentioned someone threatening you?"

Dylan nodded.

"Maybe I can help you find the culprit," Mark offered.

Dylan was surprised and willing to listen. "Oh? How's that?"

"I know someone who's been threatened by you for years. I'll keep an eye out for you."

Dylan was intrigued. "Threatened by me? How could I be a threat?"

The man shrugged. "Believe it or not, man."

Dylan demanded, "What's his name? Who is it?"

The man calmly answered, "Don't worry about that right now.

I'll have a chat with him. If it's him that's messing with you, I'll get it settled. I know where to find you."

Dylan felt left out of the loop. "Look, I have no idea what you're talking about. I'm not aware of any enemies. If I did something to make someone that angry, I'm fully unaware of what I did, so whoever you're talking about, please let them know. I'm willing to meet and talk about it, whatever it is."

"I doubt that'll be necessary."

Lynette smiled at Mark. "Thanks. We appreciate your help."

"Yes, ma'am. I've gotta be going now." With that, the man left.

Dylan's face revealed both confused frustration and intrigue. "What just happened?"

Lynette grinned. "You just got your peaceful meal. May we resume?"

He shook his head in awe of the strange encounter. Despite the questions he had, one thing stood out to him. "Lynette, you called me 'husband.' And you told him your name was Lynette Vanberg." He smiled, pleased.

She tilted her head with a grin. "Yeah, I know. So what? That's who I am," she said confidently.

He smiled. "That makes me happy."

Lynette spoke warmly. "Me too."

Chapter Nine

DYLAN SAT ON HIS OLD, CREAKY PORCH SWING, breathing in the crisp evening air. Lynette had left with little Asa in tow for a visit with sweet, merciful Marcy. Dylan was glad that Lynette knew a kind and mature woman in whom she could confide without fear of rejection. *Father, give Lynette a good day and encourage her. Please help us heal.* It was a prayer he repeated multiple times per day. He shook his head as he pondered the mess of their circumstances. The irony of redemption in the middle of chaos made him want to laugh and cry at the same time.

Dylan stared at the front yard, remembering that day just over five years ago. He was haunted by visions of ghostly images of himself falling to his knees in the grass, begging his wife not to leave. He wondered how a man could be totally engulfed by the one thing that really mattered, so much so that he would make a fool of himself in front of his neighbors. He supposed that love and desperation carried the power to strip a soul bare, revealing its awkwardness and imperfections. Remembering those moments stabbed him in the gut, taking his breath away momentarily. *Why does it still hurt so much? Will the pain ever go away?* His jaw tightened in an effort to stay in the present. *Forget the past.* In Lynette's absence, he wrestled the demons triggered by unwanted memories. Being apart from her felt too familiar, too much like the

THE WINDOWS OF HOLLY

times he would rather forget.

Dylan needed a distraction, and certainly a sweet one at that. He stood from the old swing and shuffled his feet across the wooden porch, already imagining the thing that soothed him: the smell of freshly brewed tea. His mouth watered in anticipation of that amber liquid mixed with a bit of sugar. *Straight from Heaven, it is.*

As he approached the tea drawer, he made note of the broken fleur-de-lis handle. *There's still so much to fix around here.* The weight of broken things pressed on his heart. "At least it still functions," he muttered. He slid the drawer open and lifted his two favorite teas to his nose. English breakfast tea and Earl Grey. The mix was comfort to his soul. "It's a good thing I don't like alcohol." He shook his head. "I'd be a mess."

He placed the teakettle over the fire, glad to be alone in this ritual of pain relief. A sharp knock on the door interrupted his flow. "Oh man," he sighed. He reluctantly made his way to the door, trying to muster up a jubilant greeting for the unknown visitor. Upon opening the door, it took him a few seconds to recognize the woman standing before him.

"Dylan!" She leapt toward him, wrapping her arms around his neck.

"Kelsey?" He hoped he remembered her name correctly.

With her hands on his shoulders, she threw her head back, smiling, and slurred, "You remember me!"

Oh great. She's drunk.

She leaned into him. "Preacher man, I've missed you. We never got to finish what we started." She grabbed his head and pressed her lips into his. Dylan struggled to push her away. "Aw, c'mon, Dylan. Let it go, baby."

"Kelsey! Stop!" He firmly pushed her shoulders away from his, but her grip around his head was too strong. "Kelsey, stop it!"

96

Dylan reached for her arms, attempting to pry her off. She pressed her red high heel against the doorframe, kicking her body weight into him. Losing his balance, Dylan fell backwards with Kelsey on top of him.

She laughed hysterically. "Oh, baby. I knew you'd be excited to see me." Shocked by the fall, Dylan tried to gather his thoughts and devise a plan of action. "C'mon, preacher man. Let's go to your room."

Breathing heavily with frustration, Dylan tried to push her away once more. "Kelsey, that's enough!" Kelsey moved from laughter to sudden, intense anger. Still lying on top of Dylan, she looked him in the face, pointing her finger. "Don't you dare push me away. I'll get up when I'm ready!" Once again, she pressed her lips onto his mouth. Dylan turned his head away from her, afraid that if he unleashed his fury, he'd injure the woman and be held liable.

He tried to reason as she kissed him. He turned his head to the left and right, working to avoid her advances. "Kelsey, let's talk. Just let me up and we'll talk."

Kelsey lifted her hand and slapped him across his face. "Talk? I say a little less conversation and a little more action." She began singing the old song. "All this aggravation ain't satisfactioning me." She began laughing, rolling off of him. "Oh, preacher."

Jumping to his feet, Dylan barked, "Stop calling me preacher!"

Kelsey sat up on the floor, hair disheveled, lipstick smeared. In the process of making his escape, her black skirt had made its way up her thighs. As Dylan stood, huffing and puffing from the shock of it all, he looked up, door wide open, to see a black sports car in front of his house. As soon as he saw the car, the driver peeled out. "Great! Just great, Kelsey. You made a spectacle for the neighborhood to see!" He slammed the door closed and picked up his cell phone from the sofa.

THE WINDOWS OF HOLLY

"Who are you calling, Dylan? Don't call the police," she slurred.

He tried hard to calm himself, but his face burned red with frustration. "I'm not calling the police!"

"Who are you calling?" Kelsey began to whimper.

He spoke into his phone hurriedly. "Jackson! Thank God you answered! Can you come over immediately?" A look of relief flooded Dylan's face. "Thanks, man." He hung up.

Kelsey whimpered like a spoiled child. "Dylan, I'm sorry. I'm sorry. I'll leave."

"Look at you, Kelsey. You're totally drunk! How did you even get here? I can't let you leave. You'll end up killing someone or yourself! And what are you doing in Holly? I haven't seen you in, I don't know, a year? Two...maybe three years? I can't even remember how long ago!" The details of the last five years bled together in his memory. "Why are you here?"

Kelsey stood up slowly, brushing her hair from her face. She slurred, "I was at my friend's bridal shower. She lives in Holly. Isn't that funny?" She mustered up a chuckle.

Dylan sighed. "You being here like this is not funny."

The teakettle whistled. Dylan quickly ran to shut it off.

Jackson knocked on the door. Dylan ran from sound to sound, addressing the demands. Jackson's knock was a welcomed demand.

Kelsey looked surprised. "Your friend is here already? That was fast!"

Dylan huffed, "He lives across the street." Opening the door, he sighed with relief. "Thanks for coming, man."

Jackson nodded. "No problem. What's going on?"

Dylan pointed at Kelsey, who was standing in a stupor, gazing at Jackson with a slight grin.

She whistled. "Mmhm. Well, who are you, handsome?" She

walked toward Jackson with her hand outstretched.

Dylan intercepted. "Sit down, Kelsey."

Turning his attention toward Jackson, he explained, "This is the woman from Marshall City I told you about. You know, the date night?"

Jackson raised his eyebrows. "Oh?"

Dylan continued, "She just showed up here, drunk out of her mind. I want her to leave, but obviously, she can't even drive. I don't know how she even made it here."

Kelsey giggled. "Drive? I didn't drive here, silly. My friend dropped me off."

Dylan's face remained red with irritation. "You don't just drop in on people unannounced, Kelsey. There's a reason I never called you back." He shook his head. "I needed to get my head straight and move on. I have a life. You have a life, and you need to move on."

She held her mischievous smile. "Yeah, yeah, yeah." She wobbled her head flippantly. "I'm here having fun and I thought you'd make it a bit more exciting`. You remember that night, Dylan? Kissing me? Touching me?"

Before she could finish her speech, Dylan interrupted, firmly. "Call your friend and tell her to pick you up right now."

She rolled her eyes. "Aw, man. Always the party pooper, Dylan. I see that Mr. Perfect is still without a wedding ring. It's no wonder." Drunkenness prompted her relentless taunting. Her eyes opened wide. "Oh, I get it. You're gay. I could turn you," she winked.

Ignoring her efforts to provoke a response, he stayed on task. "Call your friend to pick you up right now. If you don't, I'm calling the police."

She sighed, reclining on the sofa, positioned dramatically as a woman in distress. "Oh, Romeo, where art thou? All right, Dylan

THE WINDOWS OF HOLLY

Vanberg," she sighed. She reached into her black, sparkly clutch to retrieve her phone. "But it's your loss."

Jackson stood, speechless. As his eyes caught Dylan's intense gaze, he couldn't help but grin. Something about their childlike camaraderie broke Dylan's frustration. Humor seeped into the folds of the situation, and unable to hold it in, they burst into laughter simultaneously.

Jackson attempted to maintain a level of sensitivity, but he was overtaken by the hilarity of the ridiculous dramas that seemed to be part of Dylan's life. "I'm sorry, dude," he laughed. "But how does all this crazy stuff happen to you?"

Dylan threw his hands in the air. "I don't know, man! I don't know."

Kelsey stared at them, slightly offended. "Well, I'm glad I could give you a good laugh." She dialed her friend to get a ride.

Dylan looked into the kitchen. "All I wanted was a peaceful, reflective evening with a glass of tea. And . . .," he stretched his hands out toward Kelsey, "here ya go."

At that moment, Lynette walked in the door with Asa. Her eyes fell on Kelsey reclining on the sofa with smeared, red lipstick, tight black skirt, and her seemingly permanent mischievous grin. Lynette looked at Dylan, taking note of the red lipstick rubbed across his mouth. His hair was sticking up in various places. Her eyes turned toward Jackson, who watched with eagerness to see how things would play out.

"Lynette!" Dylan exclaimed before she could bring herself to ask what was going on. "You're back."

As her eyes surveyed the scene, she looked confused.

Knowing she needed an explanation, Dylan explained, "Lynnie, this is Kelsey." He leaned in close to Lynette's ear, not wanting to say it out loud. "The date I told you about."

Without missing a beat, she blurted, "The one you made out

with?"

He answered reluctantly. "Yes." He desperately wanted to change the subject. "You just left a few minutes ago. What are you doing back so soon?"

"Well, Dylan," she responded half sarcastically, confused by the looks of things. "I forgot the diaper bag and my cell phone, so I came to get it. Apparently, it doesn't take you but a few minutes to, well," she paused. "I don't know what. So you and Kelsey are together?" She squinted her eyes in confusion as she placed Asa's carrier on the floor.

Dylan replied quickly. "No! I haven't seen her since that night." He was both desperate to get the point across that he was not involved with Kelsey, yet he was slightly pleased to hear a hint of jealousy in Lynette's voice.

Lynette reached for Dylan's face, wiping lipstick from the corner of his mouth. "You must have missed her."

Kelsey piped up with garbled words. "Hey, chick. First of all, I didn't know he was with anyone, and secondly, he's not interested in me." She rolled her eyes to make light of it. "I'll be leaving shortly. Oh, and I'm Kelsey." She touched her chest like Tarzan trying to communicate his name.

Dylan chimed in. "This is my ex-wife, soon-to-be wife, Lynette."

Kelsey's eyes widened in awe as a smile crept over her face. "Well, that's the sweetest thing I've ever seen. Dylan Vanberg, you got your woman back!" She aimed her finger at him like a gun. "Ka-pow! Good for you. And I see you two made a baby."

Her words stung Dylan's heart. *I wish he was mine.*

Kelsey continued, "Lynette, I can't blame you for coming back. Dylan here is like the king of kisses. That's why I stopped by, but he doused the fire. Pshhh. Just like that." She flung her arms in the air. "Slung the whole bucket. Water everywhere." She grabbed her stomach. "I think I might be sick."

Jackson helped her up, ushering her to the bathroom.

Dylan muttered, "She'd better not make a mess in there." He turned his eyes toward Lynette, hoping she would understand the fiasco that was unexpectedly set before her.

Lynette pursed her lips tightly, unsure of what she was feeling. As her eyes studied Dylan's lipstick-smeared face, she smirked.

Dylan wasn't sure what emotion he should be prepared to receive. "What are you thinking?" he asked.

Lynette began to chuckle, using her hand to wipe the color from his face. "You, sir, lead a most dramatic life." She pulled a tissue from the diaper bag to clean his lips. "I wanted to tease you about the kind of woman you picked, but then I remembered my choice in Owen, so I have no place to talk. I can't cast any judgment."

He threw his hands in the air. "And all I wanted was tea! Peace and quiet and tea, for the love of God! But this is what I got instead. I literally put the water on for tea when she knocked. She blew my whole evening."

Lynette's adoration for her ex-husband instantly expanded. She placed her hands on his cheeks and drew him in for a long, gentle kiss. Dylan melted into her. He pushed his hands through her hair, pulling her head closer, longing to make up for the lost years. After a minute, Lynette withdrew. "My God. She's right."

"Who's right?"

She smiled. "Kelsey said you're the king of kisses. It's true."

Dylan stroked her hair. "That's the corniest thing I've ever heard."

She pinched his cheek. "You always were the best." She winced at her own words. *I forfeited so much. Five years lost.* She tried to brush the thought away. "I'll get you that tea."

He smiled. "You're a saint."

As Dylan and Lynette turned to make their way into the kitchen, they caught sight of their image in a mirror. Lynette stopped him. "Look, Dylan. Look at us." They gazed at the mirror. Her chin trembled beneath her smile. "I never thought I'd see us together again, yet here we are. Amazing."

Dylan witnessed the melting of her heart, the longing of her soul. "It's as it should be." He rested his head on hers. "Perhaps with a heck of a lot of baggage, but I think we'll be okay."

A grin painted Lynette's face. "Us," she giggled. "And you with another woman's lipstick all over your face." They laughed hysterically. "Is this really our life? Where are the hidden cameras? This can't be real."

He smacked her backside. "I'm down with this life."

Jackson hollered from the hallway, "Dude! I hear her pukin' in there! I'm sorry, but I don't think I can handle this." Jackson stumbled into the kitchen as if he'd been shot. "I have a weak stomach. Whatever Kelsey's releasing in your bathroom, I sure hope it lands in the toilet. There's no way I'm going in there, man."

Dylan joked, "But that's what friends are for, Jackson." He winked. "Right?"

Jackson shook his head adamantly. "Heck no."

Dylan grinned. "Greater love hath no man than this, that a man lay down his life for his friends."

Jackson grabbed his stomach. "Well, I just lost my religion. Her sounds of regurgitation are enough to make anyone forget there's a good God above."

Lynette broke into laughter. "I don't know. The chaos in this household is evidence that He holds all things together, in my opinion. If it wasn't for Him, none of us would be here right now." She delighted herself in the truth. "I think we're evidence of a good God."

THE WINDOWS OF HOLLY

As Dylan resumed the tea making he'd begun before Kelsey's arrival, he quipped, "Held together like a smashed piece of pottery with super glue. No, it's more like Crazy Glue to keep this crazy life intact." The amusement on his face caused his eyes to shine. "With as much glue as we require, we're definitely flammable."

Lynette cringed at his words. She watched him as he put the tea bags to his nose, breathing in the aroma. *Is my return too much for him?* She wondered whether or not his quips carried a hint of resentment.

Catching her eyes, he recognized a deep sadness. His smile disappeared.

Dylan wondered, "Something wrong, Lynette?"

She shrugged. "I'm sorry for all the mess."

He assured her, "It's nothing." But she knew it was everything. "Don't go there again."

Jackson felt like an intruder being present, so he decided to dismiss himself from the kitchen. "I'm going to check on Kelsey. Pray that I don't throw up." He left the room.

Lynette moved toward Dylan as he twirled the tea bags around on their strings, waiting for the water to boil. "Hey." She touched his arm. "I've given you a lot to be angry about, so I'm not going to be surprised one bit when that anger surfaces. You have the freedom to be angry, but if my presence is ever too painful for you, just tell me. If my presence makes you angrier..."

Dylan interrupted. "Stop. Your presence is pleasure. As far as being angry goes, it's not because you're here. It's mostly anger at myself for being so darned blind in the beginning. I hate the man I used to be."

She frowned. "The man you used to be was wonderful. The man you are now is amazing and beautiful in more ways than I ever knew. Don't hate yourself." She sighed. "If anyone should hate themself, it's me. I hate who I used to be."

104

Dylan breathed out heavily, letting the weight of self-hatred disintegrate into the air. He recognized the danger zone of self-loathing and knew it would only produce death. "We shouldn't let this feeling bring us down. You know that whole thing about, 'if you hate your brother or sister, you're a murderer?' I suppose if that pertains to hating self, then we're murderers of ourselves, right?"

Lynette raised her eyebrows in wonder. "I suppose. Except that we're already dead, right?"

"What do you mean?" Dylan cracked his knuckles.

She recalled the messages that Dylan preached shortly before their marriage imploded. "Well, you know that whole thing, 'I've been crucified with Christ. It's no longer I who lives, but Christ who lives in me.' Is that how it goes?"

"Yep."

She communicated her theological thought. "So if that's true, then you can't exactly murder yourself with your hatred, but it'd be more like you're murdering Christ since He's the one living in you?"

His eyes flashed with surprise. "Whoa! That's a pretty harsh way to put it. I don't know. I'd have to think on that one."

She continued, "It sounds extreme, but if He really lives in us, then it would make sense that to hate ourselves is like treating Jesus with hate."

He stared in thought. "You've got some wild thoughts in that head of yours." He pondered her words, adding, "Humanity already killed Him once. He can't be murdered again. He conquered death once and for all."

She replied in deep thought, "True. So maybe our self-hatred isn't a murder of God, so to speak, but it's certainly an assault on Him. To hate yourself would be to deny who He is and what He's done. If He chose to live among humanity and subject Himself to

THE WINDOWS OF HOLLY

their violence and hatred once, you'd think He'd choose to remain far away from them, yet He chose humanity again by deciding to live within us. He lives within our chaos, but above it." She tilted her head inquisitively. "Blows my mind. What kind of crazy, messed-up love is that?"

Dylan's mouth revealed his amused delight. "It's the kind of crazy love that has us standing here right now, in chaos, in our own home, where my one-date-woman shows up and literally attacks me." He shook his head. "I mean, in walks my ex-wife with her son who's not mine. Yet it's all ours. Our story. Our home. Our life. And that baby boy is even ours somehow." He placed his hands over his temples. "Sometimes I'm so overwhelmed with gratitude for where we're at and sometimes I just want to crumple up in a ball and cry my soul out. It's ironic. The cocktail of life, I guess. Joy mixed with pain. Pleasure mixed with disappointment." Dylan worked hard to keep amusement above sadness. "Kinda makes you crazy drunk on life," he laughed. "But I'm thankful for it, I suppose. The inhibitions are gone. The façades are gone. My heart is awake, painfully awake. I feel things I've never felt before. It's good for me, you know?"

Listening to Dylan reveal his array of emotions made Lynette glad for his vulnerability, yet she swallowed hard to keep guilt and shame from arresting her soul. She understood the gratitude that Dylan spoke of, and she understood the sting as well. *Where is your sting, oh death? I think I may have found it. Regret. Utter regret that I cannot change. And I chose it.* She wished she could pull Dylan inside herself and saturate him in everything that was good. *Is it possible for the offender to become the protector and nurturer? Can the prison become the place of freedom?* Lynette wrapped her arms around Dylan, burying her face in his chest. "I promise I will never hurt you again, Dylan Vanberg." Her words flowed like a rush of life into his chest, crumbling rocky terrain and kissing his wounds with compassion.

He nodded. "And I'll do my best to never cause you to feel alone again."

As the teakettle whistled, the doorbell rang. "The sounds of freedom," Dylan exclaimed. One's for tea and the other's for the removal of Kelsey. Yes!" He laid a celebratory kiss on Lynette's lips. "And hey. No more self-loathing. Okay?" She agreed.

Chapter Ten

THE TOWN OF HOLLY RESTED like a neatly decorated Christmas village in a glass bubble, silent and still. Frosty air breathed gently across the dark landscape, beckoning sleepers to dream. Porch swings were empty, only holding the memories of the day that had passed. Christmas lights twinkled along porch railings and rooftops, flickering hope.

Jackson and Lucy were wrapped together in her favorite plaid, flannel blanket. She had fallen asleep daydreaming about the moment she would meet her baby face-to-face. "Just a few more months," she'd declared to Jackson with excitement, before falling into a deep, happy sleep.

Across the road, Dylan and Lynette slept in an embrace, letting the cares of the world slip away. They had discussed what others might think of them staying in the same home, but they decided their marriage vows from years prior were enough to keep their covenant intact even though paper certificates would say otherwise. Besides, she was still early post-baby, and they were committed to healthy decisions. "The Father knows our hearts and that's all that matters," Dylan assured her. "I never renounced my vows. That's how I see it."

His words filled her soul with bliss as she allowed slumber to overtake her. Dylan pondered the power of redemption and renewal as he fell quickly into a dream world.

As he drifted into another dimension, Dylan carefully stepped on the fallen leaves beneath his feet, trying to be quiet as he inched forward to find the voice that called his name. As the foggy sky began to darken, the forest seemed to embrace him, inviting him to come further.

"See in Me," a voice echoed. "Come and see." Multicolored leaves cracked as he walked into a small, circular clearing. His eyes fell upon an unusual sight. A shaft of golden light pierced through the scraggly, tall pines, creating a spotlight on the ground. Inside the light stood the one whose voice Dylan heard. The silhouette of a man came into sight. He studied the man from head-to-toe. Shoulder-length brown hair flowed down his back, and he wore a long-sleeved shirt which appeared to sparkle like multicolored, stained glass. Light flashed within the glassy apparel. Dylan noticed the man's loose, khaki pants tucked into black combat boots. *Who is this odd person?*

The man stood facing an unusually large artist's canvas that rested on a wooden easel. The canvas held a glorious picture of majestic, colorful mountains towering above a crystal-clear river that flowed into a breathtaking waterfall. The waters poured into a multi-colored stream of liquid, casting a rainbow over the river, its colors reflected in the sky above.

The man reached his hand toward the canvas and uttered words that Dylan couldn't understand. At the sound of his voice, colors swirled upon the canvas. The picture shifted and changed. Dylan held his breath in awe. *Is this man actually painting with his words?*

Dylan continued watching as the man created with his breath. After a minute or two, the man stepped back and crossed his arms as he studied his creation. "Yes," he uttered. "It is good. Very good!" He tilted his head back and began to laugh. He looked at his painting with sincere admiration. "You're absolutely perfect! You are mine. I am yours. How beautiful you are!"

The man slowly stepped toward his painting. Leaning forward, he placed his hands on his knees, bending toward the canvas and breathed on it. Stepping back, he laughed with pure pleasure. Instantly, the painting began to move. Every image on the canvas became fully alive and three-dimensional: breathing, moving, and pulsing with life. The man was overjoyed. He began to spin around, arms spread wide, and face tilted upward, as he declared, "In our image and after our likeness!" Dylan couldn't see his face clearly, but he knew the man was smiling. "All of this is yours," he spoke to the painting.

Beautiful, bright colors shot out from the canvas like laser beams. They swirled into multiple rainbows and began to take form, stretching into the woods. Sounds of rushing waters rustled through the trees. Jewels of many colors appeared, covering every inch of the forest floor. The pine trees seemed to awaken. The dirt moved, seeming to breathe beneath the glimmering beauty. Everything was alive and aware of another realm.

The man stood, surrounded by living color that erupted from his painting. Dylan hid behind a tree, peering out at the spectacle, breathless with excitement. A flood of peace filled him with joy! He placed his hand over his mouth to hide the laughter that erupted from his lips. *What is this bliss?*

He relished the ecstasy until a screech pierced through the air. Dylan grabbed his ears, trying to protect himself from the painful sound. The screeching continued for a few seconds, leaving his heart and his head pounding. Terror struck his heart as he watched the swirling rainbows transform into blackness. First gray and then black. Everything within the painting began to fade as it pulled the gray into itself. Seemingly reaching for darkness, inviting it in, the canvas heaved like a monster, sucking everything back into itself.

THE WINDOWS OF HOLLY

The multidimensional life was now trapped inside the canvas, pulsing slowly, like a dying heart.

The artist stood firm, reaching his hands toward the canvas. He spoke gently. "Don't leave me, my love. I'll never forsake you." The man turned his body slightly. Dylan saw tears falling from his cheek. The man fell to his knees, keeping his eyes locked on his creation. "All you are is all of me. The darkness is not part of us. Why do you hide?"

The canvas appeared to struggle for breath as tornadoes of gray and black twisted inside it. The edges oozed something black, like grease and oil, which fell onto the ground. The colorful gemstones and majestic mountains were hidden by the darkness. The dirt became lifeless. The sky darkened, and there was stillness, then heaving.

"Just be still and know..." the man uttered. Dylan couldn't hear everything he whispered at the painting, but he felt the man's longing for his creation. Dylan's heart was overwhelmed with grief. He continued to watch. The man stared at his painting, watching with sadness and compassion. *It's like love itself staring into the face of death.* The canvas pulsed, as if bitten and now infused with anger, resentment, and hatred.

As the black venom continued spilling out, the dirt, trees and rocks crackled with a sizzling sound as they burned away beneath the poison. Dylan realized the painting was killing the forest, and if it continued flowing out, everything would die. He jumped out from behind the tree and yelled at the artist, "Do something! Destroy it before it destroys us!" But the artist remained still and quiet.

"You have to do something now!" Dylan's eyes were filled with fear, and he was losing his breath to the threat. "Listen to me! Can't you hear me?" Dylan ran in front of the man and knelt before him, pleading. As he looked into his eyes, he was instantly captivated by immense pools of peace that engulfed him with love. Dylan began to weep, overcome by the light that filled his soul. In that moment, everything was perfect. Everything was good. The pains of life were forgotten.

The man placed his hands on Dylan's cheeks and he pressed his forehead to Dylan's forehead. Face-to-face. He wept tears of relief that his mind couldn't understand, yet his heart understood.

The man said, "This is the way, Dylan. See in Me."

As waves of wholeness melted into Dylan's heart, he found himself on his back on the forest floor, peering into the gray sky above. He was losing his focus on the artist and canvas as the world around him became narrow and hazy. His attention was drawn to the heavens. He felt himself lifting into the sky, far above the earth, yet somehow, still attached to the life he had always known.

As he ascended, he was aware of an indescribable presence. It was a tangible power, the most joyful, perfect love he'd ever felt. His body trembled in its presence, not from fear, but from being absorbed in an invisible substance beyond understanding. This substance was unlike anything he'd ever experienced. It was love. Pure, perfect love.

The pain of recent years diminished into the light. The demons that tormented his soul were silenced. The roar of rage became a faint cry. The churning turmoil that existed in his soul became a gentle river.

Dylan became aware of three beings leaning over him, peering into his soul. He felt their warmth and heard their voices and laughter, yet he couldn't see their faces clearly. Their hazy forms were encircled by brightness.

Dylan sensed the world far behind him, and it seemed tiny in comparison to this new realm that enveloped him. The voices spoke of love. Although he lacked clarity, lost in a dream world,

THE WINDOWS OF HOLLY

he knew he was being celebrated. His arrival brought joy to the beings that surrounded him.

For a brief moment, he remembered the pain that lay below him on the spinning globe, but the memory of it was wiped away as a hand gently entered his chest. "Watch this," a voice said. The sound of a fast-moving river surrounded his head and warm waters purged his heart. There was no pain. Just peace. The waters flowed, bringing relief and healing. Occasionally, a painful memory would thrust its way into his mind and heart, but as quickly as it came, the waters washed it away. The debris and marks of life's disappointments became light as a feather, completely obliterated by an indescribable love.

Waves of love swept away darkness that he didn't know existed within him. Claps of thunder sounded as anger's bite broke its hold. Tentacles of bitterness slowly shriveled away, unlocking their grip on his bones. Immense love filled his entire being, saturating the deepest places of his heart. A rush of life shot through Dylan's veins, awakening his spirit to the reality of a life he never imagined existed.

As healing waters rushed through his heart, every battle scar of his soul vanished and the broken shards of betrayal were pushed out, leaving his body vibrating with light. Like waking from anesthesia, his awareness painted a blurry picture of three people laughing hysterically.

Dylan felt his body descending back into the forest. He slowly opened his eyes and found himself face-to-face with the odd artist who was still pressing his forehead to Dylan's. "This is the way," the man said. He breathed on Dylan's face. The artist stepped away and faced his raging canvas that had been consumed by darkness.

Dylan sat up slowly, watching in awe, while fighting fear that threatened to rise inside of him. The canvas, still swirling like an

114

angry hurricane, moved toward the artist, blowing venom at its creator. The man threw his arms wide, and with an embrace, he surrendered to the painting, allowing it to devour him completely. "No! No!" Dylan screamed, with tears pouring from his eyes.

Like a ball of fire and rage, the painting poured out its wrath on the man who gave it breath. Dylan wept as he watched him absorb the darkness. The ball of fire expanded. Black liquid poured from the angry sphere. As it wrapped its arms around the man's body, suddenly, a flash of light illuminated the whole forest. Dylan blinked his eyes, waiting for his sight to return.

Soon, Dylan's eyes adjusted, and he watched as the man's hands became red with blood. Droplets of red fell from his forehead. The artist, breathing hard, grabbed each side of the canvas with his hands and pulled the painting into his chest until it disappeared. As the artist became one with his creation, the leaves on the forest floor swirled around them, the trees swayed, and the ground shook.

The air shifted as silence penetrated the forest. Dylan directed his attention to the man who barely moved beneath the weight of the painting he had drawn into himself. The man opened his arms, revealing the canvas. It became quiet and still. The man sat up, running his hands over every inch of the painting, admiring the textures and designs that he'd created.

As he touched the canvas, beauty returned. Darkness began to fade, color returned, and it morphed into its original form. The artist inhaled, pulling the violence from it, into his lungs. Light was in his mouth as he spoke, "You have died with me. Now you are raised with me."

Peace rested upon the landscape. A towering pine tree stood before him. It opened its arms like an easel, and the man rested the painting there. "Now you and I are one," the man said. Once again, life and beauty were living and moving, breathing within

THE WINDOWS OF HOLLY

and from the canvas as it took its place in the forest.

Birds of every kind filled the trees. Dylan heard sounds coming from the woods that surrounded them. He turned to see what it was. Moving quietly through the forest, animals approached the scene in joyful awe of the man and his painting. "This is unbelievable," Dylan mumbled to himself. All of nature seemed to celebrate what had happened.

The scene began to fade away from Dylan's vision. He felt himself being pulled backwards, *into oblivion,* he thought. He wanted nothing more than to stay in this place, the place where the artist lived in the forest, but he was carried away by a force that he couldn't resist. Blurry shapes appeared to move as he fought to make his eyes focus. As his vision cleared, his bedroom ceiling came into view. No forest. No artist. *Dear God, what was that?*

Dylan sat up in bed, breathing hard. His movement stirred Lynette awake. "Dylan, what's going on?"

"Oh my gosh. I just had the craziest dream." His bare chest rose and fell rapidly. "It was amazing."

Lynette turned aside to retrieve her bedside journal and pen. "Here. Write it down before you forget it." She plopped the journal in his lap. "Gotta catch it while it's fresh. Trust me. If you don't write it down, you'll forget it by morning."

"Don't you wanna hear the dream?" He was desperate to share the awesome experience.

She could barely keep her eyes open. "I do, babe. But I'm so exhausted, I'm afraid I'll fall asleep while you're talking. Write it down and you can read it to me in the morning." She kissed his cheek and plopped her head down on the pillow.

Dylan carried the journal into the kitchen, fully awake, infused with energy from the supernatural experience. He poured himself a glass of water. "What a freaky dream," he mumbled to himself.

He put his pen to the paper, recording every vivid detail. The

116

dream was so real, he could easily recall every moment and emotion it evoked. Tears began to stream down his cheeks as he recorded each profound scene. His heart was drawn like a magnet to the mysterious man, the artist, the creator. Dylan knew him to be God. "See in Me." Those words were seared into Dylan's being, challenging him to see differently. He knew it wasn't about seeing into the creator, as if looking into someone, but it was about seeing as if Dylan were the creator, seeing as the artist sees. *See in Me.* Dylan knew there was something about union with the great Spirit, the one God. *I live in Him. I breathe in Him. I'm alive in Him, therefore I can see in Him.* "God, what does that fully mean, to see in You?"

Visions of Owen flashed before him. He couldn't comprehend the strange sensation of peace that visited his soul this night. It was a deep and profound peace that seemed to erase the dis-ease of betrayal and soothe the heartbreak and trauma that Owen had inflicted upon his soul. In that moment, he saw Owen as the canvas that became dark. When he pondered the passionate desire of the artist to see his painting exist in color, life, wholeness, and beauty, he knew that he, too, must desire the same.

He knew he was vulnerable to darkness and destruction if he allowed himself to be bitter. Dylan had witnessed many who chose that path. It wasn't worth paying the price. "I forgive you, Owen." Hearing himself say those undeserving words sent waves of liquid peace through his being. He knew he would need to choose those words regularly in the years to come.

His thoughts turned toward Lynette. "I choose to see Lynette in You, God. I see You in her." In his mind, he saw her face and watched as it morphed into a child's face. Bright-blue eyes revealed a trace of loneliness, yet a shining smile exposed childlike wonder and willingness to do good in the world. Dylan's heart melted as he saw his bride as an innocent little girl.

THE WINDOWS OF HOLLY

Compassion filled his heart for the woman he loved. *Forgive me for ever letting her feel alone.* "Never again," he promised out loud.

Suddenly, a thud from outside grabbed his attention. "Again?" Dylan quickly ran to the front door. He whipped the door open just in time to see a hoodie-wearing figure jump into a black sports car. Dylan grabbed his car keys from the key holder and darted for "Old Blue." *I knew I loved this car,* he thought as the V8 engine responded to the pressing of his foot.

The red taillights of the offender disappeared as they turned off Main Street. Dylan increased his speed. "You're not getting away!" He completely forgot the dream that had touched him deeply. His attention was turned to capturing his enemy. After living in Holly for over a decade, Dylan knew every road, alley, nook, and cranny. He was confident he would find his adversary.

He caught sight of the car turning onto Sycamore Road. Dylan declared, "You've done it now, buster! That's a dead-end." A smile crept across his face. As he turned onto Sycamore, the car was nowhere to be seen. His smile diminished. Frustrated, he smacked the steering wheel. "Shoot!" The street wasn't very long. Only a dozen homes lined the narrow way. Silence. No movement. No sound. Dylan slowly drove past each home, eyeing the driveways, looking for any sign of the black car. *He must've pulled into a garage. At least I know which street he lives on.*

Passing by the dark purple Victorian house, he remembered visiting a couple there. Shortly before his time as a pastor came to an end, he reached out to the family that lived there. "What were their names?" He tried hard to remember. He knew they attended the church for a few months before his marriage unexpectedly imploded. *It's all a blur. A fog. Why can't I remember their names?*

Occasionally, Dylan struggled with an amnesia of sorts. It

seemed post traumatic stress affected his memory. He tried not to recall the horrid details of infidelity that had driven him into that place of forgetting. The trauma of betrayal, it seemed, had erased facets of his life. *It's probably not worth remembering anyway.*

Feeling drawn to the purple house, he stopped his car and put it in reverse. Backing up, Dylan parked in front of the old home, forcing himself to recall the names of the couple inside. "I wonder if they still live here?" Peering down the driveway, he took note of the detached garage to the right of the house. The light that pressed its way between the cracks of the garage door quickly disappeared. *Someone's in there! Maybe it's him.* Dylan turned the engine off and waited for someone to emerge from the garage. Surely there was no other way out unless there was a back door. Certainly, whoever turned out the light had to walk to the house and would be visible.

Dylan waited and watched. Ten minutes passed, and not a soul revealed itself. He sighed heavily. "This is stupid." He turned the key in the ignition, forcing himself to leave the scene before his eyes gave way to sleep. "Charlie and Alexis Brown! That's their names. How could I forget Charlie Brown?" He grinned, shaking his head at the ridiculous fact that someone would give their child such a name. Dylan remembered the balding, forty-something man who carried the name of one of his most beloved cartoon characters. As Dylan worked to remember, the faces of Charlie and Alexis clearly appeared in his mind. He relived that moment when Charlie confided in him that he was battling drug addiction. *Poor Charlie. Whatever happened to him?*

Dylan arrived home, immediately catching sight of the object that caused the ruckus outside his house before he fled on a wild goose chase. "Another rock with a note. Real clever." He shook his head at the lack of creativity on the part of the mysterious offender. Dylan picked up the paper-wrapped rock and removed

119

THE WINDOWS OF HOLLY

the rubber bands that held it together. "What do you have to say this time?" He sighed as he walked into the house. Sitting on the couch, he uncurled the paper.

Divine Retribution Comes
Your Own Actions
Will Destroy You
Nemesis Exposes
Who You Really Are
Payback Is Hell, Preacher
Yes?

The attached page revealed a picture of Kelsey standing in front of Dylan as he answered his door. A second photo captured the moment when Kelsey forced a kiss on his lips. A third photograph centered on Kelsey's mini-skirt-clad derriere on top of Dylan. Fire shot through his body. "This guy's a genius," Dylan noted. As a newspaper journalist, he slightly admired his enemy's ability to formulate a story through photographs that tell an erroneous, convincing narrative.

"That son of a gun." He shook his head, puzzled, disturbed, and slightly amused by the efforts of this elusive ghost. Dylan was more intrigued now than threatened. What was meant to scare him was becoming a game. *I don't have a reputation to protect.* A rush of freedom darted through his veins. Dylan still wondered if the old purple house contained the culprit. *But there's no reason why Charlie and Alexis would be after me. Besides, I don't even know if they still live there.* He shrugged his shoulders as his mind raced. *I'll find out tomorrow.*

Chapter Eleven

IN ANNIE'S CAFE, Dylan eagerly awaited Jackson's response to the crazy dream that Dylan described. Jackson sat wide-eyed. "Dude, you're not going to believe this." Jackson leaned forward, grabbing the edges of the old formica tabletop. "I had the same exact dream."

"What? When?" Dylan leaned in, exhilarated. "Are you serious?"

Jackson tried to recall the time period in which his dream occurred. "I don't remember exactly, but it was around the time when Lynette left." Jackson hated to bring up that painful moment, but he would forever remember the intense dream in conjunction with the day that Lynette ran off with Owen.

"So you dreamed this same dream? I mean, was it identical to what I'm describing?"

"Totally identical, man. I'm not kidding."

Dylan processed the information for a few seconds. "Okay, so you had this dream when everything fell apart. Why would I be having it now? And what does it mean? Is everything going to fall apart again?" he wondered.

Jackson encouraged his friend. "No, man. I thought through the details of the dream many times, and the way I saw it, there's redemption. Everything was made right again. I think the artist is the Creator, God Himself. His creation turned dark but the creator embraced it anyway, taking its poison into himself. When he breathed on it, everything was set right and became more beautiful. So don't be afraid. I think it means the fullness of things being made right is happening now. You're at a pivotal point. I see it as a positive."

"I hope you're right. It's just interesting that I had the dream at the same time that someone's out plotting my destruction. I mean, I was writing the dream down when the guy threw the rock at my house." He shook his head. "There are so many unknowns; it's overwhelming. I've got my ex-wife living with me. I'm helping her raise her son that belongs to another man. We're still in love with each other. Drunk Kelsey shows up, forcing herself on me. This weirdo is creepy enough to stand outside my house with a camera and capture it all. I mean, how long was he waiting? Where was he waiting?" Dylan's eyes widened with revelation. "Holy cow! Do you think Kelsey is involved with this guy? Maybe they set the whole thing up!"

Jackson raised his eyebrows in wonder. "Perhaps. Maybe, but why would Kelsey have any reason to bring you down?"

Dylan shrugged. "I don't know. Because I wouldn't sleep with her?"

Jackson shook his head. "No, that's not probable. Besides, that was so long ago. If she wanted to cause trouble, she would have done something back then. I don't think she has anything to gain from this."

"I suppose not." Dylan sighed.

The little bell on the café door clanked as someone entered. Cold air blew in, meeting the warmth of steaming mugs of hot chocolate. Curt trudged in, donning his camouflage jacket, bright orange undershirt, and work boots that appeared to be a hundred years old.

"It's beginning to look a lot like Christmas," Dylan remarked.

Jackson grinned. "Yep. There'll be snow and mistletoe."

Dylan quickly interjected, "Curt and mistletoe don't mix. Dear God, for the sake of all women, don't let that man near the mistletoe!"

Jackson went to bat for the underdog. "Aw, c'mon, Dylan. There's someone for everyone. And Curt needs some love."

Dylan watched Curt stomp his lumbering feet on the floor mat. Curt worked hard to remove his favorite jacket, revealing the white, round flesh of his belly. Dylan wrinkled his nose. "I don't know, man. It'll take one special woman for that one. I don't think he's washed that jacket in, like, ever. From the looks of it, he's had that rag for decades."

Jackson smiled. "It must be special to him. Either that, or he can't afford a new one."

Curt successfully removed his jacket and plopped his bottom into his favorite chair. Huffing and puffing, he made eye contact with Dylan. "Hey, Dylan. How's it goin'?"

Pleasantly surprised by Curt's friendliness, Dylan's face lit with a genuine smile. "Going well, man. And you?"

Curt scratched his head, grimacing. "I'm quite surprised to hear you're doing well, Dylan."

Puzzled, Dylan asked, "Why's that?"

Curt reached into the pocket of his jacket and retrieved crinkled papers. "From the looks of it, you've gotten yourself into some trouble, mister." He unfolded the papers, revealing photographs of Kelsey and Dylan. "See for yourself."

Dylan jumped up quickly, snatching the papers from Curt. His hands shook as he read the familiar font.

A stench in town has let us down.
Oft admired, but leaves a frown.
Revealed is folly

THE WINDOWS OF HOLLY

In the windows of Holly.
It's time to bring him down.

Curt interjected. "Looks like this guy's been up to some peepin'."

Dylan looked at the second page. "What the heck?" His eyes studied a photo of himself kissing Lynette in the bedroom. Across the photograph, his name was written in large letters.

DYLAN VANBERG

Dylan's jaw tightened as his face turned red. "That freak has been looking through our windows!" A second photo showed Kelsey kissing Dylan in the doorway of his home.

Curt scratched his bearded chin. "Yep. And he's putting all them photographs in everyone's mailboxes. Ain't that against the law?"

Jackson stood to his feet, grabbing the papers from Dylan's hands. "We're going to the police with this now."

Dylan shook his head. "No! Not yet."

Jackson was confused by Dylan's delay in reporting such a crime. "Dude! This could be more serious than we thought. Someone's spying on you, invading your privacy, and putting this crap in everyone's mailboxes! You have to report it immediately."

Dylan stared straight ahead. "Give me a few minutes. I'll be back." He headed to his car like a bolt of lightning. In two seconds flat, he was peeling out of the parking lot.

Curt's concern was evident as he watched Jackson, waiting for some kind of response. "That poor fella's sure been through some awful messes, hasn't he?"

"More than you can imagine. And he deserves none of it."

"Where do ya think he's goin'?" Curt asked.

124

Jackson sighed. "I have no idea." *God help him.* Jackson stepped back to his table, eyeing the leftover bits of breakfast and Dylan's untouched second glass of iced tea. Anger seeped into his face as he pondered the fact that someone who'd done nothing wrong was being taunted by evil. "Dang it!" He slammed his fist on the table. "Why do things keep happening to him?" He quietly begged God to defend his friend.

Curt piped up, "Whoa, whoa there. You'd better calm yourself, boy. Those photographs certainly are scandalous, but Dylan done did all that to himself. I mean, it's his choice what he's doin' with the ladies."

Jackson glared at Curt. "Who are you to judge? You don't even know what's going on in his life. He's done nothing wrong. That girl on top of him, she attacked Dylan and he was trying to get her to leave."

"So you say." Curt raised his eyebrows. "If I could get a woman like that to attack me, I'd let her." He chuckled. "Maybe Dylan didn't let her, but there's still the photo of him kissing his ex-wife, not to mention, who is still married. Who can say the two of them weren't cheatin' together on Owen?"

Jackson's face flamed. "You know he didn't do that."

Curt relented slightly. "I know, but I'm just sayin' that a picture's worth a thousand words."

Jackson huffed. "You don't even know what that means, and attitudes like yours won't help Dylan. If you have any decency in you, you'll do whatever you can to help clear his name in this community. He's done nothing but good for everyone he meets. All he gets in return is pain." Jackson's eyes filled with hot tears.

David and Marcy entered the café, sober faced, bearing sadness. When David saw Jackson, he immediately recognized that he was in the company of someone who felt exactly the way he did. Their eyes met and not a word was spoken. They knew. It was easy to read the look of someone who felt helpless to stop the undeserved destruction of a loved one.

"David," Jackson said.

Without replying, David made his way to Jackson, throwing his arms around him. They hugged wordlessly. David patted Jackson's back. "Thank you for being his friend, Jackson," he said, his voice cracking. "You're a good, good man. You stick with him, okay?"

Jackson stepped back, stiffening his jaw in an effort to control emotion. "I'd never do otherwise."

David tried to encourage him. "Surely something really good is coming Dylan's way. I just have to believe that. No one goes through that much pain without gaining some kind of reward. He has a powerful defender who loves him."

THE PURPLE HOUSE

Dylan parked his car in front of the purple house on Sycamore Street. The night before, he had a hunch that the mysterious offender lived there, and that hunch hadn't left him. Now that photographs were surfacing, Dylan needed answers immediately.

Though the driveway was empty, he hoped there would be a car in the detached garage. He stepped onto the creaky, wooden porch, keeping his eye on the door as he approached. *C'mon, please be home. Someone answer the door.* His trembling fist rapped on the ornate wood, rattling the antique glass. Several seconds passed, so he knocked once more. Nothing. No signs of life.

What time is it anyway? Dylan reached into his pocket for his phone. It wasn't there. *Shoot.* He tried every pocket on his body, but the phone was gone. *It must be in the car.* Dylan thought about checking the car, but he was too consumed with searching out the person who was attempting to destroy his reputation. Bounding off the front porch, he marched his way to the garage, questioning his own decisions. *What am I doing?* Desperation drove him to snoop around. Dylan peered through a window on the side of the garage, hoping to get a clue. *Yes! A black Camaro! That's gotta be it.*

As a child, Dylan dreamed about being a great detective, solving crimes and mysteries. Now he was doing it for real. The excitement erased reality from his mind, removing him from the constraints of time. The fact that Lynette would be expecting him home in twenty minutes was eliminated from his thoughts.

A N N I E ' S C A F é
Jackson struggled with fear for his friend. He tried finishing his meal, hoping that if he waited at the café long enough, Dylan would return as he said he would. Jackson decided to call Dylan. When the call went through, he recognized Dylan's ringtone coming from the booth. Following the sound, he reached into the crevice of the seat to extract Dylan's phone. "Shoot. He left his phone," he muttered to himself. Jackson sighed deeply. As he pondered his next step, Dylan's phone rang. Lynette's smiling face dressed the screen. *What am I going to tell Lynette?* He answered the phone. "Hey. It's Jackson."

Lynette was surprised to hear Jackson's voice. "Oh, hey, Jackson. How are you?"

He hoped to hide his concern as he tried to explain. "I'm here at the café, and Dylan accidentally left his phone behind."

"He used to leave his phone everywhere. Sounds like he hasn't changed much in that department. When he gets here, I'll let him know you have it. How long ago did he leave?"

Jackson's stomach sank as he considered the fact that if Dylan had driven straight home, he'd be there by now. *She's going to be worried. I have to tell her.* "I don't think he was headed home, Lynette. I'm not sure where he went."

THE WINDOWS OF HOLLY

Worried, she questioned hastily, "What do you mean? What's wrong? I can tell something is wrong."

He drew a deep breath. "Well, Curt showed up here with papers that appeared in his mailbox. Someone took pictures of Dylan and Kelsey when she showed up at the house. Also, there's a picture of you and Dylan together. Someone's trying to stir up trouble. Dylan left in a hurry, but I don't know where he was going."

Anxiety pierced her stomach. "Oh my God. Who would do that? And why?"

Jackson hoped to reassure her. "Try not to worry. It'll be fine. You know Dylan has a good head on his shoulders."

She wanted answers. "I don't understand. The photos were in Curt's mailbox? Just his mailbox?"

Silence lingered. Again, she questioned, "Jackson, were they just in Curt's mailbox?"

Jackson hesitated. "I don't know," he replied unconvincingly.

She pressed. "Jackson! Talk to me. I need to know. Did anyone else see this?"

He sighed. "David and Marcy got one too. I don't know who else."

The flicker of anxiety that threatened to come was now running at full speed in her veins. Lynette's throat tightened, her breathing increased, and she struggled to control the lightheadedness that made her feel like fading out of this life.

Jackson could hear the upsurge in her breath. "Lynette, stay calm."

Tears erupted from her eyes. "Jackson," she said breathlessly. "I feel like I'm crumbling. I can't handle this," her voice cracked.

Jackson felt guilty for answering her questions, but he knew he had no choice. He spoke matter-of-factly. "You're going to be okay, Lynette. I'll call Lucy and tell her to come over right away.

I'll be there shortly as well. Just focus on your baby and let everything else go. I promise, it's going to be okay. Dylan is smart and he's been through worse. He can handle it."

She whimpered, "How can you be so sure?"

A holy confidence engulfed Jackson. "Because God wouldn't bring you two this far just to let you be destroyed. Don't give in to fear over these things. God's got your back."

THE PURPLE HOUSE

Dylan couldn't handle the thought of backing off now. The black Camaro sat alone inside the old detached garage. *I need to know whose car this is. I've got to get inside!* His world narrowed. Nothing else existed but this moment, and it was his moment to get answers. He couldn't leave it alone. "No one can rob me of my peace," he mumbled to himself. Dylan convinced himself he had every right to enter the garage and try to gain access to the car. After all, someone was invading his privacy, so he would invade his. *This guy took it too far by placing photos in the mailboxes of Holly's citizens.*

Dylan wouldn't stop until he got answers. *Surely the keys are in there.* He walked around the corner of the garage and noticed a door. *Yes!* But the door was locked. Dylan paced around, staring at the garage door. He considered using a coat hanger to disengage the safety release, but he didn't have any tools or supplies with him that would work.

Dylan scanned the area, making sure he was still alone. The old, towering pecan trees provided a sense of invisibility. Reaching the window, Dylan caught sight of his own reflection. "Revealed is folly in the windows of Holly," he quipped. Chuckling at the thought of his harasser's attempt at poetry, a surge of fear hit his stomach.

What am I doing? I haven't even prayed about this. Dylan used

THE WINDOWS OF HOLLY

to pray about nearly every decision, but life's disappointments caused him to cast things to chance, or rather default to, "whatever God wants to do. Stuff happens anyway." Often, he felt as if life were steamrolling him for the sake of entertainment, that he was a fragment of humanity tossed about by the winds of life for the pleasure of some wicked, unseen force.

His hands trembled as he tried pushing the window up. *Unlocked!* To his surprise, the window greeted him with an easy invitation. It was a tight squeeze, but Dylan hoisted his body into the small opening and wiggled his way through. A rickety, wooden worktable provided a resting place for his elbows as he drew his legs inside. Childlike exhilaration pushed the underlying voice of wisdom aside. Dylan needed to feel like a real man, a strong man. He needed to be in control of something in his life. Pursuing the perpetrator was his opportunity to take dominion over the circumstances and defend his reputation.

The old, musty smell evoked memories for Dylan. Flashbacks of work time with Grandpa William filled his mind. He closed his eyes as he remembered his grandfather's oil and gasoline-filled garage. *What is it about these old garages?* Dylan breathed deeply, wondering how the sense of smell contained great power to arrest one's attention and carry the mind to another era.

Opening his eyes, he instantly returned to the mission at hand. He steadied his feet on the dirty, concrete floor, locking eyes on the passenger door of the car. He walked confidently toward it, momentarily running his fingers along the handle. *Nice. Slick.* He gripped and pulled, only to find that it was locked. "Dang it! C'mon. I didn't get this far for nothing."

He quickly rounded the corner. "Be open," he demanded. Reaching for the driver's door handle, Dylan was stunned as something cracked beneath his feet. He found himself descending in slow motion, watching as the bottom of the car door moved past his face and blackness engulfed him. Everything seemed like a strange dream, yet he knew it was real. He lost his breath for a second as his body crashed onto a hard surface. "Ahhh!" Dylan let out a loud cry. Numbness mixed with occasional shots of pain. Confusion consumed his mind as his vision faded.

Chapter Twelve

*A*S EVENING APPROACHED, Jackson and Lucy prepared dinner in Dylan's kitchen, hoping their friend would walk in at any moment and life would resume normality. Lynette paced around the living room, bouncing Asa and keeping her eyes on the door for Dylan's arrival. Jackson convinced the ladies that their best option would be to give Dylan time. After all, he had said had his mind was set on something and he was wise and wouldn't do anything foolish. Now that two hours had passed, Jackson silently considered calling the police, but he knew they wouldn't see a problem with a man being away from home for a couple of hours.

"Jackson," Lynette broke the silence. "Something's not right. I just know it. We need to call the police." Her confident insistence startled him.

Jackson agreed. "Okay. I think you're right, even though they won't think anything of a grown man being gone for two hours."

She insisted. "I don't care what they think. If they won't help, then we have to do something." She walked quickly toward the phone. "We can at least tell them about the photographs and taunting."

Lucy continued chopping squash and zucchini, working to resist the growing fear that gnawed at her stomach. Her pregnant belly pressed against the countertop. *God, help me not to stress the*

baby, and please let Dylan be safe. Surely You're with him. She
sighed as she considered the chaotic storms that had infiltrated the
Christmas House over the last few years. *Restore. For the sake of
everyone, please restore.*

Her hand pressed on the handle of the knife in rhythm with
each thought that bombarded her mind. Always leaning toward the
positive, Lucy fully expected something good to arise. Her bright,
blue eyes were often the beacon of hope for the people of Holly.
Now those eyes resisted tears of fear.

Jackson stepped behind Lucy, wrapping his arms around her.
"Lucille Belle, I promise everything will be all right." Jackson
knew she needed to hear those words.

Gratitude and comfort flooded her heart. "I believe you."
Jackson pressed his face into her neck, brushing his fingers
through her silky, black hair.

She set the knife on the cutting board and wiped her hands on a
dish towel. Turning to face her husband, she smiled. "You know, I
was just thinking about this house and all of the good memories it
holds. The Christmas gatherings, the songs, the parties. This is a
place of celebration. It may have been empty for a while, but I
believe celebration is coming again. It has to come. I mean, just
think about it. Dylan and Lynette were destroyed, yet look at the
pieces coming back together again. I know things aren't the same
and it's complicated as heck, but at least there's hope, you know?
I'm determined to see this house become what it used to be. I
mean, even better than it used to be. See the Christmas tree and the
decorations?"

Lucy pointed toward the living room. "That's the starting point,
Jackson. It's coming to life again." Tears filled her eyes. "And
nothing will happen to Dylan Vanberg. Not on my watch. We're
going to live in this town and spend decades looking across the
street at this house, and we'll watch the Vanbergs live a happy,

wonderful life. Our children will play together. That's what I want more than anything right now."

Jackson hugged her tightly. "This is exactly what made me fall in love with you."

She smiled. "Thanks, love."

Lynette entered the kitchen, still carrying Asa. "Sheriff Bennett is on his way over. He has questions to ask you, Jackson, since you were the last person with him." She groaned, stretching her gaze toward the ceiling. "Oh my gosh, I hope I'm doing the right thing." She exhaled, expelling her doubts. "I mean, Dylan could walk in at any moment. Maybe he's okay. Maybe it's nothing, but my gut tells me otherwise."

Jackson assured her that her decision was a good one. "You're doing the right thing."

She was pleased with his agreement with her actions. "That's what Sheriff Bennett thinks. He said he's known of Dylan for several years. Apparently, he visited Hope Fellowship a few times. He said he appreciated Dylan's sermons. It's nice to know there's some level of connection. I think he'll take our concerns seriously."

Asa squeaked as he stretched his little fists into the air.

Lucy turned toward Lynette. "You haven't put this little guy down for two hours. Let me take over." Lucy reached for Asa. "Hey, sweet little guy. Come see Aunt Lucy."

Lynette thanked her for her offer. "I didn't even realize I've been holding him the whole time. I guess he makes me feel secure." Lynette took a seat at the dining table. "Oh my gosh, it feels good to sit down."

Lucy grinned. "No joke. You've been pacing the floor, getting a workout. I'll get you some water. You'd better stay hydrated, especially since you're breastfeeding." Lucy looked at Asa. "Right, Asa?"

135

THE WINDOWS OF HOLLY

Lynette was grateful for the Sawyers. Their relentless love and support were treasures she would not take for granted. "Thank you for being here for us. I just love you guys more than I could ever accurately express."

Jackson and Lucy smiled. He informed her, "The feeling is mutual."

THE PURPLE HOUSE

Dylan slowly returned to consciousness, forcing his eyes to focus. Dusty beams of evening's light floated above him. The smell of oil and gasoline awakened his senses. He instantly remembered why he was in the musty, old garage. *The car.* But now he was lying on his back in what he guessed was a small cellar or oil pit of some kind. *Of course he'd have one of these. Anyone with a car like that would.*

Dylan tried to sit up, placing his elbow on the ground for support as he steadied himself. As he attempted to place his feet firmly on the ground to stand, pain shot through his left leg. "God!" He cringed, clenching his teeth together. Determined to stand, he tried once again. "Agh! God!" A wave of nausea rolled over him. Panic set in as he realized he was stuck in his enemy's garage without the ability to stand on his own two feet. Through rapid breaths, he tried redirecting his thoughts to solutions.

My phone. His hands fumbled in his jacket pockets, but he knew he'd left his phone behind. "Stupid!" Dylan felt like a fool as he considered that moments ago, he'd regarded himself as a brilliant vigilante. "Idiot!" *God forgive me for my foolishness. Please help me out of here.* He twisted his torso to the right, hoping to roll over onto his stomach. *Maybe I can crawl.* But any movement overwhelmed him with pain. *Okay, I've got to be still.* His pounding heartbeat convinced him he had no choice but to calm down so he could think straight. *God, help me out of here.*

Dylan rested his head on the cold concrete floor and closed his eyes. He knew he couldn't fix things in his own strength.

Breathe deeply. He pressed his mind into submission as he imagined a bright-blue, healing presence from Heaven. *Come, Holy Spirit.* Long ago, Dylan found that by setting his focus on the reality of another realm, the realm of Heaven, a tangible peace would fill his body. This was certainly a time when he needed peace, and he was desperate for that realm. Inhaling deeply, he imagined the presence, the energy of God entering his body and moving all the way down his legs. *Okay. Okay.* He coaxed his mind into a state of calm. *I can't get out of here and that's okay.* He forced his thoughts toward a superior reality, finding the strength to surrender. *Inhale. Exhale. Inhale. Exhale.* He imagined life and wholeness entering into his lungs with each breath. As he exhaled, he forced his fears to leave his body.

Eyes still closed, delirious from being knocked out, the artist from Dylan's dream appeared in the recesses of his mind. While his leg and ribs throbbed with pain, his spirit pulsed with light. *It's you.* Tears formed in his eyes, making their way across his temples. His insides fluttered with vibration. "Holy Spirit," he whispered. Shards of light flashed past him as he breathed deeply. Forgetting where he was, he soared into another place. *Home.* Perfect peace enveloped Dylan. It was the place where disappointment was erased, pain was forgotten, and anger vanished. Time was no more. Only the eternal reality vividly remained.

Peaceful whispers passed by his ears carrying joy-filled laughter. A field of green came into his vision. Love rushed into every fiber of his being, drawing him deeper into the heart of God. *It's You.* There was no want, no need, no lack. In this place, the spirit was free from every hindrance. Self-condemnation, regret, accusation, guilt, and shame were completely obliterated by the

THE WINDOWS OF HOLLY

all-consuming light.

As Dylan moved, silky grass caressed his feet, and he couldn't help but notice the brilliantly colored flowers that released quiet, joyful sounds. There was no effort in walking and moving. His spirit was light as a feather and hypersensitive to everything good and beautiful. Floating toward the bright-blue horizon, Dylan saw the artist once again. His clothing was different than it was in the dream, however. He was clothed in light. His long, dark hair flowed gracefully, as if underwater. Radiant love overflowed from the man enrobed in the brightness of perfection. Their eyes locked, fully engaged in wholeness. In love.

The artist spoke. "You are in Me and I am in you. Now, see in Me. See as I see. Let your eyes be full of light." He pressed his hand toward Dylan, palm out. A wind blew over Dylan, lifting him off the ground, penetrating his being with light. The ecstasy of Heaven caused him to close his eyes, as if taking a picture to lock the experience inside himself, never to be forgotten. Dylan's spirit moved backward, making its way to the temporal realm. Slowly, the feeling of need hit him once again. *I need to stay here.* "See in Me." *Can I just stay here?* "Yes. Wherever you are, you are always here." *But how can that be?*

Hazily, Dylan opened his eyes as his body's pain reminded him where he was. The familiar smell of gasoline and oil permeated his nose. There was barely any light left as the trees outside captured what remained of the sun's light. He winced from the pain. *Do I wait for someone to find me? Perhaps my enemy?* His manly instincts told him to fight for a way of escape, but his spirit relented. A sense of being in the right place brought him comfort. He wondered how it was possible to feel peace under such frightening circumstances.

Despite the pain, the right side of his mouth formed a grin at the sheer ridiculousness of the situation. *I guess You've got me where You want me, huh, God?* Dylan thought it was ironic that by chasing a suspected enemy, he'd literally landed himself in a pit. He knew Lynette must be in a panic by now. *God, help her.*

DYLAN'S HOUSE

Lynette fought to keep herself from trembling, but fear for Dylan consumed her. Waves of peace came intermittently but were interrupted by the relentless doubts of her mind. In her spirit, she felt he would be all right, but the what-ifs bombarded her. *No one is promised tomorrow.* Life taught her that nothing could be counted on or taken for granted. She knew she didn't deserve Dylan's love, and now that she was back in his home, she feared the mistakes of her past were reason for him to be removed from her life. *God, please don't take him away from me. Please, Father. He has to be okay.*

Sheriff Bennett listened to Lynette and Jackson carefully, making note of every detail. His heart went out to them. He knew their story, even though Lynette hadn't mentioned the specifics of their past. Everyone in town remembered the fiasco that happened five years before. Most weren't too quick to forget when the preacher's wife left the preacher for a deacon.

The sheriff also remembered Owen Smith from long ago. Owen's ex-wife, Cybil, had called the police department during a midnight fight many years ago. Bennett was the officer on duty who responded to the call. His memory of Owen consisted of a drunken, disheveled man in a stretched-out, white cotton undershirt. *Isn't that always the case?* He thought Cybil was far too elegant and beautiful to be with such a beast. When he heard the news about Owen getting remarried, he was shocked that it was to the pastor's wife from Hope Fellowship. *How does such a loser get two pretty wives? Now look at this poor woman.* He tried hard to drop his judgments as he came up with a plan to help find

Dylan.

Sheriff Bennett sighed. "All right now. I think we got all the details I'll need." He glanced over the paperwork. "Do you think it's possible that he purposefully left his phone behind so no one could contact him or interfere with something he was about to do?"

Simultaneously, Lynette, Jackson, and Lucy spoke an emphatic "No!"

Jackson explained that the phone had obviously fallen into the crevice of the booth, and it would be uncharacteristic of Dylan to be irresponsible, and there was no way he'd cause Lynette to worry. Lynette explained that his phone was always on him, and that he'd been especially attentive to her and the baby, therefore, he wouldn't have done such a thing. "He would have called me to let me know he wouldn't be home," she assured the sheriff.

He acknowledged the information they gave. "Okay then. You all sound pretty certain. Being that he doesn't have his phone on him, we obviously have no way to track him. I can put out some calls to see if anyone has seen his vehicle. The officers and I can drive through town and keep an eye out. If you hear anything or if something comes to mind, be sure to call me right away."

Lynette wasn't satisfied. "We need to do something right now. What can we do?"

"Make some phone calls to alert friends and coworkers. Perhaps you can drive around and look for his car. Holly's a small town, so your chances of finding his car are pretty good." He shrugged. "That is, of course, unless he's left town."

"Like I said before," interjected Lynette, "I think we've called everyone we could think of, and no one has seen him."

Jackson stood to retrieve his keys from his pocket. "Lucy, can you stay here with Asa in case Dylan shows up?

"Of course," she replied.

140

Jackson reached his hand toward Lynette. "Do you want to search with me?"

Lynette was immediately on her feet, ready to go. "Yes. Lucy, there's some pumped milk in the refrigerator for Asa. Do you mind watching him?"

Lucy's bright-blue eyes gleamed with hope. "I don't mind one bit," she said, smiling. "You go find your man. Asa and I will pray."

THE PURPLE HOUSE

Three hours had passed since Dylan left Annie's Café. He wondered how long he'd been there. The sun abandoned him to darkness. Any attempt to move his leg caused pain he couldn't bear. He was afraid to stand, imagining that his leg would break in two. Gritting his teeth together, he decided his only option was to lie still and hope that someone with good intentions would find him.

Click. Click. "Hello?" Dylan called out. "Hello?" He heard shuffling feet, slow and foreboding. *God, I hope it's some innocent, old person.* Feeling like a trapped fly in a spider's web, he waited for the revealing of his captor. Dylan dared to make himself known once more. "Help me, please. I need help." No one responded, but the footsteps drew closer. *Click.* A bright light came on. Dylan squinted as his eyes adjusted to the brightness. His heart rate climbed. *A captor or a savior?* He hoped for the best.

The sound was upon him. A shadowy face peered out from beneath a dark hoodie. The image leaned down from above, pressing its gaze into the pit. Dylan dared to speak up. "Listen, I know I shouldn't have been in here. I was looking for someone and I fell. Please, will you help me?" But the slim, dark image remained silent, maintaining his menacing stance. Dylan begged, "Sir, please have mercy. I promise I'll leave you alone. Can you

THE WINDOWS OF HOLLY

please just call an ambulance?"

The man turned away without a word. The aching challenged Dylan's ability to hold it together. His chin quivered and his lower lip curled at the possibility that he may tortured and killed. Squinting from pain and fear, tears began to roll down the sides of his head. Dylan was angry at himself for being so weak, especially in the presence of his accuser. He was a strong man, but the circumstances caused him to wonder if he'd just thrown away the possibility of being with Lynette again, of having a second chance. *What if I don't get out of here alive?* He pressed himself to hold it together. *Be strong. Stop being a baby.*

Click. Click. Thud. Dylan turned his head to the left. The wooden stairs came into sight. The sinister intimidator moved with calculated intent to cause alarm. Dylan made note of the Puma symbol on the black sneakers as they approached him. *Should I say something?* He worried the person might smash his head in if he dared to utter a word. *Holy Spirit, help me. Body, do not fail me.*

"Well, well, preacher man," the man said. "Looks like you've gotten yourself into a mess. Seems you're always in a mess, doesn't it?" The man paced around Dylan, keeping his face down, out of the light.

Dylan replied, "Seems that way. Who are you?"

The man cleared his throat. "No one that you ever cared about. Did you ever care for anyone but yourself, preacher?"

Dylan sighed. "I'm not a preacher."

"You were when it mattered to me."

Dylan demanded, "And who are you? Let me see your face." Dylan could tell he was young. Maybe twenty-something.

"You probably wouldn't remember me. I was just a back-row peasant in your little money-making church."

Dylan couldn't help but nearly laugh with amusement at the

young man's choice of words. "Money-making? That's hilarious," he scoffed. "Dude, don't you know most preachers live at poverty level? Money-making? Not that little church."

The young man knelt down at Dylan's left side. He leaned in closely as he pulled the hood off his head. Dylan stared into his eyes. Deep, sad, brown eyes held his gaze. Long eyelashes were still, unmoving, as the haunting eyes pierced his soul. Dylan studied the young man's face. Clenched, chiseled jaw: the face of an athletic supermodel.

"You look familiar, but I can't remember your name," Dylan admitted. "Are you Charlie's son?"

The young man raised an eyebrow. "You can't remember my name, but at least you remembered my dad's. That's surprising, being that you hardly gave my family the time of day. But then again, who can forget a name like Charlie Brown? Am I supposed to be impressed, preacher?"

Though Dylan was frustrated by the pain in his body and the game of intimidation, his heart was filled with compassion for this family that he had failed many years ago. Staring into the young man's eyes, Dylan felt his despair. The young man had only identified himself as a back-row peasant. Those words broke Dylan's heart. "You're not a peasant. You have never been a peasant. Please, will you tell me your name?"

"Why does it matter to you now, preacher?"

Dylan squeezed his eyes shut. "Please stop calling me preacher. My name is Dylan. And I'm so sorry for ever letting you down. I tried my best, but I let a lot of people down, and I'm sorry you were one of those."

The young man stood to his feet, crossing his arms. "You mean like your wife?"

His words were a sword. Dylan mustered up a response to the taunting question. "Yes, like my wife. Sometimes you think you're

THE WINDOWS OF HOLLY

doing everything right, and then you wake up one day to realize you've done wrong by the one you love the most. By the time you realize where you dropped the ball, it's too late to fix it."

"And what did you do to make your wife run off with another man?"

Dylan shook his head. "Why are you asking me these things? I don't understand."

The young man spoke sneeringly. "Because I want to know what it is about you that drives people down the path to hell. I want to know how it's possible that someone who supposedly knows God ends up leaving a path of destruction behind him. How does a man of God leave people to suffer? So answer me. What did you do to make your wife run off with another man?"

His accuser's words caused Dylan to feel he was in the presence of Satan himself. He knew he didn't owe any explanations, yet he knew he was encountering a deeply wounded individual. Dylan hoped this wouldn't be his last conversation on earth, but he feared it might be. He had to make it count. Dylan spoke through pain. "I did what too many pastors do. I gave the church more than I gave my own bride. I spent more time with others than I did with the one I promised to cherish."

Dylan gritted his teeth as pain shot down his leg. His vision was fuzzy, but he fully intended to stick to the conversation with the hope that the tormented young man would understand. "I didn't listen to her, and when she needed me the most, I was too busy trying to fix everything for everyone else."

The man spoke with disdain, "For everyone else except my dad."

Dylan's soul ached as he wondered how many people he had let down. "I remember your mom and dad coming to my office for advice. It's been so long ago that I don't recall the details, but I referred them to someone who was licensed and equipped. I was

144

just a pastor, not a professional counselor, so I'd send people elsewhere for help if it was above my ability. May I ask, what happened to your dad?"

The man lashed out. "Why do you care?"

Dylan winced from the harshness of his words. Dylan replied gently, "Believe it or not, I do care. Whatever I did or didn't do has driven you to taunt me and destroy my reputation with the entire town. I've gotta say, those photographs were pretty good. You must have waited around for a long time to capture those shots." Dylan could feel his pulse throughout his body. He wasn't sure how much longer he could lie there without passing out from the agony.

"Well, preacher. If you really want to know, my dad kept drinking and doing drugs. He couldn't handle the pain from his motorcycle accident. He needed painkillers constantly. Mom brought him to you for help, but that was a waste of time. Long story short, dad ended up leaving us for a man. Can you imagine that? He left town to live with him. Turns out the guy's a pharmacist. Doesn't take a genius to figure out what drove him into that relationship."

Dylan groaned. "I'm so sorry. How long ago did he leave?"

"Two months ago."

Dylan was puzzled. "The way you told the story, I thought he must've left years ago. I don't understand. How was it my fault?"

The man breathed rapidly as he explained. "If you had a connection with God, you should have been able to save my dad. He'd still be here, sober and out of pain. Unless, of course, God is a jerk too."

Dylan asked once more. "Please. What is your name?"

"Nick," the man offered without hesitation.

"Hey, Nick. I promise you, God is not a jerk. He doesn't want your dad to hurt. He doesn't want you and your mom to hurt."

Nick clenched his fists. "Yeah, well, I want you to hurt!" With that, Nick kicked Dylan's fractured leg. Dylan howled with agony as he writhed on the hard, cold floor. Tears streamed from his eyes as he struggled to stay conscious. The image of Nick standing over him grew fuzzy as waves of nausea rolled over him. "God!" He cried out.

Nick leaned down, glaring at him. "Oh yeah. Call out to God and see if he'll help you, preacher! He didn't help us. You actually think He'll help you?"

"Nick, Nick," Dylan struggled to speak between gasps. "Please." Dylan wanted to ask him to stop hurting him, but he feared his request would only be an invitation for more torment. Trying to slow his breathing and regain his composure, Dylan worked hard to communicate when he would rather pass out. *If I pass out, he might bury me alive.* "Nick, I wish I could have helped your dad."

Dylan breathed hard. "I'm so sorry for what's happened. Pain drives people to do things they would normally never do. Pain makes people desperate, and they'll do anything for relief," he panted. Your dad must have been hurting so much, he didn't know what else to do. I know you're hurting too." Dylan groaned with pain. "Man, I knew I couldn't be the one to help your dad. That's why I sent them somewhere else. I'm so sorry I didn't know how to give him what he needed. Addiction usually requires professionals. I wish I could have done something."

Nick seethed. "But if you were connected to God, you could, right?"

Dylan tried to make sense of things. "I talk with God every day, and I do my best to listen to Him, but that doesn't mean I have all the answers. It doesn't mean I knew what your dad needed. I suppose I'm blind in some areas."

Nick demanded answers, taunting Dylan with things he used to preach. "But isn't He the light of the world? Isn't He supposed to live inside of you? If the light lives within you, how can you be blind?"

Dylan gulped. "I'm only human, Nick. I suppose the light was there, but I got in the way. We have the ability to ignore the light." He winced from the jab in his side. "Making our own way can be like putting blinders on at times. I don't know, man. I don't know what you want me to say. I'm sorry. I wish I could change your situation. Why are you holding me responsible after all these years?"

Nick didn't answer.

Dylan continued, hoping to make a connection with the young man. *If I'm about to die, I need to go out on a good note.* He figured vulnerability was the best choice for the moment. Perhaps that would touch Nick's angry heart. "Life is unfair. It's full of pain." His chin quivered beneath the ache in his body and soul. "But I think it's full of beauty too. Maybe all the pain is what highlights the beauty. Otherwise, we might miss it all together and not even notice it. You're right, Nick. I let people down. People let me down too, man. All the time. When Lynette chose someone else, it shredded me inside and out. I felt like I was going to die. I couldn't see light. It was like all the color in the world was gone. I hated waking up in the morning to face a life I didn't want."

Dylan drew in a breath. "And now I finally have a chance, man. I finally have a chance to be with the woman I've always loved and actually do it right this time. But instead I'm here," his voice cracked, "in an oil pit in an old garage with someone who probably wants me dead. Tell me, Nick, is this where my life ends? Huh? Do I get another chance to see something beautiful happen?"

Nick paced around Dylan like a lion. He stepped toward a shelf and began knocking tools and cans to the floor. "Do I get a second

THE WINDOWS OF HOLLY

chance?" He pounded his fists against the wall. "My mom sits in the house staring at the television when she's not at work. She's like a shell, barely alive. And guess who's gotta pay the bills that my dad doesn't pay. Me! Mom and I are left carrying everything while he lives with his boyfriend." Nick's anger broke into sobs. Dylan listened to the sounds of a son longing for his father, a bitter, mournful wailing. Dylan's soul bore the young man's pain and he began to weep with him, two humans longing for their families to be restored. The echo reverberated in their ears.

Nick dropped to his knees at Dylan's side. "I don't know how to take care of my mom. What am I supposed to do?" Nick's visage changed. Dylan saw a gentle little boy who wept for home. His hardness disintegrated. *It was a mask. That's all.*

Dylan reached up, resting his hand on Nick's shoulder. "I'll help you get a second chance. Let's get out of here and help your parents."

Relief flooded Nick's face. "Seriously?"

Dylan nodded.

Nick feared that he was being tricked. *This guy could have me put in jail.* "But after what I've done to you? I don't know, man. What are you trying to do to me?"

Dylan pleaded. "I promise, Nick. I'll help you as much as I possibly can. I'll do my best."

Nick knelt on his knees, frozen. Dylan knew the young man was calculating his actions and the potential consequences.

"Look, Nick. I promise I won't press charges. If you'll just call for help, please. I'll drop the whole thing like it never happened."

Nick was unsure. "You would do that?"

Dylan reassured, "Yes."

Nick questioned him. "Why would you do that?"

Dylan's head throbbed, but he tried to stay with the conversation. "Because your life is valuable. The last thing you

148

need is a criminal record. How could you help your mom with a criminal record?"

Nick mulled over the details in his mind. "But if I call for help, what do I tell them? They'll want to know why you're in my garage."

Dylan thought for a moment. "Let's tell them I came over to buy that awesome set of hubcaps I saw before I fell into this mess? I'm just the idiot buyer who showed up early, went into the garage and happened to step into the pit. You be the hero and call for help. Trust me. I've got you covered."

Nick weighed options in his mind, calculating the potential fallout of each choice. He figured his only possibility of escaping the mess was to get Dylan help and hope he would truly be merciful. Nick's other options would only lead to a potential jail sentence. He quickly reached for his cell phone and dialed 9-1-1.

Chapter Thirteen

ETWEEN JACKSON, MARCY, DAVID, LYNETTE, AND LUCY, surely half of the town heard that Dylan had not returned home when expected. News traveled quickly. Still, no one had seen any sign of him.

Jackson continued driving Lynette through town, searching for Dylan's car. Lynette sighed. "C'mon, Old Blue. Where are you?"

Jackson looked puzzled. "Old Blue?"

She smiled. "Yeah. That's what he calls that old Volvo of his. You knew that, Jackson."

"Ha! I guess I forgot."

Lynette's cell phone rang. "Hello? Yes." Barely three seconds passed before she hollered, "Oh my God! He's okay?"

Jackson's heart was relieved. *Thank God.* He listened as Lynette asked questions and repeated an address.

She beamed with relief. "Yes, thank you! We'll be right there," she exclaimed. Her hands shook as she hung up. "Jackson, that was an emergency operator. Dylan's at a house on Sycamore Street. Apparently he fell, but he'll be fine. Someone called EMS and asked them to contact me."

"Thank God!" Jackson's mind scurried with questions, but he knew this wasn't the time to ask them. He and Lynette sat in strange silence as they drove toward Dylan.

THE WINDOWS OF HOLLY

One of the wonderful things about Holly was that its size allowed a person to drive across town in less than eight minutes. Jackson and Lynette made it to Sycamore Street in just under five minutes. "There's Old Blue," Lynette squealed with excitement as they approached. Before Jackson could come to a complete stop, Lynette leapt from the car, running straight for the house. Blue and red lights flashed from the ambulance and fire truck.

"Back here," a woman directed her. "Behind the house, in the garage."

The woman looked familiar. Lynette hesitated for a moment upon seeing her, but Lynette's priority was to be at Dylan's side.

"Thank you," she responded politely before rushing to the scene.

As they entered the garage, she was shocked to see paramedics walking down the stairs into the pit. "Dylan!" *What the heck was he doing in here?*

One of the paramedics motioned for her. "Come on in, ma'am. He'll be fine. We're just trying to figure out the best way to get him situated on the stretcher and get him up these steps. You can come down. Just stay to the right, close to the wall, so we have room to move around."

Lynette peered down into the hole, catching Dylan's eye. He forced a smile. "Hi, Lynnie." She knew he would do his best to lighten the mood, so she decided to follow suit.

"Well, hello, Dyl," she grinned. She wanted to melt into a puddle of tears at the sight of him, but seeing Dylan in a vulnerable state convinced her that, for his sake, it was time she demonstrated strength. "They'll have you out of here soon, babe."

Despite the cold air, she could see beads of sweat across his forehead. His beautiful dark hair was disheveled, and the creases on his face told her he had battled pain for a long while. *Poor guy.* Lynette made her way down the steps and stood to the right as she

152

TRACI VANDERBUSH

was directed. She watched and listened, making note of the words exchanged by paramedics. "Possibly fractured" and "suspected break" were used. Her heart sank. *Oh, Dylan. What were you doing here?*

She noticed the slim, young man that stood across from her inside the dreary, dim pit. His hands rested in the pockets of his hoodie. He looked her way and nodded. Lynette thought he looked familiar. *Where do I know him from?* She always had a sharp memory. Faces and names flipped through her mind, and suddenly, she remembered.

She addressed him confidently. "Nick Brown?"

Surprise crossed his face. "You remember me?"

"Sure, I do. Is this your house?"

"Yes, ma'am."

Lynette inched her way behind the paramedics to position herself for her own detective work. "Nick, what was Dylan doing here?"

Before Nick could answer, Dylan managed to chime in as he was being lifted up on the stretcher. "Lynnie, I was buying something from Nick. I'll tell you all about it later. I was clumsy. Took a wrong step and ended up in here."

She knew Dylan well enough to know when he had someone's back. Dylan was protecting Nick. She nodded with understanding. "Well, Nick. I'm glad you were here. Thanks for looking out for my guy."

"Sure," Nick replied nervously.

She moved closer to the sheepish young man. Putting two and two together, she read the guilt on his face, figuring he must be the mysterious offender. Lynette remembered that his family had faced trouble in the past, which meant young Nick was in turmoil. She read the situation clearly and hoped to offer Nick something to hold onto. Her feminine intuition was on overdrive. *This kid*

153

THE WINDOWS OF HOLLY

needs to be forgiven.

Leaning in, Lynette whispered, "You know, I don't mean to sound preachy, but I was just thinking. Sometimes everything seems to be falling apart, but then we get surprised. A good kind of surprise. When you think you're falling into a pit, you're actually falling into an opportunity for something good to happen. We make mistakes, like taking a wrong step. I've been there so many times," she shook her head in wonder. "What's crazy is that every single time, I end up finding that I have a loving Father in Heaven who doesn't want me or anyone else to hurt because of my mistakes. Somewhere along the way, He makes my mess into a path to a clean slate. He's like magic, transforming everything into a story worth telling. That's probably what's going on here." She winked.

Gazing at the floor, he muttered, "Maybe."

As they waited for Dylan's deliverance from the pit, she asked, "Nick, where are your parents?"

He sighed. "Mom's working. Dad isn't here anymore. He left us two months ago."

Lynette placed her hand on his back. "I'm so sorry." His tense body relaxed at her touch. Lynette's gift for melting hard edges off hardened hearts was still intact.

Nick let her know the promise in which he placed his hope. "Dylan said he would help."

She assured him, "And he will. That's just like my Dylan."

"Why do you say 'my Dylan?'" Nick blurted out. "You're married to Owen, right?" The bitterness was tangible despite the slight softening of his demeanor. Nick didn't understand the things he had witnessed through the windows of the Vanberg home. He still had questions about Lynette's return, the intimacy between her and Dylan, and the random appearance of the mini-skirt clad woman who threw herself at Dylan. Nick's pursuit of scouting out

Dylan's place definitely raised more questions and judgments than he ever imagined.

Lynette had absorbed the painful fact that her choices affected more people than she wanted to admit. She couldn't blame Nick for coming across rudely. She tried to explain. "Owen left me and our baby. He's divorcing me. Thankfully, Dylan opened his arms to me. I'm really lucky; he's never stopped loving me, and to be honest, I still love him." She hoped her quick summary of an explanation would reduce the level of judgment she felt coming from Nick.

Lynette understood Nick's anger. She knew she had thrown Dylan's life into chaos shortly after he began meeting with Nick's parents. She was sure Dylan would have done more to help the Brown family had his own life not imploded. And it was her fault.

A rush of guilt punched Lynette in the gut. Another regret to add to her list. *How many people suffered because of me?* She turned to face Nick. "I have no doubt that Dylan would have helped your family, Nick. It's my fault. He didn't do anything wrong. I did. I was stupid. I don't know where my brain was. I let my heart go to a bad place. It was just a bad place and it was unfair to Dylan. I turned his life upside down." Her eyes moistened. "And in doing so, I turned yours upside down as well. For that, I'm eternally sorry."

Nick's face softened. It didn't take much to brush away his hard exterior. He shrugged. "Who's to say that my dad would have changed? I don't know. Maybe Dylan couldn't have fixed things. Dad might have run off with his boyfriend anyway." His jaw stiffened at the thought.

Lynette's eyes filled with compassion. "I'm so sorry."

"Aaaah!" Dylan's cry of pain shook Lynette. She darted toward him as the paramedic adjusted his position.

A medic assured her, "It's okay, ma'am. He'll be all right."

155

THE WINDOWS OF HOLLY

Dylan saw the terror on her face. He gritted his teeth, breathing quickly. "I'm…I'm okay." He forced a fake smile to lighten her anxiety.

Lynette followed behind them as they slowly ascended the stairs. "Can I ride with him in the ambulance?" she called after them, with a sound of desperation.

"Yes, ma'am," the medic replied.

As she emerged from the pit, she saw Jackson standing near the old Camaro, waiting patiently.

He called to Dylan, "Hey, buddy. I'm here. You're gonna be all right." Dylan responded with a pained smile. Jackson fixed his attention on the face of his friend, noting his vulnerability. Cold air rushed through the garage, reminding him that winter had descended upon them. *Why is it always cold when the worst things happen?* The dark thought whisked through Jackson's mind before landing on the fact that many good things also presented themselves in the cold of winter. He recalled the words of his sweet Lucy: *What is good and right is truer than what is wrong.*

As Lynette stepped into the ambulance, her eyes caught sight of Alexis Brown, the familiar woman who had directed her to the garage. Alexis sat alone on the front step of the purple porch, staring at her feet. "One moment," Lynette said to the ambulance driver. She ran toward Alexis and knelt down in front of her on the cold concrete. Alexis's eyes opened wide with surprise as Lynette took her hands. "Alexis. I remember you," she said with a smile. "Thank you for helping Dylan."

"You're welcome," she said.

Lynette knew she and Dylan had disappointed this family long ago. Though the situation was beyond their abilities to cure, guilt seeped into her soul. "I know I let you down. Please, if there's anything I can do to help you, let me know."

Alexis shook her head. "It's not your fault. You'd better be

156

going now."

Lynette hugged her before turning away.

ANNIE'S CAFÉ

On cold December nights, Annie's Café was the hub of connection for the town. The tiny grocery store was a close second, or perhaps the post office, but nothing compared to the warmth and conversations that happened at Annie's. Every November and December, one of the topics of the town was whether or not Arnold, the café manager, used magic or easily accessible ingredients in his "special" hot cocoa. It seemed no one could replicate the magical concoction. The owner always looked forward to Arnold's cocoa because it attracted the entire population of Holly.

Lucy would normally be waiting tables on most December nights, but tonight she rocked baby Asa at the Vanberg home as she waited to hear news of the damage done to Dylan from his fall into the pit. She gazed at Asa's perfect little face and pondered what the baby in her womb might look like. *Hopefully as perfect as this little one.* She decided she would much rather rock a sleeping baby than weary her feet with the pressure of meeting the demands of hungry adults at the café.

The café rumbled with conversation as residents rolled in. Old Emma Gray happily announced the arrival of her daughter, Kathleen, and grandchildren. Ever since she was reunited with the daughter she'd given up for adoption, a special kindness and compassion filled her heart. Living a life free from her big secret had transformed her into a new person. Once the town grump, now she stood in the café with a smile on her face as she made sure everyone knew that her baby girl was in town along with her grandbabies.

Burt and Elsie worked quickly to pull together a couple of

THE WINDOWS OF HOLLY

tables for Emma and her family. The jingle bell above the door announced the entrance of Mike and Curt, never mind the fact they were just there three hours before. When the duo had a day off, they'd spend it at Annie's, playing dominoes and indulging themselves in desserts. Burt rolled his eyes at the sight of Mike and Curt. "Pshh. There they are again," he lamented.

Elsie grinned. "C'mon, Burt. Give 'em a break. Where else do they have to go? Where's your Christmas spirit?"

Burt mockingly mouthed words back at her. "Well, it ain't Christmas yet, missy."

Elsie shook her finger at him. "It's close enough. Just over two weeks away!"

Burt cringed. "Don't remind me. That means my mother-in-law is coming, God help us all!"

Finishing the arrangement of the tables, Elsie made sure that Emma and her offspring were seated.

Mike noticed Burt's grumpy face as he approached them. "Hey, Burt. You're lookin' a bit crotchety tonight. What got your hind end a-sizzlin'?"

Burt shook his head at Mike. The two would often engage in a battle of less-than-witty wits, but Burt wasn't feeling it tonight. Burt explained, "We're busy tonight. I've got in-laws arriving tomorrow. The heater went out at my house, and now the oven appears to be on the fritz. That's what got my hind end a-sizzlin'."

Mike's eyes flashed a hint of care. "My goodness, Burt. Maybe your house is freakin' out because it knows your mother-in-law is coming," he joked. "I can help you with that heater, you know."

Burt looked surprised. "Seriously?"

"Yep. That's kinda my trade. Except it's the trade for which I don't get paid. I know how to fix a heater like I know how to pick my nose. It just comes natural."

Burt grinned. "I'm not sure I like the analogy, but I'd

158

appreciate it if you'd take a look. Are you available tomorrow morning, like seven o'clock?"

"Sure am," Mike replied.

Burt pointed at him. "But no picking your nose in my house. And I'm banning you from the beans tonight."

"Deal." Mike shifted the conversation. "Any news on Dylan Vanberg?"

Burt gave him the update. "All we know is he had a fall and he's at Marshall City Hospital getting checked out."

Mike shook his head. "Poor guy. He's had a heck of a month so far. It seems like everywhere Lynette goes, a hurricane follows."

Burt chuckled. "Sounds like my ex-wife. You know that wreckin' ball song." He laughed. "She came in like a wreckin' ball!" He wiggled his hips.

Curt hollered, "Whoa, Mike. Don't you start dancin' now! We don't need to see that performance of yours."

Elsie piped up, "Spare us all!"

Chapter Fourteen

YNETTE BALANCED A CUP OF HOT TEA on the arm of her living room recliner as she nestled into it, enveloped in her fuzzy, white robe. "Good morning, bright eyes," she said to Dylan who was laid out on the sofa.

"Hey," he said, a smile lighting his face.

Lynette exhaled. "That was a heck of a night, huh?"

Dylan rolled his eyes at the mess he'd created. "Understatement of the year."

She encouraged him, "But look at how lucky you are. I think it's miraculous you came out as well as you did. A couple of bruised ribs and two small fractures that don't even need a cast. You're one lucky rabbit. Of course, the concussion is worrying, but at least it's mild. I'm just glad you're home."

"Lucky rabbit?" He grinned. "Where do you come up with these things?"

She tilted her head. "My weird mind, I suppose."

Dylan winked at her. "But I love that about you." He smiled as he tried to readjust his position. "Ouch, ouch, ouch. The way it hurts, you'd think my leg was broken in half."

She patted his arm. "You should try childbirth sometime. Then we'll talk," she quipped. "Would you like some tea?"

Dylan gave a thumbs-up. "Have you ever known me to turn

THE WINDOWS OF HOLLY

down tea?"

Lynette smiled, "Nope. If you did, I'd be calling the doctor!" She went to the kitchen and made a cup of tea while pondering everything that happened in the last twenty-four hours. She silently thanked God for Lucy's willingness to keep Asa through the night. *And thank God for that breast pump!* She was glad she stored milk for the little guy.

She considered the craziness of life and wondered how they kept breathing. *Amazing.* Lynette thought about Dylan's kindness toward her. *How is it possible he would still love me after all these years? After all I've done? And under these circumstances?* Her eyes were quick to moisten with inexpressible emotion. She silently thanked God for him and for their close friends who carried them through difficulties.

Lynette carried Dylan's tea to the living room. "Here you go, love. When you're ready, I'll help you sit up. I know those bruised ribs can really hurt."

Dylan noticed her watery eyes. "You okay?"

She smiled. "More than okay. I'm just happy to be here with you, that's all."

He was moved by her sincerity. "I'm glad you're here too." He flashed a cheesy smile. "Here I am, laid up through Christmas and into the New Year, but I get to have you here with me. Aren't you a lucky lady?" he said with a wink.

"Yes, I am," she said sincerely.

Dylan touched his finger to his lips, grinning mischievously, as he winked at her once more. "Pardon me, nurse. Please be advised the patient you're tending to will need lots of attention."

She giggled, shaking her head. "Mr. Vanberg, it appears that your medication is taking effect."

He shook his head. "Nah. I'm just under the influence of my

hot wife."

A flash of warmth shot through Lynette at the sound of his voice calling her his 'wife.' Desire for him, in the purest sense, overwhelmed her. *I love this man so much.*

Dylan's pain medicine opened the floodgate to uninhibited words. "I can't wait to take you, nurse Lynette. Let's set a wedding date right now. Life's too short. What are we waiting around for?"

She loved hearing his words, but she hoped that once the medication wore off, he wouldn't change his mind. "I'm all for setting a date," she responded, "but you know we have to wait until my divorce is final."

Dylan pointed to his phone. "Well, let's call Owen about it. Can we speed up the process?"

Lynette was surprised by his readiness, but she knew he probably wasn't thinking straight. "I hope that's not the concussion speaking," she grinned. "But since you mentioned it, I'll tell you I've been doing some research. The way Owen laid things out, if I agree with an uncontested divorce since he and I don't have our names on anything jointly, it should be quick. We kept everything separate. The only thing is the money he promised from the sale of the ranch, but honestly, I don't want anything. I just want to be free. From what I've read, it can be done within days if we're in agreement. I mean, most likely three months, but depending on the lawyer, it could be really fast."

Dylan, not thinking, tried to sit up. "Ugh! God, that hurts," he yelped, wincing.

Lynette jumped to his aid. "Slowly. Take it slowly." She assisted him as he sat up. "Here, have your tea. It'll make you feel better."

He breathed rapidly for a few seconds as the pain subsided. "Okay, I'm fine," he puffed. "Can you call Owen now and talk with him about this?"

163

THE WINDOWS OF HOLLY

She tilted her head, trying to decipher what he was thinking. "Right now? Did you hear anything I just said?"

"Of course."

She wasn't fond of the idea of having to speak to the man who abandoned her and his own baby, but Dylan was right. In order to get anywhere, communication was required.

Dylan thought for a moment. "You know, the last five years have been a mix of hoping, believing, giving up, and letting go. Even after I let go, there were still fractions of a second, occasionally, when I would imagine us being together again. I'd blow it off because I knew it was impossible. And then, suddenly, you came home," he smiled. "The very second I saw you on our porch, I knew those dreams were glimpses of reality. Five years is a long time. I know people will say we need to take it slow because we've got a lot of baggage to deal with, and I know they'll assume things that aren't true, but I don't want to lose more time. Life is flying by too quickly. I don't feel so young and vibrant anymore."

"Dylan, you're still young! You're just a bit beat up right now. In a few months you'll be back to normal," she assured him.

Dylan continued, "Yeah, but what I mean by not feeling young is that I'm more aware of the passing of time. Every second counts."

She reminded him, "You're recovering from a fall, not to mention a concussion. Give yourself a break. Don't kick your mind into panic mode about racing against time. You need to recover before we make plans."

Dylan wanted her to know he was fully in charge of his thoughts. "Listen, this isn't the concussion talking. I've thought about this a lot. I know we have things to work through, but I want to do it together. I mean, really together. We can figure out details as we go. Besides, to be honest, what's the point of thinking through every detail? I already know I want you in my life. You're my best friend. I could choose to stop at friendship but I'd like more than that. If we went through all the counseling before getting married again, we will have spent even more time unmarried. Why not be married and work it out at the same time? If we're committed, then we're committed, right?"

Lynette smiled. "Wow. You really have thought about this, haven't you? I can't say the advice you're giving yourself would be good for everyone, but I do think it's right for us. I know I want to spend my life with you too." She smiled and tilted her head sideways, inquisitively.

"When do you want to get married?"

"Like, yesterday," he replied with a grin. "So, seriously. When I say 'call Owen now,' I really do mean today. Let's not waste time."

"Okay then." The thought of hearing Owen's voice turned her stomach a bit. "I suppose I should call before Lucy brings Asa back over."

THE CALL

Lynette's heart pounded as she waited for an answer. She tapped her pen on the notepad, ready to record every detail. With each ring, she braced herself.

"Hey," answered a gruff, reluctant voice. "What's up?"

"Hi, Owen." *Why should I even ask how he's doing?* "How are things?" She didn't really care how he was at the moment, but it made for civil conversation.

He cleared his throat. "I'm doing well. And you?"

Hearing his confidence and the news of his wellness confirmed Owen's selfishness. *Amazing how he can leave his son and say he's doing well. Nauseating.* Lynette wanted to lash out at him for

THE WINDOWS OF HOLLY

his arrogant carelessness, but she knew it wasn't worth rocking the boat, especially when she was in a good place with Dylan. *Why waste my time and energy? It's not worth it.*

"I'm doing well too." she replied.

He grunted, "You're enjoying yourself over there at Dylan's, are ya?"

Owen's directness caused alarms to go off in her mind. *Is this a threat?* Her heart skipped a beat. *Stay calm, Lynette.* She wondered if his question was a trap of some sort. She dared to ask, "Do you have a problem with me being at Dylan's?"

He replied emotionless. "No. That's where you're supposed to be."

Lynette was shocked by his statement, unsure of his motivation and intentions. "What is that supposed to mean?"

He coughed. "Nothing. Just that I think that's where you were always meant to be." His reply surprised her.

She was stunned. She believed that too, but didn't dare tell Owen that's where her heart was at home.

She breathed deeply. "I don't know how to respond to that. Are you playing games with me?"

He changed the subject. "So why are you calling, Lynette?"

She wanted to get to the point. "To talk about the divorce. I guess I need answers about a timeline, you know? How does this all work?"

Owen cleared his throat and paused for a moment. "Let me paint a picture for you. I'm looking out my cabin window, watching snow lightly falling on the tall pines. There's a buck and a couple of lady deer walking about thirty feet from where I'm sitting. A fire's burning behind me. The wood's cracklin' and I'm at peace. I don't want a long, drawn-out divorce. I just want to be done with everything so I can move on. The quicker, the better. I

166

don't need unpleasant, complicated details to think about."

"Unpleasant?" Just one thing mattered to Lynette. She had to know. "What about Asa? Do you think about your son?"

Silence.

Lynette asked again, "Owen, what about your son?"

He sighed. "Don't you think Dylan will take him as his own?"

Lynette was frustrated. "You're evading my question, Owen. What I want to know is, what are your intentions toward your son?" The depths of her soul burned with sadness and anger that he showed no desire toward his own child. "How could you so easily walk away?"

Owen sighed once more. "I don't know what to tell you. Of course I think about him occasionally, but I don't feel any connection. You wanted a baby so badly. That's kind of your thing. I suppose something is wrong with me, but I haven't really felt connected with anyone for a long time. But here, in nature, I'm at peace. When I'm alone, I can't mess anything up for anyone. No demands. Kids are demanding, and I'm not ready for that. What kind of father would I be? I'd probably screw the kid up."

A mixture of emotion flooded her eyes with stinging tears. "I feel sorry for you, Owen." Her voice trembled. "To not be able to feel...that would be awful. To not feel the kind of love for a child that makes you want to lay down your life for him, to not feel the joy of caring for someone else, to not feel what it's like to truly love; that's unthinkable. I'm sad for you because you don't know the pleasure of bending your will for the benefit of another. I can't imagine, but I'm glad you're happy up there alone. I don't think I'll ever understand your feelings toward Asa, your own son."

Owen butted in, "Look. I know Dylan well enough to know he'll care for you and Asa. So, in a sense, I'm freeing you to something better. Maybe you could appreciate me for that. I'm smart enough to recognize where I'm lacking, and I'm smart

THE WINDOWS OF HOLLY

enough to know what I want. I should've gone after it a long time ago."

Lynette chimed in, "But you're apparently not smart enough to care enough to try and fix what's lacking. It's called doing the right thing. It's simple to not abandon a child, Owen. The marriage is one thing, but your own child is another."

He replied strongly, "Maybe for you, it's simple."

She couldn't comprehend Owen's condition. "You're seriously more interested in giving your life to a mountain than a human being?" *Forgive him, Lynette. He's a poor soul.* She quieted her soul. "Okay. I respect where you are in your journey. It's clear to me that we have two extremely different goals. So thank you, Owen, for releasing me from the relationship. You're right that I'm where I'm supposed to be. You are right that Dylan will love Asa as his own."

Silence lingered for a few seconds.

Owen finally spoke up. "You're welcome. Let's just stick to talking about the divorce so we can all be free. Did you sign those papers I sent?"

She wished she had. "No. I haven't even read them all because I've been too overwhelmed." *He doesn't have a clue how I feel.*

He cleared his throat. "Well, if you'd take the time to look through everything," he started.

Lynette quickly interrupted, "Take the time? You mean, all the time I've had since adjusting to a newborn, being sleep deprived, being abandoned, and then beaten up?"

Owen continued without acknowledging her dilemma. "If you'd take the time to read through everything, you'll see that two options were laid out. One would take about six months. Hell, the other could be as quick as six days."

Lynette was flooded with relief by the idea of six days. "Six days? How is that possible?"

He explained, "If you'd read it, you'd see. It basically frees me of any obligations. If you fully agree, it's uncontested, and my lawyer said he can have everything finalized quickly."

She tried to hide her relief at the possibility of being done with him. "Okay. I'll get back to you as soon as possible."

Owen was pleased by the thought of being done with the process. "All right. Oh, and by the way, you don't have to worry about Will. He'll never bother you again."

Lynette was glad to hear that. "Good."

"Bye now." Owen abruptly hung up the phone, exhaling deeply. "Poor little whiny thing. I don't know what I was thinking taking a princess away from her glorious castle," he muttered sarcastically. "Call me the fool."

Lynette walked back to the living room with mixed emotions. *How can he not care about Asa? How did I fall in love with that?* The fact that she thought they were in love made her feel like the biggest idiot in the universe. Sadness pierced her heart at the loss of five years with Dylan. She squeezed her eyes closed for a second, breathing deeply. "Let it go, Lynette. Let it go," she whispered to herself. "You can't go back in time. You just have to move forward."

Dylan reclined on the couch from which he'd tried his best to overhear the conversation with Owen. He only caught bits and pieces, and he listened to her trying to encourage herself. Hearing Lynette's footsteps, he called out, "Trying to let it go, Lynnie?"

She exhaled long and deep. "Yeah." She wanted to vent her frustrations about Owen to Dylan, but she knew he needed to rest, and she knew for the sake of her soul, she needed to change the subject to something positive. *Marrying Dylan is what I want more than anything right now.* "So let's talk dates, Dylan."

He raised his eyebrow. "Dates?"

169

THE WINDOWS OF HOLLY

"Yep." A tear rolled down her cheek. She knelt by his side. Chin quivering, she managed, "Will you really marry me again?"

He wanted to embrace her, but his injuries prevented him from moving too much. "Oh yes." He smiled. "I've said it a million times. Yes."

On bended knees, she rested her head against his arm. Dylan ran his fingers through her golden hair. "It's been a wild ride, huh? Don't let the detour crush you. Focus on now. When the bad memories and regrets weigh on you, go to now. Stay in the now and don't worry about the future. God's got us."

"I know," she whispered. "I just wish I wouldn't have been so stupid. And so wrong. And so mean to you."

He touched her cheek. "You weren't stupid. You were lonely. And that was my fault."

She raised her head to look into his eyes. "Dylan, I was stupid and selfish. That's my own fault."

Dylan shook his head. "If you're gonna play that game, then who was stupid first? Could it have been your pastor-husband who worked at the church sixty hours a week, staying on call 24-7? Could it have been that he didn't listen to you when you asked him to spend time with you? You talk about stupid. That guy was an idiot." He grinned. "All we can do at this point is focus on now and continue the journey, making the most out of the time we've been given."

She wiped her tears away. "I just hope those five lost years will be completely given back to us. Can we live to be a hundred years old? I want all the years we can get." She smiled.

He puckered his lips. "One hundred years, huh? Well, no one is promised tomorrow, but sure. Let's go for it. Hopefully this leg heals up well, otherwise I might need a cane a bit earlier than expected." He chuckled. "Think of that. Us at the age of a hundred. That could be scary."

She grinned. "Yeah, but it could be fun."

He widened his eyes. "Hm. Do you think I'll be a bald old man?"

She giggled. "Dylan, you've got the thickest head of hair. I highly doubt you'll lose it. What about me? What will I look like?"

He whistled. "You'll be even more beautiful than old Mary Elliott. She's an elegant, classy granny with a flair for art. Come to think of it, she's quite hip in her old age. You'll surpass her, I'm sure."

Lynette liked the idea. "If I can look as good as her, that'll be just fine with me." She set her eyes on Dylan's beautiful painting above the mantle, studying the intricate details. She was amazed by his ability to create shadows and the folds in the bride's veil. "That painting is incredible, Dylan. I still can't believe you did that. Will you give me lessons?"

He tucked a piece of hair behind her ear. "It was Mary who taught me how to paint, so maybe you should ask her for lessons. Honestly, I barely remember painting those. It was therapy for me during a foggy time."

She thought for a moment. "Maybe I'll ask her."

Dylan steered the conversation back to marriage. "Okay, back on topic, lady! Wedding date?"

She perked up. "Yes! First I have to read over some paperwork that Owen sent, and we'll go from there. According to Owen, depending on what option I choose, it could be as quick as six days."

Dylan was shocked. "What? How's that possible? I thought divorces took months!"

She shook her head. "So did I. Knowing Owen, he's had this in the works for a long time. He probably paid somebody off, for all I know. He has a lawyer friend. As far as I'm concerned, the sooner,

THE WINDOWS OF HOLLY

the better."

"Just be sure you get legal advice so you don't lose anything," said Dylan. "I'm not sure the info he gave you is correct. I don't know about six days. Some states have waiting periods."

Disappointment fell over her face. The idea of having to wait pained her inside and out. "Well then. Could we do a spiritual ceremony and then do a legal wedding later?"

Dylan's eyes widened. "Wow. In our situation, I'd be cool with that, but I'm sure we'd start a theological firestorm of a debate for other people."

She sighed. "Nowadays, people do whatever they want anyway. You and I have been married to each other before, so does it really matter? In God's eyes, don't you think he sees our marriage still intact? I mean, who am I to break the covenant? I was foolish, and I may have chosen to dissolve it, but don't you think our Father doesn't need us to get a piece of paper in order for Him to recognize our marriage? It's a covenant that He's strong enough to keep, despite our inability to do so."

He grinned, intrigued by her conclusion. "Oh, girlfriend. You're pressing the envelope, but yes, I believe you're right. Like I said before, in my heart I never divorced you. I think God looks at the heart. If people can't do the same, I feel sorry for them. But don't tell anyone I said that. I'm sure I'd be crucified for making such a statement."

Lynette tilted her head in thought. "Dyl, you know that verse they always use in ceremonies? 'Therefore, what God has joined together, no human being must separate?' Or 'put asunder,' or whatever? I don't believe God joined me and Owen together. That was my own selfish doing. That was my will, not His. So if God didn't join us together, maybe that marriage really doesn't exist."

Dylan placed his hand on his forehead. "You're blowing my

172

drug-saturated brain."

She shrugged. "I'm sorry, babe. I'm just thinking out loud. Seriously though. Think about it. Didn't Jesus teach that marriage was permanent, or something like that? I mean, that's what I got out of it. Maybe God never recognized our divorce, so our marriage still remains. If I made a decision while my heart was in a really bad place, does that decision have to stick?"

Dylan thought for a moment. *She so desperately wants to be free from the choices she made.* "People do all kinds of things, and usually they do those things when their hearts and minds are not in the right place. God erases our mistakes, but on this earthly plane, there are some things that remain from the choices we make."

Lynette agreed reluctantly, "Yes, but which plane is greater? This earthly plane, or the unseen realm that's been visiting me over the last few years? I've had dreams and visions, and heard voices that have ultimately directed me back to you. At least, I believe they have. I know my heart has drawn me to you."

"Well, Lynette," he raised an eyebrow, "you have many good arguments. I guess, ultimately, it's between you and God. And me. I know for me, I always saw us as married. I've always been married to you. When I chose you once, I chose you forever. It's not that way for everyone, but for me, it is. I guess we should pray about all of this and see how things play out. I want to do things right."

Dylan sat for a few seconds as he thought about what he just said. *I want to do things right.* He snickered to himself. "I want to do things right. You can do things rightly, but that doesn't mean things will turn out the way you expected. Isn't that hilarious?"

Lynette looked into his eyes. "Yeah. I wouldn't know though, because I've usually not done things the right way."

He objected. "That's not true, babe. One mistake doesn't erase all of the good things you've done."

173

THE WINDOWS OF HOLLY

She closed her eyes, soaking in his healing words, wanting to believe him. "But maybe in the eyes of people, it does. One mistake is enough to destroy your reputation forever. It seems that people label others for life based on the wrong they've done."

He sighed. "Yes, but their judgments don't matter so much. Besides, they can pull their own planks out of their eyes. Who of us really, consistently, sees clearly?"

As Dylan asked that question, he and Lynette were both filled with the vibration of Heaven as these words rang inside their souls: "See in Me."

"See in Me," Lynette repeated.

"What?" Dylan was taken aback. "What did you just say?"

She replied, "See in Me. I hear those words a lot lately."

Dylan's eyes widened once again. "Holy cow! No way. I've heard that too. It was in a dream. Lynnie, I think God is telling us to see as He does." Dylan placed his hand on the back of Lynette's head, elbow bent behind her neck. "If we could just see as He sees."

"Then we would see clearly."

Chapter Fifteen

ANOTHER DAY DAWNED. Lynette exhaled with relief as she hung up the phone and tossed the papers on the table. *His mercies are new every morning.* She reminded herself to take things one step at a time. If she thought too far ahead, allowing details to overwhelm her, she'd lose her peace. She mumbled to herself, "Keep your peace, Lynette."

Dylan called from the living room, "So how did that go?"

She picked up her glass of tea, making her way toward Dylan. "Not bad. I just have some decisions to make." Pulling the wooden rocking chair closer to the sofa, she was both relieved by the lawyer's words yet anxious about how her decisions would affect Dylan.

"Have a little sit down," he commanded. "Wanna tell me about it?"

She sat down gently, taking in the comfort of a good companion and a good rocking chair. "There's good news, but still much to consider. And it doesn't just affect me. It affects you as well."

"Okay. So give it to me."

She turned her eyes to the bay window, admiring the swaying of the porch swing. *If only life were simple again.* "How about we sit outside? It's warmed up enough; we should take advantage of

THE WINDOWS OF HOLLY

the porch before that next cold front blows in. As long as we're sitting in the sunshine, it'll be perfect. You need some fresh air anyway."

"Sure," he agreed.

"Let me grab the baby monitor so I can listen for Asa." She left the room, watching her feet as they whisked across the wooden floors. The sight of her old floors caused her to smile. She whispered, "Hello, floors. I'm so happy to be with you again." She was sure that cleaning the floors would never be seen as an inconvenience again. It would be a delight.

Dylan focused on the rays of light landing on his painting over the mantle. The diamonds in the bridal gown captured the light, glowing with promise. *Not bad. Not a bad painting at all.* He admired his work and thanked God for the gift that emerged in the midst of his darkest days. Each stroke of the brush was salvation to him, saving him from a moment of deep sadness. He marveled over how many intricate brushstrokes it took to make up such a vision.

The *tick tock* of the tall grandfather clock reminded Dylan to count. *One, two, three, four, five, six.* He began to ponder time with fascination. *Counting. How fascinating, counting time. Time's sound. The sound of time passing.* He wondered how many ticks had sounded since the creation of timekeeping. *Is time whispering of things to come?*

Rhythms and thoughts rolled through Dylan's head. He found himself singing softly, a hymn of old that he once wrote off as cheesy. "Count your blessings, name them one by one. Count your blessings, see what God has done. When upon life's billows, you are tempest-tossed, when you are discouraged, thinking all is lost, count your blessings, name them one by one, and it will surprise you what the Lord has done." The warmth of joy rushed through his bruised body. "I gotta give it to you, old Johnson Oatman, Jr.

176

That's a good little song," he muttered. "Not so cheesy."

Lynette came back in the living room. "What are you mumbling? What's not cheesy?"

"Aw, nothing. I was remembering that old hymn about counting your blessings. I used to think it was cheesy, but I suppose things of old tend to mean more later down the road."

She brought the crutches to his side. "Here, I'll help you up. Remember not to put weight on that leg at all. We don't need you having any setbacks."

He grimaced, bracing himself for any potential pain as he moved into a sitting position. "That wasn't too bad. It's just awkward with this giant, robot leg brace. Attractive, isn't it?"

Lynette helped him position the crutches. "Uh, yeah. Incredibly." She moved the cushion for him. "Will you be working for the *Herald* today?"

"Yep," he replied. "I have some editing and lots of writing to do since the Christmas week edition is coming up. The last couple of weeks have inspired me. There are almost too many thoughts running through my head for me to grasp. The paper should be especially entertaining since I'm on pain meds." He laughed.

Lynette looked disturbed. "Gee. I guess I'm to thank for all the inspiration?"

He pointed at her. "Why, of course you are!"

She smiled nervously. "Is that good? Or bad?"

He beamed, "Lighten up, babe. It's all good."

Lynette looked to the ceiling and muttered, "Thank God." As they made their way to the porch, she was filled with gratitude for Dylan's role in being a voice for the community. "It's nice that you can work from home and reach so many people."

"Yes, thanks to Jackson," Dylan was eternally grateful for his best friend. Jackson had shown up in Dylan's moment of utter abandonment, offering comfort. He walked with Dylan through his

THE WINDOWS OF HOLLY

unwanted divorce and brought him back to Holly with a job he would enjoy: a full-time gig with the *Holly Herald* that actually paid enough for him to be comfortable in the little town he adored.

The added bonus of occasional contracts with other regional papers and businesses kept his bank account in the black. His ability to stir hearts and identify with each community earned him quick recognition. Dylan Vanberg was a name known by almost everyone in the region who read their local paper.

After Lynette left Dylan, Pastor Dean and Elder David rallied behind Dylan, going above and beyond to provide funds for a small cushion that would keep him from losing his house. They wanted to honor and care for him since he'd given many years of service to the community. He was able to keep his dream home and remain a part of the town that he loved. Even when some rejected him and spread rumors about his downfall, he still knew he was home, and Holly was where he wanted to be.

As Lynette assisted Dylan into a chair on the front porch, she covered him with a light blanket. "There's still a little chill in the air," she said, smiling lovingly.

Dylan treasured the feeling of being nurtured. His mind and body welcomed the attention after five long years of deprivation. The simple gesture of being given warmth caused his eyes to sting a bit with gratitude. "Thank you."

Lynette sat on the porch swing across from him. "This is lovely. Gosh, I remember sitting out here all the time." She allowed herself to take in the little details of picket fences, ornate architectural touches, rockers and swings swaying. "I've missed this terribly. It's funny how even the clanking chains bring back good memories." She closed her eyes, moving the swing back and forth with her feet, concentrating on the sound.

Dylan admired the way the light of the sun lit her hair. "So what did the lawyer say?" He was eager to hear the news.

178

She opened her eyes slowly. "The lawyer says if I don't want anything at all from Owen and just want the marriage to be dissolved, it can be done quickly because of the way Owen set things up with his lawyer. He's had this in the works for about a year. Can you believe that? A full year. That means he was already seeking a divorce before I got pregnant. I guess he set divorce plans aside for awhile when we found out I was pregnant. I'm not sure why he decided to leave right after I had Asa though." She shook her head.

Dylan didn't know what to say. "I'm so sorry."

"Thanks." She smiled warmly. "But I'm here now, so it worked out in my favor."

Dylan responded with a smile.

Lynette continued, "He doesn't want any rights to Asa. He just wants to walk away."

He shook his head. "That's horrible. How are you dealing with that?"

She looked at the sky as she considered the thoughts of her soul. "Well, on one hand, I'm relieved because I don't have to deal with custody issues, but on the other hand, it angers me that he could treat his son that way. How do I explain things to Asa when he gets older? How do you tell someone his father didn't want him?"

Dylan wanted to ease her mind. "I guess we can't worry about that right now. Just take it one day at a time. That's all you can do."

"Yeah. If I want to get the ranch money or fight for anything regarding Asa, it'll be a long, drawn-out deal. Here's the kicker, Dylan. He knows the only way he can get out of paying child support is if I remarry you and you adopt Asa. When we talked on the phone yesterday, Owen sounded like he expected you would take Asa as your own. He's taking advantage of your kindness, hoping for a way out of responsibility. That's just wrong."

Dylan cleared his throat. "I've already thought through this stuff. When I say I want you to be in my life, I mean both of you. I know what I'm taking on."

Lynette dropped her head, looking at the wooden planks of the porch. She shuffled through her thoughts to find a sufficient response, but nothing seemed adequate. "Dylan, that's far too much. You've mentioned taking Asa as your own, but that makes me feel awful. You shouldn't have to pay a price for my decisions, the decisions that caused you pain. Why should you take on that responsibility?"

Her doubts failed to cause him concern. Dylan spoke with the voice of God, it seemed. "Lynette, look at me." She lifted her eyes to meet his. "I love you. I always have. This baby is part of you. I am more than willing to care for both of you. All the details will come together. Stop doubting and let me carry you."

She shook her head once more. "But what if it gets too hard? What if you wake up one day and you feel differently? What if Asa looks like Owen? What if he's a brat? You could end up resenting him, and me."

He reassured her. "Look, I'm no superhero. I know my weaknesses, and I'm well aware that it'll be challenging, but I'm not afraid. I've made up my mind. It's a choice, a promise. I won't break my promise. If I have a hard time with something, we'll find a way through it. You know I'm not one for holding the actions of parents against their children. Asa is not Owen. I won't turn my back on him."

Lynette stared at him in awe. "Okay." She managed a hopeful smile. "Then I won't be afraid either."

"Good," he replied confidently.

She wanted him to know, "I'll never take you for granted, Dylan. You're a portrait of true love." She stood from the swing to kiss his forehead. "A true masterpiece."

A woman's high-pitched voice called out, "Well, well! Look at the lovebirds!"

Dylan and Lynette turned their heads to respond. They smiled at the sight of old Emma Gray. Dylan waved. "Hey, Miss Emma! How are you?"

Emma shuffled along in her house shoes, wrapped in her beloved fuzzy, red robe. "How am I? Well, I'll tell you," she said as she approached the porch steps, "I'm alive, upright, and functioning despite the dying smoke alarm battery that woke me up at one in the morning! The only way I could reach the thing was to stand on my kitchen table and smack the heck out of it with my broom handle. I was finally able to knock it down so I could get the battery out. Then the three a.m. potty-piddle-parade woke me up. Seems I always have to pee during the witching hour. I suppose that's what happens when you're nearing the age of eighty."

Dylan and Lynette laughed. Dylan joked, "Maybe that's God's way of making you exercise."

Emma shook her finger at him. "Very funny, young man!" She drew closer to them. "So how are you two lovebirds?" It did Emma's heart good to see the couple together, just like old times.

Dylan happily responded, "We're doing well. I'm a bit of a bruised mess, but I'm slowly healing up from my fall. This pretty lady takes good care of me."

Lynette offered, "May I get you some tea, Miss Emma?"

Emma smiled. "I would love some, if you don't mind."

"Not at all," Lynette gleamed. "Here, have a seat on the swing. Or would you rather have a chair?"

Emma wiggled her hips playfully. "Oh, it's the swing for me all right! I've gotta keep this body moving, keep it young, you know? The more movement, the better."

THE WINDOWS OF HOLLY

Lynette grinned as she entered the house to get Emma's tea.

Emma nestled herself on one end of the wooden swing, pulling her robe tightly for warmth. Dylan lifted the blanket off himself. "Here, Miss Emma. I'll have to toss it to you." He carefully flung the blanket her way, cringing slightly at the pain in his ribs.

Being in his presence gave her something to brag about. Emma enjoyed the friendship. "Thank you, sir. It seems you can never have too many blankets at my age." She pulled the blanket over herself. "So how are you two getting along? That kiss looked quite nice," she said with a wink.

Dylan smiled. "We're very happy. I'm so glad she's here."

Emma tried not to pry too much, yet then again, she never really minded prying. "Are things looking up for you? I mean, I know it's only been a short time, but is there talk of a future?" She flashed a cheesy grin.

"Yes, ma'am. Most definitely." Dylan felt safe talking with Emma Gray. She'd been a faithful neighbor for many years. Emma was part of what made Holly home for Dylan. He used to enjoy her more for the entertainment. Once a grumpy, nosy neighborhood tell-all, Emma had become a good and gentle friend. He didn't mind sharing his life with her. "We're getting remarried as soon as possible. Hopefully sooner rather than later. Of course, she's dealing with all this divorce stuff. It sounds like Owen wants to rush it and have no responsibility. He started the ball rolling toward a divorce over a year ago, before Lynette was even pregnant. Anyway, she's ready for it to be over."

Emma shook her head with disgust. "The sooner they're divorced, the better. That guy's always been downright beastly. I'm glad she's free of him. I can't tell you how it warmed my old heart to see you two sitting on the porch this morning, just like old times. Things have a way of coming together, don't they? Sometimes with a lot of pain, but still, it comes together."

182

Dylan wanted Emma to be the first to know his plan. "I'm going to adopt Asa."

Emma smiled. "I wouldn't expect anything less from you."

His eyes twinkled. "Well, thanks. Lynette is a bit worried about it, you know? She's worried about me resenting her or the baby down the road."

Emma reassured him, "Oh, Dylan. I've known you long enough to know that's not possible. The way you've dealt with life's punches is evidence to me that there's no resentment in you."

"Well," he shrugged, "I don't deal with all of life's punches so well. Here I am with my leg in a brace all because I chased down the mysterious rock thrower."

Emma looked confused. "What? I thought you went to buy a car part from someone and fell in his garage."

He shook his head. "Oh, Emma. That's just a fabricated story to make me look better than the actual idiot I am. I was looking for the guy who kept throwing rocks and notes at my door. I found him all right." He threw his hands into the air. "Injuries and embarrassment is what came out of that. I did fall, but not because I was buying car parts."

"Oh, I see. Well, your secret is safe with me," she assured him. "So who was the culprit? Did he hurt you?"

Dylan shifted his gaze downward. "It was just a young man I'd let down many years ago. It seems ministry failures can follow you for a long time. And no, he didn't hurt me. I took a wrong step and fell into an oil pit."

She pooched her lips out. "Did he apologize for taunting you?"

"He did. We had a good, long talk. Lynette and I are communicating with him and his mom. Everything's good."

Emma nodded with satisfaction. She didn't need to know any more. "Well, I'm glad to hear that!"

A rush of wind came unexpectedly. Chains clinked in

THE WINDOWS OF HOLLY

harmony. Bare branches crackled. Emma pulled the blanket tighter. "Whew! Winds of change, Dylan. Winds of change. I feel a rush of life coming. It's time for a new and better season, my friend."

Dylan saluted. "Amen. I bow in honor of that season. Bring it on."

Emma smiled. "Christmas is right around the corner and I can't wait! I'm so excited because Kathleen and my grandbabies will be here. Did you see the lights on my house? David and Marcy helped me decorate."

He acknowledged her efforts. "I did see that. Your home looks lovely."

Emma's eyes shined with a youthful glow. "Ever since Kathleen came back into my life, it's like the world is more colorful."

Dylan smiled genuinely for her happiness. "Well, Miss Emma, I suppose that's what redemption does. It gives us a new perspective, new vision, and reignites our ability to dream again."

She agreed. "It sure does. What a year it's been. The ups and downs with all of us extraordinarily weird characters—we make life interesting, don't we? I especially love the parts where we get second chances. That's exactly what this year has been. A year of second chances. Aren't we lucky?" She pushed her fist into the air like a marching baton. Emma was known to be a bit animated at times. Her giddy smile morphed into wrinkled lips as she crossed her eyes. She pressed her lips together, making a flatulent sound. "And then there are the Owens in the world who need many chances. We all need about a thousand chances, I suppose. Lord, help us all. And help me not to think of that man as a douche." She sighed.

Dylan tried to stop the burst of laughter he knew would be painful. He snickered at Emma's choice of words.

Emma continued, "But you know what, Dylan? You and Lynette, you were meant to be with each other from the very start. I'm all for it, and I hope you two will do what you need to do without worrying what others think. My goodness. Life happens quickly, so you've gotta dig your feet in when you find where or who you're supposed to be with. These days, it seems too many couples are scared of life, scared of choices, and they second-guess every move. By the time they get around to living, their hair is gray and falling out!"

"I can't blame them. They've probably seen too many relationships fall apart."

She continued. "Yes, yes, but that's no reason to be paralyzed by fear. Fear always paralyzes, robbing people of life. Think about it. Anything good that happens in life involves risks. Every relationship is a risk. You open up your heart to someone without any assurances that it won't be damaged. But that's what love does, right?"

He smiled. "Love does just that," he nodded. "That's exactly what our heavenly Father does over and over again."

Emma tilted her head and shook a knowing finger at Dylan. "I still see the preacher in there. I hear him right now." She winked.

Dylan laughed. "Oh man. Seriously? Is my preach still showing?"

She grinned from ear to ear. "Yes, sir. You didn't think you were done with that, did you? Second chances, Dylan. Second chances."

Shaking his head in wonder, he mumbled, "I don't know, Miss Emma. We'll see."

She giggled. "I already see it. The preach is back. Lynette is back. It won't be long."

"We have a long ways to go. She's still married to another man you know," he reminded her.

THE WINDOWS OF HOLLY

Emma flung her hand in the air as if shooing a fly. "Fiddle faddle. That's no biggie. She'll be free soon."

"Yes, but as far as the preacher thing goes, the idea of being a preacher again still makes my stomach turn. I'm content with being a regular guy, you know? It's much easier than being labeled as a minister. I like being free from constant scrutiny. I can do life without every move being questioned and analyzed."

Emma wasn't swayed. "We'll see," she remarked with a grin.

Dylan tried to convince her that it was an impossibility. "As far as preaching goes, if I ever did that again, it wouldn't be the same, and it certainly wouldn't be at Hope Fellowship. Shoot, I don't even know that it would be in Holly, Emma. Too much damage has been done here. Who would ever listen to me?"

Emma leaned her body toward him. "Now listen to me, young man. I'll tell you who'd listen to you. The broken, the bruised, and the battered. The redeemed, the resurrected, and the reclaimed. That's who! And do you know what percentage of humanity that is? I'd say about one hundred percent. At some point in their lives, they'll find themselves in one of those places. I once heard a man say he'd only trust a preacher with a limp. A limp means you've been through the battle and come out on the other side. Everyone needs to hear from somebody who's been to hell and back. You and Lynette have both been there, and together, you can make a difference."

Dylan was inspired by her speech. "You make a good point. Thanks. I needed to hear that."

She iterated, "As far as Lynette goes, she wants to be with you, and I think she always has. She just didn't know it for a time. It seems we often learn what love is by experiencing what love is not."

Dylan raised his eyebrows. "True, Emma. True.

Lynette stepped onto the porch carrying a white tray.

"Teatime!"

Emma clutched her hands together like an excited child ready to receive a gift. "Thank you, dear. I can't believe it. I'm having tea with the Vanbergs on their front porch on a December morning. How lovely. It's like a dream come true."

Lynette smiled. "This is nice, isn't it?"

"Redemption at its finest." As Emma sipped her tea, she thought about the Christmases of the past at the Vanberg home. "Perhaps it's time for a Christmas House gathering, like old times."

Lynette and Dylan locked eyes, delighted by the memory of such wonderful times. Dylan let the idea run through his head for a second, but it seemed the obstacles to such bliss presented themselves quickly. Dylan responded to Emma's thought. "I'd love to do that again. Maybe next year."

Emma didn't hesitate to interject. "Why wait? Let's do it this year!"

He cleared his throat. "Christmas is, like, two weeks away. I'm not exactly mobile, and Lynette is in the middle of some big decisions. I don't see how we could possibly pull that off. Besides, who would attend such a scandalous event?"

Emma was relentless. "Scandalous? Now listen here. Did you already forget about the bruised and the redeemed I just mentioned? Dylan Vanberg, I'm telling you, there are many people in this community who know and love you and Lynette. They know your story, and they've been through their own crazy situations. I think their spirits would be lifted if they heard there was a Christmas gathering in your home. The ladies and I would be glad to put together refreshments. What do you say?"

Lynette and Dylan looked at each other questioningly. Dylan asked her, "What do you think, Lynnie?"

She shrugged with a smile. "Well, we could certainly use some

celebrating around here. I'm okay with it. I mean, it'd be a bit
awkward for me, being that people know our circumstances. Can
you imagine the rumors that must be flying around?"

Emma shook her finger in the air. "Give them something to
talk about. Let them see you two come back together. My
goodness, Lynette. Everyone already knows Owen is a selfish oaf.
Do you think it'd be such a shock for them to find you back here
with this amazing man?"

"Good point."

Emma continued, "I think people are more understanding than
you give them credit for. Let's party!" Emma threw a fist into the
air. "You two have probably been sitting here moping over your
past and the pressures of the present. If you let your lower lip hang
too low to the ground, you'll be able to write the Lord's Prayer on
it with a mop! And no one's got time for that."

Dylan and Lynette burst into laughter. Pain arrested Dylan's
ribs, but he couldn't help but giggle.

Lynette cackled, "Where do you get these sayings?"

Emma grinned. "I suppose Beverly has rubbed off on me a bit.
Silly bird."

Dylan was grateful for her humor. "Emma, if laughter is good
medicine, then you're the best doctor in town."

Emma sipped her tea, wild-eyed as she thought of another joke
she could crack. Seeing the Vanbergs laughing together fueled her
desire to keep it going. "I was at Hope Fellowship the other day.
Pastor Dean was preaching about the importance of being more
aware of the eternal than we are of the temporal world. You know,
like being more aware of the unseen realm than the seen. Well, I
was trying so hard to concentrate on what he was saying, but there
was this couple that came walking in right in the middle of his
message. I've never seen them before. For some reason, they
wanted to sit right up front, I mean, on the very first row! That tall,

blonde Barbie doll was wearing a tight red dress. She was stuffed in it like pork in a sausage casing. Definitely not from around these parts. She waltzed right down the aisle, swinging her backside for the whole congregation to see. Poor thing; she was so knock-kneed and her husband was so bowlegged. As they walked down the aisle side-by-side, their legs spelled 'ox,' and I couldn't contain myself."

Dylan spewed tea out of his mouth, grabbing his ribs as he tried hard to contain the laughter. "Ow, ouch. Oh my gosh." He squinted his eyes from the pain and hilarity. "Ox," he giggled. "Please, Emma. It hurts!"

Lynette hurried to his side as she convulsed with giggles. "Oh, Dylan. Are you okay?"

"It hurts, but it's good. I'll never forget that. Ox." He snickered as he winced.

Emma sipped her tea nonchalantly. "Sorry about that. I'll behave myself, but only until you're healed up. Then you're fair game."

"Deal," he agreed.

Emma continued, "For now, let's get back to planning a Christmas gathering. I want to see this happen."

Lynette sat next to Emma on the swing. "I love the idea. I really do. After this crazy year, and this being Asa's first Christmas, it should be a special time. I definitely want his first to be memorable for good reasons, not for all the chaos surrounding it." Lynette's eyes glistened. "The party would be the greatest Christmas gift I could get this year. Being in our old home, together with friends. Thank you for bringing up such an idea, Emma."

Emma patted Lynette's knee. "I'll see to it that you, Dylan, and Asa have a beautiful Christmas this year. Just think of it! The Christmas House will be lit up for Holly to see." She clamped her hands together with excitement. Emma's mind ran wild with ideas. "It's going to be beautiful. We could have Hailey or Victor play the piano. Oh, and Charlie Richmond could sing 'O Holy Night.' Oh, his voice! It's like a choir of angels. Beverly and I can gather the ladies to plan the food. You've already got some of your Christmas lights up. Just a little more decorating and it'll be perfect!"

Dylan reminded her, "I'm all for it, but I don't know how I can possibly help."

Emma assured them, "You don't have to do a thing. You served Holly for so many years. Now it's time to let us serve you."

Emma's kindness filled Lynette, drawing tears to her eyes. "Thank you. This means so much to us."

Emma smiled. "Honey, no need to thank me. Just thank your Father in Heaven. It's obvious to me that He's behind the two of you sitting here together today."

The baby monitor crackled with the sound of Asa cooing. Lynette stood. "It's breakfast time for the baby. I'll catch up with you later. Please be sure to call me and let me know what I can do to help prepare. I'm so excited about this!" Lynette gave her a warm, sincere hug.

"I'll let you know, dear." Emma set her teacup on the table next to the swing. "Well, I'd better be headin' home. I'll see you lovebirds later."

Unable to stand and hug her, Dylan gave a little wave. "Thank you."

Emma steadied herself on her feet. "Now, don't you go gettin' into trouble, mister."

Dylan motioned toward his legs. "It doesn't look like I'll be going too far, so no worries." He winked.

She shook her head, grinning. "I don't know. I've known far too many men. It doesn't take legs to stir up trouble, son." She

190

hesitated. "I'd say something else, but I can't afford to have you laughing too hard with those bruised ribs. It'll have to wait," she giggled.

As she shuffled carefully down the steps, Dylan was overcome by what had taken place. "Apparently, the Christmas House is happening," he muttered to himself. A simple, childlike joy brightened his eyes. A cool whoosh of wind caressed his face as if in response to his thoughts. He closed his eyes, allowing himself to be enveloped by his maker. *Thank you. I feel You here.*

He remembered his dream of the artist in the forest. His mind focused on the expression of love on the creator's face as he wrapped his arm around the canvas and drew it into himself. Dylan squeezed his eyes tight with tears. *So much love and compassion.* He recalled how the dark, seething picture affected the artist, how the artist drew its pain into himself. He envisioned the moment when the man breathed into the canvas and it morphed into color and life once again. He felt as if he were the canvas and God was awakening him to life and color once more. *Now if I can just be like You.*

Dylan listened to the sound of Asa's tiny voice on the baby monitor. "God, please give me the strength to be a father to that little boy," he whispered.

Dylan listened to Lynette's gentleness toward her baby. "Good morning, sweet one. I'm so happy to see you. Did you have good dreams? Huh?" The sound of her voice brought a smile to Dylan's face. He looked across the street at Emma Gray's place as the old lady shuffled up the steps of her front porch. Her fanciful, furry, red robe caused him to chuckle. As he cheered her on in his mind, a slick, black BMW stopped in front of his house. *Preston?* A picture of manly perfection stepped out of the car. Perfect, dirty-blond hair, gray slim-fit suit, and shoes that shined like jewels. *Yep, it's Preston.* "Hey, man!" Dylan called out to him.

THE WINDOWS OF HOLLY

Preston glowed. "Hey!" He accelerated his footsteps, excited to see his friend. Preston once judged the preacher falsely, figuring him to be a condescending, arrogant dictator, but Preston's own pride and arrogance had driven him into a pit of hell that had left him gasping for air. At that point in his life, he became desperate for encouragement and advice. He grew fond of Dylan and was forever thankful for his help in saving his marriage from the devastation of his affair. Knowing that Dylan had suffered betrayal and brokenness, Preston's heart had softened toward him. Seeing Dylan's face reminded him there is always light in the darkness.

Preston trotted up the porch steps. "Man! I heard you've been playing *Dukes of Hazzard* without me. I had to come see what's up."

Dylan smiled, shaking his head. "There've been many reports of my latest escapades, but I assure you it wasn't a recreation of the *Dukes of Hazzard*. This time, I was actually being chased down by machine-gun-wielding spies on skis. I ended up falling off a cliff and, well, I forgot to wear my parachute."

Preston raised an eyebrow. "Hm. A bit of James Bond action right here in Holly? Who'd have thought?"

Dylan smirked, "You know it, man. Besides, I was kinda tired of Boss Hogg."

Preston laughed. "Man, it's so good to see you."

"You too," Dylan replied sincerely. "What brings you to town?"

Preston took a seat on the swing. "I had a meeting with John Clark. We're partnering together on the ethanol plant project. I ran into Mike at the gas station. He told me about your fall, so I thought I'd stop by to see how you're doing."

"Well, it's a crazy story," said Dylan. There's been a ton of action around my house this month. December's been a whopper. Did you hear Lynette is back?"

192

Preston cleared his throat for the sake of pause. The last thing he wanted was for Dylan to think he was gossip hungry. "Yes, Mike mentioned that."

Dylan told the story of Owen filing for divorce, leaving his wife and child, the assault on Lynette, the mysterious rock thrower who left threatening messages, and lastly, his mission to find the culprit which left him in a greasy garage pit with a fractured leg.

Preston let out a long breath. "Wow. And I used to think Holly was boring as heck. I've gotta say, though, I'm really happy to hear about you and Lynette. I mean, it's a tough, complicated situation, but it's quite beautiful."

Dylan agreed. "I love having her around here. It's almost like old times," he paused, "except totally different." He laughed out loud. "It's ridiculous, isn't it? So tell me about you and Kat? How are things going?"

Preston evaluated things before answering. "Honestly, we're doing pretty well considering what we've been through, after what I've put her through. Most of the time we're great, but when something triggers a bad memory, she spirals downward pretty quickly. Last night was one of the spirals." He sighed. "She said I've stained her soul. She doesn't know if she'll ever feel whole again. Like, she wonders if she'll ever feel secure and completely loved again. What do I do with that, man?"

Dylan assured him, "I've felt that way myself. Betrayal leaves a mark, for sure. When you feel the pain so deeply, you wonder if you'll ever be the same again. I mean, you know you won't be the same, but you wonder if you'll ever be able to function or think like a normal human being. Just be patient with her and give her time. Kat loves you. If she didn't, she wouldn't be with you now. You guys have beat the odds so far." He smiled encouragingly.

"Yeah, I'm not sure why she loves me, but I know she does. I'm a lucky man."

THE WINDOWS OF HOLLY

Dylan replied, "More than lucky. I'd say you're a very blessed man."

Preston was grateful. "Definitely. She's an incredible woman. Love incarnate."

Lynette's voice came over the baby monitor. "Good boy. You were hungry, weren't you? All right, let's go see Daddy."

Preston looked at Dylan, puzzled. "Daddy? She's going to see Owen?"

Dylan shook his head no. "I think she means me," he said, smiling. I'm planning to adopt Asa."

Preston was stunned. "Man, that's awesome." He shook his head in awe. "You're like a real superhero."

Dylan crinkled his nose. "Nah, I'm not that great. I just realize life is short, and if I'm going to live it with the woman I love, then I'm going to be an instant dad too." He chuckled at the ridiculousness of it all.

"Unbelievable." Preston shook his head. "And to think I used to call you a pompous preacher."

Dylan shrugged. "Maybe you were right on some levels." He laughed and then winced as his ribs reminded him of their infirmed condition.

Preston took notice of his pained face. "Sorry, man. I guess we'd better behave until you're feeling better."

Dylan shook his head. "I'm fine. Besides, laughter is supposed to be good medicine, right? I could use a heavy dose."

Preston attempted to shift the conversation to one that wouldn't produce laughter, for Dylan's sake. "So what's new? Any Christmas plans?"

"Yes, actually. As of a few minutes ago, it was decided that we'll be hosting a Christmas party here. Isn't that insane?" Dylan grinned, amused. "Throwing a party in the middle of chaos. Apparently, that's how we roll."

194

Preston looked confused but intrigued. "I'm not sure what to say," he said with a slight smile. "You live the most colorful life of anyone I know. A party is probably the perfect way to wrap it all up, but I do have to ask why you're doing it under these circumstances."

Dylan explained, "Lynette and I used to throw big Christmas parties for the church and our neighbors. Really, it was for anyone who wanted to come. People started referring to our house as the Christmas House, and it kinda became a thing. You and Kat should come."

Preston liked the idea. "We'd love to. You tell me when and I'll see if our calendar is open. It'll depend on Kat's mood too. She used to keep a full holiday calendar with parties and events, but she's being more of a homebody this year."

Dylan spoke warmly. "Being a homebody for a while isn't such a bad thing. I'm mildly enjoying being laid up right now. Home is a nice place to be. It's helped me take notice of the little things I've missed, like the ticking of the clock or the way the light shines through the windows. It's definitely given me a lot to write about in the paper."

Preston recalled, "Yeah, I saw the article you did for the Marshall City paper. I loved it. I'm glad the communities don't mind sharing your talent. You're the best community reporter I've ever seen, or rather, read." He smiled. "The way you write is different than the norm."

Dylan was pleased with the compliment. "Thanks, man. We try to cross-pollinate. Jackson and I want to bring a sense of unity to these divided towns. I've wanted to kick down small-town pride for quite awhile. It's time for us to get out of our bubbles and actually love our neighbors. We have to do it gently though. Otherwise we'll make enemies."

Preston raised his eyebrows. "I like the way you put that. I ran

THE WINDOWS OF HOLLY

into that pride today. It's crazy how city limit signs come with labels and wrong perspectives of the people who live there. Unfortunately, I come across a lot of division as I go from town to town. Can you imagine what we could accomplish if we all came together and got a vision for something bigger than taking care of our own butts and building our own little empires?"

"Yeah, it's easy to only care for our own butts, I guess."

"Yeah." Preston looked down as he twiddled his thumbs. "That's what got me into my own mess: trying to 'care' for myself. I was selfish, and let me tell you, selfishness comes with a price that's not worth paying." He shook his head.

Dylan studied Preston's facial expressions compassionately. "Yes, but thank God for redemption."

"I'm certainly thankful, but I have to admit that when Kat spirals down, I feel a bit hopeless. What if she decides she can't handle the pain and she leaves me? Like, how can she stand to look at me? When I look in the mirror, I hate who I see."

Dylan's compassion pressed him to help Preston see clearly. "Preston, you are not your failures."

Preston looked at Dylan. "But maybe I am my own stupidity and nothing more than that."

"Dude," Dylan interjected. "That's not true. If that were true, every person on the face of the planet is doomed." Dylan reached into the pocket of his robe. "Look, check this out. I'm gonna go preacher on you." He chuckled while he searched his cell phone. "I was just reading this yesterday. In First Corinthians chapter six, there's a list of all kinds of sinners. Most every person makes that list. But it says in verse eleven, 'Such were some of you, but you were washed, but you were sanctified, but you were justified in the name of the Lord Jesus Christ and in the Spirit of our God.' What you once did is no longer who you are. Are you still committing adultery?"

Preston shook his head. "No. Never again."

Dylan continued, "You've changed your path. You've changed your mind and given your life to your Father. The old identity doesn't exist anymore, Preston. Jesus said you're already clean because of the word He spoke. If you live in Him, you are made clean. Not because of anything you've done, but because of what He's done. He gives to us what we don't deserve. Grace. Another chance." Dylan put his phone back in his pocket.

Preston pondered the words Dylan spoke. Dylan tried to explain further, hoping his friend would see himself differently. "So when you look in the mirror, you should see yourself as clean, pure, righteous, and holy. I know it's hard, man. Believe me. I still beat myself up over not doing things right in the past. But I know this to be true. There's something about believing in the power of what Christ did, and the power of the Holy Spirit in us, that propels us forward into who we were made to be. Seriously, do you think God ever said, 'Hey, I think I'll make a thief today?' Or 'I think I'll create a murderer today?' I don't think so."

Preston was stunned by the question. "Of course not. I don't think He would ever do that."

Dylan continued, "Of course He doesn't. That'd be totally against His nature. Love is who He is. See, we get to look at each other through a filter of seeing each other's origin, which is God. That changes everything."

Preston understood. "I need eyes to see like that."

Dylan noticed the curtain move in the window to his right. He turned to see Lynette peering out the window, smiling. He winked at her, knowing she didn't want to interrupt a serious conversation.

Dylan assured his friend, "We're all learning to see in Christ, to see as He sees. You'll get there. On another note, would you like to see my soon-to-be son?"

Preston was delighted. "I'd love to."

Chapter Sixteen

MMA GRAY BREATHED HARD as she pulled the black flannel leggings over her puffy legs. "Dear Lord, it's like stuffing a German sausage into a balloon," she huffed. Emma had learned to talk to herself over the years to make her lonely days entertaining. She planned to meet Beverly, Lucy, and Marcy at Annie's Café to begin planning the Christmas party. "Leggings on. Check. Bra on. Check. Now for a top." She hummed as she browsed through a variety of blouses in her old, cedar closet.

Emma pulled a new, flamboyant Christmas top from the rack. "Oh, Beverly. I can only imagine what you'll say about this one. I think I'll wear it just for you." She wiggled her body as she pulled the top over her head. She stood in front of the mirror, admiring the bright red color decorated with vivid Christmas packages, candy canes, wreaths, and trees. Even little snowmen mingled in between colorful ornaments. "Top on. Check!" She wondered for a moment if she'd forgotten a bra. She grabbed her breasts. "Yep. Boulder holder intact and holding. Now, off to the races," she said as she pointed her finger into the air.

As Emma pulled into a parking space in front of the café, Burt recognized her car. He called to Elsie, "Hey, Elsie! It's gonna be an entertaining evening."

THE WINDOWS OF HOLLY

"Oh?" Elsie responded from the kitchen. "Why's that?"

"We got Emma Gray comin' in," he grinned.

Elsie smiled. "Yay! I love it when she and Bev come in. They make my tiny paycheck worth being here."

Burt continued wiping the countertop. "If Mike and Curt come in at the same time, it'll really be worth it. Those four in one room is the best entertainment in town."

"You can say that again," she agreed.

The bells clanged on the café door as Emma entered. The cool air whisked in right along with her. "I have arrived," she declared, throwing her hands in the air. "It's your lucky night."

Burt grinned. "Hello, Miss Emma. How's it going?"

She smiled. "It's been a great day, Burt! Oh, I have exciting news. Do you remember Holly's special Christmas House?

He stared blankly for a second. "Do you mean Dylan's house?"

"Yes!" She lifted her hand, finger pointing at his face. "It's back!"

Burt was pleased with the news. "Dylan's a great guy. I'm glad to hear he's opening his home again. Lots of great memories were made there."

Emma leaned in, whispering, "I'm not one for gossiping, but you know he and Lynette are getting back together?"

He whispered back, "I heard some rumors about Owen leaving her. And something about Owen's friend beating her up? Is that right?"

She held her hand to her cheek, as if to block the sound of her voice. "Like I said, I'm not one for gossiping, but that's exactly right. Dylan took her in and he's helping to care for the baby. He's a good man."

Burt gave a thumbs-up. "Be sure to let me know when that Christmas party is happening. I'll be there.".

Emma beamed. "You know I will. Can I have my regular

200

table? I've got Bev, Marcy, and Lucy coming to help plan the party."

Burt smiled. "Yes, ma'am. Your table awaits."

The bells clanged once again, announcing the arrival of another Holly resident. "Beverly!" Emma motioned for her to sit. She pulled her notebook and pen from her purple tote bag. "We've got lots of planning to do."

Beverly approached the table, taking note of Emma's wild blouse. "Emma, I see you've just returned from the North Pole. Does Santa know you stole the elves' wrapping paper?"

Emma glanced her way with a smirk. "I knew you wouldn't be able to resist. Why do you think I wore it?"

Beverly continued, "Burt, can we get some hot cocoa over here? And if you've got sunglasses, bring those along. Emma went for a visit to the North Pole, and it appears she took a tumble through the tinsel and neon wrapping paper department. She must have fallen into the candy cane factory on her way out too."

Burt was already amused by the hilarious duo. "Hot cocoa coming right up. Sunglasses I don't have, so you'll have to suck it up and enjoy the brightness."

Beverly plopped into her seat. "Well, Emma, I do appreciate your festive personality. If Social Security ever fizzles out, you can be assured, with that face and that blouse, you'll easily get a job as Santa's helper."

Emma giggled. "Thanks for the encouragement. I wore this blouse just for you and it worked." She smacked the palm of her hand on the table. "Now we move on to the most important thing. Let's plan this party!"

Beverly smiled. "I was up most of the night tossing ideas around. Can you believe it? After five long years. Wow." She shook her head with delight. "Let's wait for Marcy and Lucy before we get into the planning details. For now, we can talk about

THE WINDOWS OF HOLLY

who's invited to this shindig. We have to consider that Dylan and Lynette's situation is sensitive right now, and there'll be people wanting to come just to analyze and observe so they'll have something to gossip about."

"Yeah, that's for sure," Emma replied. "They used to open their home to all the neighbors. I don't think I'd trust them all now. I overheard Mrs. Burnside and that crotchety Layla Smith at the grocery store, on multiple occasions, saying awful things about Dylan and Lynette. I reprimanded those old bats and ever since then, they glare at me when I run into them."

Beverly tapped her fingers on the table. "We'll definitely need to be able to distinguish between those who care about Dylan and Lynette and those who don't. We certainly don't want this Christmas gathering to become a judgment zone. Lord knows this town has enough gossipers." Beverly reached for Emma's notepad and pen. She proceeded to write "Number one on the list is: Avoid diarrhea inducers."

"Diarrhea inducers?"

Beverly pushed the notepad back to Emma. "Yep. We can't have any of those in attendance."

Emma questioned, "What are diarrhea inducers, Bev?"

Beverly answered confidently, "Well, have you ever known people who make your stomach turn? You know, all it takes is one word out of their mouths and suddenly, boom! Diarrhea. It's people who are lifesuckers. Instead of filling you up with goodness, they make you sick."

Emma shook her head. "Oh, Beverly. The things you say . . . but, yes, I know what you mean. I had a mother-in-law who was like that, God rest her soul."

Beverly chimed in, "And I'd bet God rested your belly ever since she departed this earth?"

Emma giggled. "Well, yes. It's been at ease for quite some time now."

The bells on the café door announced Marcy and Lucy's arrival. The two ladies were vibrant and excited about planning the Christmas gathering at the Vanbergs.

The café was filled with an atmosphere of joyful expectation and gratitude. Dylan and Lynette were once the lifeblood of Holly. Something about their recent reunion shifted the air, infusing belief and hope into Holly's residents. News was traveling quickly, some of it true and some of it not, some of it twisted and skewed with details changed here and there, but everyone knew that Dylan and Lynette were reunited.

Marcy and Lucy approached the table. Lucy caressed her pregnant belly, acknowledging the presence of life that filled her soul. As the women sat together, joyful expectation of the future penetrated their hearts. The café held an air of resurrection as a few simple ladies gathered with the intent to create magic.

Lucy's dark hair framed her soft, white face. Her favorite red lipstick decorated her face like a red ribbon on an elegant gift. Her blue eyes sparkled with joy.

Burt approached the table with a tray of hot chocolate. "Why, Lucy Sawyer. You're glowing like the sun. Pregnancy must be treating you well," he said.

She beamed. "Thank you, Burt. You're so kind."

He sat four hot chocolates on the table. "I went ahead and brought a round of my magical cocoa for everybody. I added a touch of butterscotch and cinnamon. I promise you'll taste Christmas."

The ladies thanked him.

Marcy gently grabbed Burt's arm before he could walk away. "Burt, we're planning a Christmas party at the Vanbergs. Will you come?"

He smiled. "Marcy, I wouldn't miss it. As long as I'm not

THE WINDOWS OF HOLLY

working this joint, I'll be there." He cleared his throat as he pulled out his notepad. "Ladies, tonight's specials are King Ranch chicken, pork with apples, or roasted rosemary chicken. Each entrée comes with two sides, as if you didn't already know that." He winked. "I'll be back in a couple of minutes to take your order." Burt stepped away from the table.

"It's King Ranch for me," Lucy exclaimed.

"I'll second that," said Beverly.

Marcy tilted her head with a chuckle, "And I'll be the third."

Emma sighed. "I don't wanna be the oddball. I was leaning toward the pork with apples, but if you're all having the King Ranch, I'll do the same."

Beverly couldn't resist. "Emma, my friend. You are an oddball. But so am I. It doesn't matter what you choose to eat. You just enjoy yourself and get whatever floats your boat."

Emma wore a smirk as she rolled her eyes dramatically. "Well, what floats my boat tonight is the pork and apples. If I go with King Ranch, I'll be visiting the water closet throughout the night."

The ladies giggled.

Marcy suggested, "Now that we know what we're ordering, let's get this show on the road. We have a party to plan! I want to make sure we contact Mary Elliott. It's a bit difficult for her to get out as much lately, but I know she'll want to be part of this."

Lucy lit up. "We should have her paint something for Dylan and Lynette!"

Marcy clasped her hands over her heart, smiling. "Oh my goodness. What a fabulous idea! They'll love that. Mary enjoys doing meaningful projects."

Lucy interjected another idea. "Rose Reynolds used to donate foods from her restaurant for the Vanbergs' Christmas gathering. I remember one year, she brought her amazing lasagna. I'll contact her and see if she's willing to help."

204

Marcy jotted the idea down on her notepad. "Excellent idea."

Emma wasn't so sure. "I don't know. I like the idea of a traditional Christmas meal like turkey, ham, potatoes, and all the fixins."

Beverly piped up. "Emma, Rose's restaurant is Italian, and if she's willing to bring free food, let her! Just pretend to be Italian and enjoy it. Free food is free food."

Emma crinkled her nose. "I suppose you're right, but I'm no Italian!"

Beverly tilted her head inquisitively. "What exactly are you anyway? I've never asked."

Emma replied matter-of-factly, "Scottish or Irish, or some combo of the sort, according to my father." That must be why I've always enjoyed a sip or two of Scotch."

The ladies were shocked. Marcy's eyes widened. "Emma! Really? I had no idea."

Emma grinned. "It's not a regular thing, so don't worry about that. I've never been into alcohol, but there's something about a good Scotch. It evokes fond memories of my grandfather. Every now and then, he'd sip a Scotch. I asked him why he drank that nasty stuff and he said, 'Emmy, one of the most powerful things in the world is a good story. You see, Scotch is my favorite storyteller. It sits and ages in a barrel for years. When you drink it, if you pay close attention, you can taste the story it tells. You wonder what it heard while sitting in those old oak barrels. I'm not saying you need to drink it of course. Your mama would kill me.' Grandpa and I had lots of great conversations like that."

Marcy wondered, "So how often do you drink Scotch? I never would have guessed."

Emma held up two fingers. "About twice a year, when nostalgia hits."

Beverly chimed in. "Well, let's hope that's all. I can't imagine

THE WINDOWS OF HOLLY

what your wardrobe would look like if you became a regularly inebriated human being."

Emma waved her fist at Beverly. "Bev! I'm never inebriated. That's one thing I can't stand. I've known far too many drunks, and I never want to be like any of them."

Marcy attempted to steer the conversation back to their original purpose. "Okay, ladies. Let's talk decorations first and then we'll move on to food. I like Lucy's idea. Anything we can get at no charge would be a great blessing. The point of the gathering is to celebrate."

"Absolutely," agreed Lucy.

PASTOR DEAN'S FIELD

Just outside Holly's city limits, Pastor Dean stood in the middle of his cotton field. *Almost time to harvest.* Even though he felt called to the ministry of helping sinners become saints along their journey of life, the passion that filled him the most was farming. Being a farmer in the south was much different than his experience with farming in the north. He appreciated the ability to stand in his field in December; the fact that there was something to harvest during that winter month was a blessing that made him glad he was now a southerner.

Something about the smell of soil and the power to place seeds in the ground and watch them flourish gratified his soul. Anticipating the harvest process brought him satisfaction that surpassed the pleasure of pastoring. Each year, planting the seed reminded him to sow well in life through kindness, compassion, mercy, and grace. He firmly believed in the principle of sowing and reaping.

When the burdens of being a pastor weighed too heavily on his well-worn heart, he ventured into his field, walking each row and inspecting the growth. He made it a habit to pray for specific people during the length of his walk along each row. "Father, the Brown family needs your touch right now. They're hurting so deeply." He watched his feet move through the dirt as he spoke into the air. "Just as you've given me great harvest and produced abundance from a tiny seed, please reach into their lives and take the little seed of faith that's in Nick's heart. Turn it into goodness and rescue their family. Even to those who have no faith, your love is there to embrace them."

He looked up to the sky, taking a deep breath. "Father, forgive Charlie and have mercy on him. Open his eyes to see clearly. Free him from the addiction that's kept him bound and lost. Fill him with your Spirit and, well, God," he sighed, "may Charlie become addicted to You." Dean smiled to himself as hope surged through his veins. "Lord, would you do a Christmas miracle?"

His hopeful thought was quickly arrested by the memory of two church members who lost their battle with addiction. He was afraid he'd always be haunted by the memory of Darius Baker's face. The man's tearful plea to be freed from alcoholism wasn't enough to free him, and no matter how hard Dean tried to walk him through the valley to wholeness, it seemed the demon of alcohol was too strong. Dean knew that wasn't true, but at times, it sure felt that way. Eventually, Darius's liver gave out and he fell asleep, never to wake up again. The memory of him pricked Dean's heart. "Oh, Darius," he sighed. "You're finally free and at peace. I just wish you could've stuck around and found joy in this life."

The memory of that loss took his mind to another face he could not forget: the face of a young man who'd left this life way too soon. "Oh, Elijah." He let out a long exhale. Dean shook his head as he recalled the image of the twenty-year-old resting in a casket. Elijah was a wild spirit, full of life and personality, brimming with creativity and passion. Elijah carried a deep desire to do good in the world, but someone destroyed his opportunity to accomplish what was in his heart with the offer of heroin at an impressionable age. *Just one hit. Just try it.* That one hit enraptured every cell of his body, gifting him with a momentary enlightenment that made every bit of fear, doubt, and sadness disappear. Elijah promised himself he would never do it again, but when difficulty arose, his body screamed and clawed at him to do it just one more time. It was a never-ending cycle.

When Elijah's mom couldn't find him one day, she called Pastor Dean for help. She suspected her son may have relapsed after several months of being "clean." Dean would never forget the moment he found Elijah's car on an abandoned farm. The second he laid eyes on the man's motionless body, his heart sank to a despair he didn't know he could feel for someone outside his family. That experience left its mark deep within him.

Beginning to walk alongside another row of cotton, Dean continued pondering those losses. He stopped to kneel in the cool, loose dirt. "Oh, Father. Help Elijah's family today and in the days to come. Parents should never outlive their children. It's just not right." The thought pierced his heart. He thought of his own children. "How can anyone survive such loss?"

Tears began to fall down his cheeks, plummeting into the dirt. Dean was a strong man, yet a tender man. *Surely men of every kind need to periodically take a moment to fall into soil and let themselves mourn and wonder why.* Today was one of those days. Dean needed to allow himself a cleansing of pain. His mother used to tell him tears were a necessary washing and were required to live this life with compassion and mercy. He didn't understand the need for crying, but as he grew older, it all started to make sense.

The weight of loss and disappointment, even the ones he'd surrendered and accepted, seemed to reveal their imprints in his soul. No matter how joyful his soul, seasons of pressing into life's difficulties that made his heart raw and human would emerge at the most unexpected times. Shedding tears brought an inexplicable relief. Eyes closed tightly to prevent the flood from coming too abruptly, but the dam gave way. Dean wondered how it was possible that such a waterfall had managed to stay inside for so long. "Oh, Father." He let the cry of his heart flow from his being.

A few minutes passed and he opened his eyes, now sensing peace and the presence of God. "See in Me," a voice whispered. Dean shifted his body in order to examine his surroundings only to discover he was certainly alone. It was him alone, with cotton and dirt. "See in me," he repeated. Dean turned his attention back to the dirt where his tears had gathered. He took notice of how soil mingled together with his tears, turning to mud. *Tears of man. Dust of earth.*

Dean thought of God bending low to form man from the dirt. He wondered if God wept over man. Dean plunged his finger into the mud, swirling it around. He created small circles, then bigger circles. Around and around, spreading the tears into dirt, creating more mud. He licked his lips, tasting the remnants of salty tears. *We are the salt of the earth.*

Dean remembered studying salt and its incredible healing abilities. *Long ago, salt was as good as money, a means of exchange that only the wealthy possessed.* He considered the use of salt for preservation. Our presence preserves the earth. *God, Your presence preserves the earth and all within it. We are the salt of the earth.*

"See in Me," a voice whispered again. Dean examined his surroundings once more and laughed aloud. "Of course no one is here. Okay, Father. I'm listening." He looked to the sky for a moment, then returned his gaze to the mud created by the emotion of his heart. Immediately, he thought of the blind man in the Scriptures. He recalled how Jesus spat into the dirt and made mud,

THE WINDOWS OF HOLLY

placing it on the blind man's eyes. *What a strange thing to do. What an offensive thing to do.* The man's vision returned. As Dean admired the mud at his feet, he wondered. *Should I? Why not?* He dug his fingers into the mud and slathered it across his eyelids. "Give me eyes to see." He waited.

While feeling the amusement and pleasure of God, he also felt the ridiculousness of such a gesture. "Lord, my congregation would think I've gone mad," he muttered. But he lingered and listened. His heart was full as the remembrance of healings, salvations, and victories danced through his mind. "Help me to never forget. Thank You, Father. I know you've got the Brown family. C'mon, Lord. Let's bring Charlie home."

Chapter Seventeen

ET ANOTHER COOL DECEMBER MORNING, Dylan exhaled as he sat in the recliner, thankful that he could tolerate the discomfort of his injuries enough to avoid pain medication. It seemed he and Lynette were experiencing accelerated healing. Dylan supposed their reunion was medicinal to body and soul.

He breathed a thank you as he propped his computer on the cushion in his lap, willing himself to write a brief encouragement for the *Holly Herald* holiday section. He brainstormed, thinking about his current circumstances and figured that, perhaps, other Holly residents were also dealing with unbelievable life issues during this holiday season.

Dylan summarized his own ridiculous circumstances in his head. *Divorced pastor. His ex-wife shows up with her baby in tow. They're still in love with each other. Local, disgruntled kid tosses rocks and threatening notes at his house. Pastor races off to find the perpetrator. He finds the kid's place, falls into a pit, fractures some bones, and gains himself a concussion. He's laid up while ex-wife, who he plans to remarry, takes care of him. The town's ladies plan a Christmas celebration at the couple's home.* Dylan shook his head at the unbelievable, scandalous scene that was his life. He wondered how he could be filled with gratitude and

THE WINDOWS OF HOLLY

offense simultaneously. He supposed some part of him still lacked
love.

He composed himself, intent on getting serious about bringing
hope to his readers. He wondered if they would even read what he
had to say. *What rumors are being spread around, especially after
Nick's little mail delivery with those stupid photographs?* He
sighed at the memory of the images Nick captured of Kelsey
kissing him. Dylan shook his head, trying to shake off remaining
bits of anger and resentment toward Kelsey and Nick. *I can't
believe he put those pictures in peoples' mailboxes. Dumb kid.* But
once he thought of Nick's dad, Charlie, leaving the family for a
man, and feeding his drug addiction, Dylan's resentment once
again gave way to compassion for Nick.

Dylan closed his eyes, slowly taking in a shallow breath,
shallow because the pain was still there, in body and soul. "How
can I bring hope, Father? My life's a mess."

Dylan pondered acts of mercy, how God presented mercy even
when man was undeserving. "You, God, who saved us and called
us with a holy calling, not according to our works, but according
to Your own purpose and grace which was given to us in Christ
Jesus before time began." The Scriptures meant more to Dylan
now than when he was a distinguished, highly regarded, "perfect"
pastor.

He squeezed his eyes closed, as if to force his internal sight to
see and realize the power of those words. "Not according to our
works, but according to Your grace," he whispered. "It's the grace
which You gave to us before time began." The reality of grace
caused him to vibrate with life. "You knew we'd screw up, but
You loved us and wanted us anyway." Dylan shook his head,
overwhelmed by such love.

He continued meditating on the goodness of the Father that he
once thought abandoned him. "God, You gave grace to Noah.

When he was drunk and naked, You covered him. King David lusted, stole, lied, fornicated, and murdered. Still, You were there for him. And holy cow, look at me and Lynette. You're still here." He wondered if God really could be insane. "Who else would love like that?" Words echoed in Dylan's ear, *You would.* The sound shocked him.

Dylan knew his own struggle to push past the disappointment and pain of his wife's adultery, yet he was willing to take her back and adopt the baby conceived with the man who betrayed his friendship. "Oh my God. Am I insane?" Again, words echoed in his ear, *I'm within you. See in Me.*

Dylan began to write:

It's Christmas time in Holly. The barren branches and crisp, cool air remind us of our fragility and strength. Holidays often come with a mixture of joyful anticipation of reunion that clashes with anxiety and sadness. Each of us is tasting various facets of this journey of life. While some experience one facet, others experience another. Though different, we are still united as one, bearing hearts, souls, and minds that know the ups and downs of living. Depending on where we are in the journey, we have different perspectives of life, of living, and of the Christmas season.

During this time of gift buying and celebration, most of us practice the art of window shopping. You can't help but notice the beautifully decorated windows throughout the town of Holly. The talents and artistic abilities of our residents are displayed more noticeably as the holidays approach. Perhaps you've taken notice of the silvery snowflakes dangling above handcrafted, miniature houses in the window of Sanders Printing Company or the classy, black grand piano topped with a snow-enveloped, golden candelabra in Wilson's Music Store. We are a privileged community to have these visions to behold as we go about our daily lives.

THE WINDOWS OF HOLLY

Windows draw us into another place, inviting us to see another perspective. These windows remind me to ask myself what perspective I bring to those around me. What do I invite them to see and experience? In my own life, daily decisions, experiences, and unexpected twists and turns have either broadened a good perspective or threatened to taint my vision of myself and others. As a community, together, we can either choose to strengthen or weaken each other. What a gift we have been given!

This Christmas, I'd like to encourage everyone to strengthen one another's perspective, realizing that you are a window. There is power in being a window.

Too often, we see and make judgments about people without knowing their stories. We believe we know their stories, but perhaps we don't have all the pieces. Good things can appear to be bad; bad things can appear to be good, depending on who is looking and how they are perceiving. As a reporter, I know very well the power of media to paint pictures that may or may not exist. Reporting comes with great responsibility to shape and form mindsets, to create windows through which people view life. Being windows, we must be aware of the etches in our lenses as others will see through us.

What do Holly's windows hold this Christmas? Trauma, anger? Perhaps restoration, grace, and love? If Holly's windows hold something less than beautiful, may her panes be changed and her lenses be perfected in love. How can Holly create windows of joy? Each of us carries the ability to create a joyful invitation for passersby if we make a conscious decision to focus on creating a life-giving perspective. It's not about creating a false perspective, but a revived and renewed one. Daily, there are good things happening in our little town, and I'd like to thank each of you, whether you're a homemaker or business leader, for being a part of making a community that infuses hope into its residents and visitors. As we dive into Christmas festivities in the week to come, may light and love be evident in the windows of Holly.

Dylan ran his fingers through his hair, grabbing the sides of his head. "Shew-wee," he exhaled. He figured he must have been holding his breath for the duration of his writing. He wondered how vulnerable he should be, especially after being publicly humiliated by Nick's scandalous photographs. *That young man painted a pretty dark picture.* Despite Dylan's doubts about writing the article, he knew what he needed to do. *Write it, Dylan.*

He didn't want it to be blazingly obvious that he hoped his community would see him favorably. He desperately wanted people to know the picture of Kelsey kissing him was not what it seemed, but the photo spoke for itself. It spoke a lie that would be translated by the eyes of those who saw it. Even though Dylan was trying to get away from Kelsey, there they were with lips pressed together. Then there was the other photo of him kissing Lynette, whom most knew as Owen's wife. *People must think I'm a womanizer. They probably think I broke up Lynette's marriage.* Dylan dropped his face into his hands. *God, I keep telling myself I don't care what people think, but apparently I do.*

Lynette entered the room. "Good morning, Dylan."

His face lit up as he laid eyes on her. "Wow, you look amazing! What are you all dolled up for?"

She was elated by his pleasure. "I answered an ad for Mr. Sanders' print shop. I've got an interview this morning!" She smiled. "It's just a part time gig, but Lucy said she'd be glad to babysit for me."

Disappointment flooded Dylan's face. "You just had a baby. Not to mention, you got tussled around by a madman. You're still recovering from all of that. Why are you applying for a job?"

She worked to maintain a positive, upbeat attitude as she explained, "I'm capable of working and I want to earn my keep.

THE WINDOWS OF HOLLY

Asa and I will not be a burden to you."

Dylan wanted to jump to his feet in protest, but his injuries held him back. "Lynette." He spoke her name with compassion. "I'm not one to tell you what you can and can't do, but I will tell you that everything within me is opposed to this idea. At least for now."

Lynette reassured him, "The job doesn't begin until January. You know how Mr. Sanders is. He's an organizer and planner who's always several steps ahead of the game."

Dylan shifted his gaze to his painting of the bride. He admired the beautiful, sparkling diamonds in her train.

Lynette waited for a response. "Dylan, what are you thinking?"

He kept his focus on the painting. "See that bride? She's radiant, isn't she?"

"Yes. It's a beautiful painting," she responded.

He continued, "This is how I see you. Not bruised and battered. Not abandoned." He pointed at the painting. "Not a woman who has to rush out and get a job at a print shop 'to earn her keep.' I don't think you understand, Lynette." He turned to look at her. "You're not a burden. If you believe you're a burden, you're going to make yourself a burden by trying not to be one. Can you just rest in being you? In being here? In being a new mom? Can you just allow us time to heal before we start entertaining budgets?"

His plea softened her soul. The posture of his heart and request caused everything within her to bow to his desires. The supplication that was evident in his eyes stabbed at her to never cause him pain again. Lynette didn't know how she would live with the damage she caused, and she wouldn't dare add to his list of disappointments. Her confident, determined countenance became humble and submissive. Gratitude for his love turned to waterworks. She was surprised and embarrassed by the sudden shift in persona as she melted like putty in his hands. "Yes," she replied. "I can do that. You're right. I know we need time to heal. Honestly, I'm absolutely exhausted, but I just didn't want to burden you. That's all."

He motioned for her to come to him. "Let's just be. I have enough in savings that will get us by for a while, so no more worrying about money, okay?"

She knelt by his side, laying her head in his lap. "Okay, but do you know how much diapers cost?"

He raised his eyebrow. "Are diapers too much for God? I mean, the crap of humanity hasn't yet outweighed His abilities."

She grinned at his witty response. "Thank you for the reminder."

He ran his fingers through her hair. "There's nothing to thank me for."

She gasped, "Are you kidding me?"

"Nope." He touched her mouth, tracing her lips. They lingered in silence for a minute. "Lynette?"

"Yeah," she responded.

"How has everything shifted your perspective?"

She wasn't sure what he meant. "What do you mean? Like what, specifically?"

Dylan ran his hand down her arm as he considered the questions in his mind. "I don't know. I mean, you go through life, stuff happens, and it changes the way you see things."

She thought for a moment. "Well, I used to judge people who made stupid decisions. I thought I was smarter than most people. I guess I had a superiority complex, but that's changed." She shook her head with disgust. "When I started compromising, I really didn't care about anyone. I don't think I even noticed other people. It's like I had tunnel vision and I was the one at the end of the tunnel. Waking up from that is hell."

She paused, reliving the moment when her vision began to

THE WINDOWS OF HOLLY

clear. "When I began to see the trail of debris I left behind, I tried justifying it, but I knew there was no excuse. Now I have to live with what I've done."

"So how does that change how you see people?"

She looked at him, tilting her head. "I definitely have no room for judging them. I see others as better than myself. I see God differently too. For a time, I think I was angry at Him, maybe in a passive-aggressive kind of way. He seemed distant and indifferent, but now I'm overwhelmed by His kindness. He was actually carrying me when I fell. I'm the most undeserving of His grace, yet He brought me back to you. If He did that for me, how could I want any less for anyone else? Every person is worth loving, worth saving. And when it comes down to it, we're really all pretty much the same."

Dylan breathed deeply. "I get that." He pondered the transformation of his first love. "I heard someone say that sin doesn't change the way God feels about you, but it changes the way you feel about God."

"Oh so true."

Dylan questioned her further. "What about how you see yourself now? Can you forgive yourself?"

She bit her lip as she considered what he was asking. "I'm not there yet. I know I need to forgive myself, but I'm not there." She shook her head. "I don't know if I'll be able to completely get there in this lifetime."

"Well," he encouraged, "I hope you do. Life's too short to live it full of regrets. Guilt and shame are ravagers of the soul. And the mind." He thought about it more. "And the body and spirit." He shook his head. "Woman, you've gotta get there. If you don't, you're destined to be a mess," he said, chuckling. "Forgive yourself. Free yourself from your own judgment. Jesus took care of it all, you know."

218

She took a deep breath. She considered her former self-righteous attitude and how it produced pride and arrogance that stole her vision. "So stupid. What a pompous butt."

Dylan inquired, "Who? Me?"

She laughed. "Of course not! I was talking about myself."

Dylan chuckled. "I was kind of a pompous butt myself, so maybe it rubbed off on you. See! Maybe it was my fault all along."

She grinned at his gesture of trying to relieve her self-condemnation. "We were so young when we got married. I guess we didn't know a whole lot."

Dylan twirled her hair around his finger. "Girlfriend, I've done enough counseling with couples over the years to know that age doesn't matter. People can marry at thirty, forty, and fifty and still have mounds of issues. I'm glad you and I married when we did. Might as well start early and fix the kinks along the way. Besides, waiting until later in life requires being even more flexible. You get set in your ways and then, suddenly, you have to adjust your way of living to include someone else. I don't think it matters when a person marries. There'll always be issues."

Lynette smiled. "Yeah, everyone is different. You're right. No matter how old or young, no matter what background, there's bound to be challenges. That's just life."

"Yep," he agreed.

Lynette found herself admiring the intricate, ornate mantle over the fireplace. She and Dylan always loved the artistry and detail of Victorian architecture. "I'm such a beauty addict," she declared.

"I knew that about you long ago. Don't you know that's why you married me? I'm such a perfect specimen of man, you couldn't resist."

She looked into his eyes. "There's definitely some truth to that," she replied, and winked.

THE WINDOWS OF HOLLY

Dylan confessed, "I'm a beauty addict too. I mean, look at you. After five long years of separation and hell, I still want you."

She smiled with delight. "Thank you. But now I have stretch marks and I think my rear end is lopsided."

"Lopsided?" He raised an eyebrow. "It's definitely not lopsided."

She questioned, "How do you know? You haven't seen it."

He tilted his head, wearing a mischievous grin. "Lynette, you have no idea how many times I've checked you out when you're not looking. You're definitely not lopsided."

She received his confession with pleasure. "You've been checking me out?"

"Is that such a surprise?" He raised his eyebrows up and down, throwing a kiss into the air.

Lynette laughed. "You're cute." The ticking of the clock caught her attention. "I'd better call Mr. Sanders and cancel the interview. I hope he won't be offended."

Dylan assured her, "Offended? Mr. Sanders? No way. Besides, that guy adores you. I'm sure he'll be disappointed, but not offended."

Lynette stood to her feet, thankful that Dylan lifted the weight of employment from her shoulders.

Dylan grabbed her hand before she could walk away. "Hey, thanks for cancelling. I never want to stop you from doing something you really want, but I'm glad you'll be sticking around here."

She patted his hand. "Honestly, I didn't really want that job. I was just trying to be helpful."

"I know." He smiled. "My little beauty addict needs a good, long break. Just enjoy life and focus on creating beauty. I've got tons of canvasses and plenty of paint around here."

She clasped her hands together with gratitude and her eyes

brightened. "I would love that!"

As Lynette walked away, Dylan reached for his computer to study what he had written. He read his closing line aloud. "As we dive into Christmas festivities in the week to come, may light and love be evident in the windows of Holly." He pondered how this could be accomplished. *I've gotta live these words, especially if I'm publishing this.* He thought about the upcoming Christmas party. He wondered who might be there. He had no assurance of not having enemies present in his home. *Who can I really trust? Can light and love be evident in me, even toward people who might not be true friends?* Dylan remembered the words "You prepare a table before me in the presence of my enemies." He considered the fact that there would be analyzers and criticizers, but he knew it wasn't his job to figure out who was who. His job was to love people and let the rest work itself out.

Dylan peered out the bay window, watching the swing shift back and forth with the breeze. "Be like the swing," he mumbled to himself. *Let the wind move you. Let the Spirit lead. Let mercy lead.* He saw Jackson and Lucy step onto their porch across the street. *Looks like Jackson's heading to the office.* Jackson wrapped his arms around his pregnant wife and kissed her deeply. Dylan smiled. "Father, please don't let them go through the hell that we've been through." He guessed that Jackson was much smarter than himself, and he knew Lucy to be a woman of great loyalty. *They'll be fine. After watching us go through this, I'm sure they'll be careful to avoid those pitfalls.*

Dylan's cell phone rang. "Hello?"

Emma's squeaky voice excitedly greeted him. "Well, hello, young man! How are you doing today?"

Dylan smiled. "Not bad for such a mess."

"Well, I'm the queen of mess makin,' and I can promise you that you'll come out of it just fine. Oh, if you only knew how many impossible situations I was in, you'd be amazed that I'm still alive. But I have a little suggestion for you."

Dylan was curious. "Yeah, what's that?"

"You'd better milk it for all you can. You let Lynette take care of you," she said with a whisper. "It'll be our little secret."

Dylan laughed. "Okay. Advice acknowledged. So what's on your mind today, Emma?"

She cleared her throat. "The ladies and I have a great plan for the party. We just need to know what night works best for you and Lynette. We were thinking either December twenty-second or twenty-third. It'd be a great way for people to kick off their own Christmas festivities," she said excitedly.

Lynette returned to the living room. Dylan told Emma, "Lynette just walked in. Give me one second and I'll ask her. Hey, Lynnie?"

Lynette bounced to his side with a big smile on her face. He could see that she was feeling lighter after cancelling her interview with Mr. Sanders. "Hey, babe. Emma would like to know which night works best for the party. The twenty-second or twenty-third?"

She was delighted to have something to look forward to. "Oh fun!" She held her hands together over her mouth, pulling her chin upward in decisive thought. "You and I haven't really talked about Christmas Eve plans yet, but I'm thinking if we do the party on the twenty-second, that will give us a full day in between to get ready for any plans we might make. What do you think?"

"Sounds good to me. Let's do the twenty-second," said Dylan.

Emma proclaimed, "Oh goodie! I was hoping you'd say that. Now, the bigger factor. If there's anyone you don't want us to invite, let us know as soon as possible. And that means by tomorrow. We need time to let people know."

Dylan and Lynette were silent. The gathering sounded fun and redeeming, but they wondered if they hadn't really thought this through. Dylan piped up, "We'll let you know, Emma. Thanks for all your hard work."

He locked eyes with Lynette as he hung up the phone. "Are we absolutely mad?" He pursed his lips.

She raised an eyebrow and crossed her eyes comically. "Yes, we are," she said, giggling. "I'd say we're a bit batty."

He wondered, "Do you want to back out of this insanity?" He half hoped she would say yes.

Lynette lifted her shoulders in a hesitant shrug. "Well," she breathed deeply. "I have mixed feelings. I'm scared and I'm excited. I mean, on one hand, it's so redeeming, you know? I mean, after all we've been through, here we are together in our home, and it would be wonderful to celebrate Christmas just like old times. It's important to me to make Asa's first Christmas extra special."

"I agree," Dylan interjected. "So why are we afraid?"

She walked toward the fireplace, seeking an answer from deep within. "Maybe we're afraid of getting burned," she replied. "We're about the most scandalous thing in Holly. How do we know who's really a friend?"

Dylan thought for a moment. "Yeah, I considered that. But we can either let our circumstances push us into a place of fear, which will paralyze us at every turn, or we can embrace where we are and who we are and just be us. Honestly, don't you think most everyone is glad you and I are back together?"

"Probably. But I'm the violator in the story, you know? I'm the one who left you, so I'm sure I have enemies who feel you deserve better. And you do deserve better."

He looked at her lovingly. "Oh, Lynnie," he sighed. "You deserve better too. I hate that you're in this situation."

She was touched by his kindness. "I brought it on myself. How

THE WINDOWS OF HOLLY

can you say I deserve better? Any normal person would be happy that I'm in this crappy situation. It's what I get for being an idiot."

Dylan shook his head. "First of all, I'm not normal," he said, smiling. "Secondly, we all make bad decisions."

She disagreed. "No, not like I have."

He was relentless, refusing to let her spiral downward in self-slaughter. "You're not the worst person in the world. You know that, right? There are many people in your shoes. It's just a blindness that comes from wounds."

She interjected, "There's no excuse for what I did. Lots of people carry wounds without being unfaithful. I was just utterly selfish."

Dylan knew it was time to change the subject. "How about we don't go down this path of self-mutilation? Enough of that kind of talk. Let's have some tea. I'd like to make it myself, so could you help me out of this chair?"

"I can make it for you," she offered.

He insisted. "I appreciate that, but I need to stay active and keep this healing process moving. If you don't move it, you lose it."

Lynette placed her hand under his forearm to give him stability as he slowly raised himself out of the chair. As she helped him to the kitchen, she couldn't stop thinking about the guest list for the Christmas party. "So what about the guest list, Dylan?"

He spoke what he knew was right. "Love your neighbor as yourself, right? So would I want to invite myself to a Christmas party? Sure I would."

Lynette smiled. "Preacher."

He grinned. "That's not preaching. That's really just logic."

"True," she acknowledged. "And it's completely illogical for us to even throw a party." She giggled. "There's nothing logical about this."

He agreed. "Yes. All the more reason we should be logical in treating others well. We've got some making up to do. We've missed five years of doing good. We should lay ourselves aside, forget about our reputations, and not worry about looking like Ward and June Cleaver. To be honest, I think that was part of our problem."

She was curious. "What was part of our problem?"

Dylan continued his thoughts. "Thinking we had to be perfect all the time. I really thought I was pretty darned perfect. I was so caught up in trying to help everyone else do life right, I didn't realize how I was screwing up my own life. I'm not willing to live under that façade again. Life's too short. We need to be real with each other."

"I understand that."

Dylan continued, "As much as I'm kinda dreading this Christmas party, I'm also looking forward to having a chance to be real with everyone. Just think about how people must have seen us in the past. They probably thought we had and did everything perfectly, and some may have felt embarrassed about their own lives. I don't ever want anyone to feel that way around me. So, yeah, I think we need to let this party happen. We need to invite everybody just like we used to. Community leaders, local business owners, our neighbors on this block, and even our former church members. Let them see reality. We have nothing to hide."

Lynette swallowed hard. "Wow." She thought about possible criticisms she might face. *All of those people.* "Okay, I'm with you." She exhaled loudly. "I feel a bit like I'll be on display, but I guess I have to get over that. It's not about me."

Dylan shuffled through a box of tea bags, searching for the perfect flavor to bring him momentary happiness. He reflected on how she must feel like a bug under a microscope. "Can you handle it?"

THE WINDOWS OF HOLLY

"Yeah, I can. If this gathering brings hope to even one person, any judgments will be worth facing." She placed two coffee mugs on the table. "We really need to invite Nick and his mom too, you know?"

Dylan breathed deeply. "Talk about facing any judgments. That'll be mine to face."

Lynette reminded him, "Nick forgave you for not being able to help his dad. I think he understands that now. I saw tenderness beneath that hard exterior. Nick won't be a problem."

Dylan wobbled his head with uncertainty. "I know, but I'm not sure what his mom thinks of me. She barely speaks. Hardly says a word. For all I know, she wants to murder me."

"Dylan, I highly doubt that. From my brief interaction with her the other day, I get the impression she's just shell shocked and grieving, not angry. Can you imagine what she's been through? She tried helping Charlie through his addiction for years. Their whole marriage was a battle and then he leaves her for a man. It's no wonder she looks lost."

Dylan knew that was true. "Poor woman. I wish I could've changed things for them somehow."

Lynette still felt guilty about unraveling things for Dylan, especially at the apex of his ministry. She gazed out the window, wondering how many peoples' lives were affected by her decision to be with another man. "You could have helped them if it wasn't for me turning your life upside down. It's my judgment to face. Not yours."

Dylan was determined to see life through the eyes of the Christ he'd long claimed to love and serve. "Lynnie, what if it's neither of our judgments to face? What if Jesus already took that judgment for us?"

She tilted her head, struck by his words. "Where do you get these things? You always shock me with these crazy-deep spiritual

226

questions."

He grinned. "I'm not trying to be spiritual, just factual."

"Well, whatever it is, I love and appreciate it. That's an incredible thought, but there are consequences and I'm fully aware that I have a price to pay."

Dylan was concerned for his ex-wife. "He paid the price for every wrongdoing, Lynette, and yes, there are consequences, but those consequences are not God punishing you. Consequences are the natural affect of certain choices. But I fully believe your heart is positioned in a good place now. God's right there, holding your hand through every trial and every decision." He paused, letting his words sink into her soul. Dylan knew she must be warned. "Listen to me. If you're expecting bad consequences, Lynette, you're going to attract bad things to yourself. You've got to know and believe that you have a good Father who has chosen to forget the wrongs just as He said He would. You know the whole 'as far as the east is from the west' thing? Either it's true or He's a liar."

She processed the words of the man she trusted.

Dylan continued. "And you know Jeremiah's writings, 'I have plans to prosper you and not to harm you.' So don't attract negativity. If we're going to survive this whole thing, you and I have to be a strong team. That means keeping our minds in a positive place. Life's too short not to attract good things. You and I need to team up on every level: body, spirit, soul, and mind." He grinned as he recalled one of his favorite childhood shows. "Hey, do you remember this? 'Wonder twin powers! Activate!' I loved that show."

Lynette chuckled. "Oh my gosh! I remember that."

He hoped to inspire her with childlikeness. "Let's be like that, okay? I mean, except for the being brother and sister part. When I said we need to team up in body, spirit, soul, and mind, I was especially excited about the body part." He winked.

THE WINDOWS OF HOLLY

Lynette picked up a straw from the table and threw it at him. "You're so bad."

"And you like it, don't you?"

She narrowed her eyes and tightened her lips, attempting to appear serious, but her effort failed as a smile erupted.

Dylan pointed at her. "Uh huh. Look at those blushing cheeks," he gloated.

She was thoroughly entertained by Dylan. *Gosh, I've missed this.* "Well, Dylan. I hope you're into cottage cheese and stretch marks, because this body isn't what it used to be."

As always, Dylan knew just what to say. "Your body is beautiful. Besides, you are not your body. And just so you know, I do like cottage cheese," he quipped. "You know how passionate I've always been about food."

She shook her head. "You're too much, Vanberg. Seriously, I'm glad you have such a good perspective on everything. That's one of the things I've missed so, so much." Her eyes sparkled as she regarded the man she loved. Lynette flipped through images of her last five years of life, contrasting them with her current state. She couldn't recall herself smiling much while she was with Owen. *I feel so different now. So happy.*

Dylan wondered what was going on inside her head. "What are you thinking about?"

She tried to convey her thoughts. "I've spent the last five years living around constant negative comments, complaints, and arrogant rants. I'm not kidding; it became a daily thing. I felt like I'd died inside. The only thing that kept me going in that relationship was the hope of having a baby. I know that sounds dumb, but I thought having a child would be the only way I could experience joy again. I knew I didn't deserve anything better than Owen, but the thought of getting to be a mom was like air to a drowning person. When motherhood kept eluding me, I took that

228

as evidence that I deserved punishment. Now I have Asa *and* you." She choked back her emotion. "And this grace absolutely undoes me. I feel like a wad of blubbering gratitude lately."

Sitting next to her at the table, Dylan took her hand and smiled. "Blubbering gratitude is one of the most rare and precious treasures of this world."

Lynette tilted her head back, looking at the ceiling as she took a deep breath to compose herself. *Quit being so emotional all the time, Lynette.* She dropped her head back down, eyes level with Dylan's. "Grace like this is also one of those rare treasures. I'll never take it for granted. Thank you, Dylan." She leaned forward to wrap her arms around his neck. "I love you so much." Her lips decorated his cheek with kisses, finally resting on his neck.

The sensation of her kisses and the smell of her hair caused Dylan to close his eyes and linger in the moment. His whole body awakened. He turned to whisper in her ear, "I love you too." He lifted his hands to hold her face in his palms, pressing his lips gently into hers.

Chapter Eighteen

MIKE AND CURT MADE THEIR REGULAR LUNCH VISIT to Annie's Café. The two grungy men were happy to get a break from their plumbing project at the local supermarket. Curt blurted out, "That dang toilet's stuck in there like a hippopotamus in an inner tube."

Mike shook his head. "Curt, that analogy makes no sense. How is the toilet like a hippo in an inner tube?"

Curt smeared butter on his biscuit. "Well, I mean, it's nearly impossible to pull it outta the floor. I think old man Pendleton must've poured a bucket of Gorilla Glue on that floor when they installed it."

Mike swallowed his food. "It's just the old, rusted bolts that are difficult. Once we get those suckers out, it'll pop right outta the floor."

Curt disagreed, shaking his head. "No, I'm telling you, I tried rockin' the thing back and forth, and there's no budging it. It's stuck solid to the floor. It's gotta be Gorilla Glue."

Mike scratched his head. "Curt, you're a real nincompoop. That toilet was probably installed in the 1940s. Gorilla Glue wasn't invented until the '90s."

Curt was impressed. "How do you know that? Was it your mama that made it?"

THE WINDOWS OF HOLLY

Mike rolled his eyes. "No, but your mama probably sat on that toilet and that's why it's stuck to the dang floor."

"Hardy har har." Crumbs fell from Curt's lips as he scoffed.

Lucy approached the table, pregnant belly clad in a red-and-white apron. "How are you guys today?"

Mike nodded in acknowledgment of her presence. "Ma'am, we're doing well. And you?"

Lucy glowed. "I'm great." She placed her hand on her tummy. "We can't wait for this little one to arrive. Jackson is so excited. Just a few more months to go."

"We're excited to meet the little feller," Curt offered.

"Or little miss," she replied. "Is Elsie taking good care of you today?"

"Yes, ma'am. Now if she could just get Curt to stop smacking so loudly, this eating environment would be perfect for us finer food connoisseurs."

Lucy chuckled. "Oh, Mike. You're always a hoot." She winked at Curt, then shifted her eyes away from him before the appearance of Curt's messy mouth made her nauseous. "Have you guys heard about the Christmas party at the Vanberg's place yet?"

Mike swallowed his food before answering. "Lori from the supermarket mentioned it today. Seems the news is spreading like a wildfire."

Lucy smiled. "You know you're invited, right?"

Curt shook his head. "We thought we was, but we didn't know for sure."

Lucy explained, "That's because the ladies haven't made all the phone calls yet. Miss Emma wanted to send invitations, but they decided to make calls instead since it's such short notice. December twenty-second is right around the corner. Mark it on your calendar. Will you come?"

Mike took a swig of his tea and wiped his mouth. "Well, pretty lady, I think it's quite possible we'll be there. It's not like Curt and I have multiple invitations to parties or such. Besides, I have to admit I'm curious to check out the situation. I haven't seen Lynette in a long while and I hear she's got a baby." Mike shook his head. "That's one heck of a situation, but you know," he paused for a few seconds, "I'm glad she's not with that knucklehead, Owen. I'm not sure what she ever saw in him. I mean, I know of his ability to smooth talk the ladies. He's always done that. Once he wins them, it isn't long before he crumples them up and throws 'em away."

Curt interrupted, "Yeah, and when he sees something he wants, he won't quit until he gets it."

Lucy was uncomfortable with the conversation, afraid to be caught up in gossip, especially when it involved people she loved dearly, but she was pleasantly surprised by their softness toward Lynette. They didn't cast judgment on her, but Lucy was compelled to remind them of the Vanbergs' humanity. "Well, just so you know, Dylan and Lynette are not animals on display in the zoo. I hope you'll come to the party to celebrate, not to gawk. They already feel awkward, and I don't want anyone adding to the awkwardness."

"You're right. No spectating. How did we get invited anyway?"

Lucy patted his shoulder. "You got invited because that's how Dylan and Lynette are. On top of that, you're kinda buddies with Beverly and Emma," she said, laughing.

"Buddies? Hmph." Mike grinned.

Lucy understood their strange, witty friendship. "Yeah, yeah. You know you love your buddies. Without Emma and Beverly around, your times at the café would be rather boring."

Curt snickered, "I tried to tell him he should hook up with Bev."

Lucy tilted her head, trying to envision such a connection.

THE WINDOWS OF HOLLY

"That'd be interesting." She laughed. "But no, I don't think so."

The bell chimed as more customers entered. Pastor Dean and Elder David were beaming as they continued their conversation from the parking lot. David held a newspaper in his hand. "Dean, I'm just so proud of Dylan for the way he's handled things. What a great perspective he brought in this article. And, man, I'm totally behind your idea to contribute to the Christmas party. Having their old congregation show support would mean so much to Dylan and Lynette. They really need that right now."

The two men took a seat at the bar. Pastor Dean preferred the old, round barstools over a table or booth. Nostalgia was to blame for that. The fond memories he carried of his childhood, hanging out at his Aunt Maggie's old café, kept him infatuated with small town life. Coming to Holly was an invitation he welcomed easily.

Stepping into Hope Fellowship soon after the scandal of an affair that involved a deacon and the pastor's wife was quite a challenge. He would never forget the first time he stepped behind the pulpit, being the target of suspicious, questioning eyes. Walking into a system that included entitled people with an overabundant sense of ownership caused him to drop to his knees often. Thankfully, there were teachable spirits that embraced him, ready to move forward into a more hopeful season. David had become one of Dean's most faithful supporters. The elder board was still intrigued by the transformation of David from dictator to defender.

Lucy approached the bar with pen and pad ready for their order. "Hey, David! Hello, Pastor Dean. It's good to see you today."

The men lit up. David deeply admired Lucy for being a light in the community of Holly. It was her kindness that played a role in the softening of his heart. "Hi, Lucy. How's Holly's favorite baby coming along?"

She smiled at his question. "We seem to be doing well. The doctor says baby is right on schedule."

"Wonderful," he replied.

Lucy continued, "Speaking of being right on schedule, your wife is a brilliant planner! I can't wait for the party. Can you believe it?" Her joy was obvious.

David agreed. "Yes, Marcy never ceases to amaze me. The woman's got skills—a regular Martha Stewart."

Dean chimed in. "We're looking forward to being there. I just told David today that the church board has agreed to help fund the party. We want Dylan and Lynette to know we're for them."

Lucy fixed her gaze on the two men, touched by their kindness. Her eyes filled with tears. She placed her pen and notepad in her apron pocket and leaned in to hug Pastor Dean. "Oh my gosh, Pastor Dean. Thank you. Thank you so much." She let go of him. "I'm just blown away. What a wonderful thing to do. After all Dylan has been through, this is exactly what he needs. And Lynette too."

Dean smiled. "Yes. That's why we're going to make this occasion extra special."

"Excellent," she beamed. "So what can I get you guys for lunch?"

David and Dean studied the chalkboard that hung above the mirror behind the bar. "Mmm. So many great options today. What would you choose, Lucy?" Dean inquired.

"Most definitely the buttermilk cornflake baked chicken. You can't go wrong with that."

"Then put me down for that one," said Dean.

"Me too," David concurred.

Lucy made her way to the kitchen. Dean tapped his fingers on the countertop, pondering tasks to be tackled. "So, David."

"Yeah?"

THE WINDOWS OF HOLLY

Dean leaned in, seeking counsel. "I need some advice on how to deal with a couple of situations." He sighed. "I have two church members irritating me. To be honest, it's more than irritating. It's gnawing at my stomach and keeping me awake at night."

David wrinkled his brow. "Only two? You lucky man!" The men laughed. "Who do I need to take to the woodshed?" he said, making an attempt to lighten his friend's load.

Dean grinned. "I'm talking about little old ladies."

David shook his head. "Little old ladies, huh? Well, I guess we're in really big trouble then. So what's going on?"

"It's stupid, insignificant things really." Dean rubbed the back of his neck. "I shouldn't let it bother me, but man, it's irritating as heck. Beatrice is arguing with my nursery workers over trash cans and diaper pails."

David laughed. "Of course. There's a dying world out there, but someone's gotta be the one to cause problems over diaper pails. It seems there's always one in the bunch. Dean, you know those kinds of people exist no matter where you go, right?"

Dean cracked his knuckles. "Yes," he sighed. "I've been doing ministry long enough to know that, but you'd think people would grow up and stop nitpicking, you know? It's crazy how that stuff can eat away at you and make you wake up in a sweat, wishing you could run away from ministry."

"Yeah, I know." David rubbed the bridge of his nose. "I suppose that's why several hundred ministers leave the pulpit every month. I've heard varying statistics on that."

Dean continued, "I mean, here's what I'm dealing with right now. I've got nursery workers who've faithfully worked ever since I came here. They never bother me for a thing. Two weeks ago they requested two new diaper pails and two new trash cans. No big deal, right? But Beatrice is a bigger penny-pincher than I realized. Why the congregation voted her in as treasurer is beyond

236

me. People say she's good with money, but this woman is going way too far with her frugality. She denied their request and told them to simply bleach the pails and cans to avoid being wasteful. Those cans are probably twenty years old!"

David was amused. "Small town church drama. I must say that I've been to Beatrice's home and I'm pretty positive that everything in that house is at least seventy years old, including her trash can."

"Dear God. This is why we should do home inspections before anyone can be voted in." Dean laughed. "Dude, why didn't you warn me?"

David shrugged. "She's just a little, old lady. I guess I forgot how dangerous they can be."

Dean continued his story. "Beatrice has denied the nursery workers repeatedly, so I finally broke down and bought what they needed myself, paid out of my own pocket. I figured an intervention was necessary to avoid an all-out war. Honestly, this isn't the first time I've paid for things I felt the church needed. It's easier than battling Beatrice. One can only handle the look of disapproval and condescension so many times."

David shook his head. "That's not right, Dean. It's not your responsibility to buy items for the church. I'll talk with her and make sure you get reimbursed."

Dean nearly panicked. "Oh no, no, no! I'm not willing to waste precious time with her biting at my heels. I've got bigger things to deal with. I'd rather just buy it and stop the fighting."

David thought he would attempt a bit of humor. "I suppose we could take up a collection specifically for the trash cans and diaper pails. We could entice them by offering to place an engraved gold plate bearing their names on the cans. Maybe Beatrice would like to have her name on a diaper pail. 'This diaper pail joyfully provided by Beatrice Griswold.' Or maybe we could dedicate it in

THE WINDOWS OF HOLLY

memory of someone. You never know. People are that silly about things when it comes to spending money in the church."

Dean snickered. "You're not kidding. Seriously, though, I stopped the situation from going over the line. Nancy was threatening to leave a dirty diaper in the drawer of Beatrice's treasury desk. I had to do something. Can you imagine what would've happened if Bea came into the office and found a nasty diaper in there?"

David laughed. "Well, that would've gotten her a diaper pail, I'd bet. But with Beatrice involved, it'd certainly make the newspaper. You know how she is about submitting little snippets to the *Holly Herald*. She would have reported it in the crimes section, claiming she was assaulted by a diaper at Hope Fellowship."

Dean laughed. "Yes, she would. Thank God we have Dylan and Jackson at the *Herald*. They've played damage control many times."

David sipped his tea. "So what else are you dealing with?"

Dean closed his eyes, taking a deep breath. "Miss Eleanor." He shook his head. "God bless Miss Eleanor. The day that lady learned how to use the internet was the day my e-mail inbox trembled. Every single day, David. Every single day, there's an e-mail about what I should be doing about worship, the song choices, the placement of offering envelopes, the need for plants in particular spots on the platform, the need for ten million different kinds of funds to address needs, and how I should improve hospital visitations. She even questioned me about what my wife does throughout the week." He sighed. "Do you want me to keep going?"

David looked surprised. "Man, I had no idea. I thought Miss Eleanor was just quiet and sweet as can be."

Dean's eyes widened. "Are you kidding me? That lady is

anything but quiet and sweet. She appears that way to people around her, but behind the scenes, she's an ornery one. I know she's lonely since her husband passed away. She tries to busy herself. Her downfall is that she feels a sense of ownership after being here for several decades. Do you know if Dylan dealt with that?"

"Not that I'm aware of," David replied. "But I don't think Dylan let us know about everything he was dealing with. Obviously."

Dean continued, "Nothing is ever right for Eleanor. Church growth bothers her. Someone always take 'her' seat, as if she owns that particular chair. You'd honestly think she's sitting in worship with a sheet of paper, critiquing every note that's being sung. All I want to do is worship God, gather people together, and focus on our creator. I want to infuse people with hope to do life in a way that produces love, joy, and peace, but I'm surrounded with pointless, petty distractions."

David agreed. "I'm right there with you on that."

Dean continued unleashing his feelings. "Sometimes I want to take these people, put them on an airplane, and send them to Liberia, where they can watch people who are struggling to stay alive. Maybe that would shift perspectives. We're so danged pampered, wrapped up in a bubble of self-absorption. I mean, seriously, nitpicking peeves me no end. People are starving, but God forbid that we have to share a chair." He threw his hands in the air, breathing out heavily.

"Yep. I know."

Dean gulped his iced tea and continued his introspection. "And I know it shouldn't bother me, but last Sunday, I preached a message from the heart. I'm talking about the kind of message I poured my soul and spirit into all week. I stayed up until three in the morning making sure that I could convey it correctly. I wake up early on Sunday, focused on what I feel is from God, and after I preach it, Dick Walker comes up to me and starts talking about how the platform wasn't installed correctly. He went off on how the pulpit needed to be sanded around the edges, blah, blah, blah. Absolutely stunning! You can speak words of life to the heart and spirit, and it can mean nothing to some people."

David shook his head. "Part of the reason Dick did that is because he wanted his brother to make a pulpit for the church, but the board had already chosen someone else."

Dean acknowledged that fact. "I know, but that was years ago! Why, out of the blue, is it suddenly an issue again? And why on that particular day?"

David tried to encourage him. "When you bring something to the congregation and your heart is really in tune with God, releasing that truth is a challenging invitation to people whose eyes and minds are stuck on the things of this temporal realm. Their disappointments, bitterness, resentment and anger get pricked when truth is spoken. It stirs them up. Instead of taking it personally, you've got to let it go and be patient with their process. I believe it's God trying to free them from something. Whether or not they let Him is their choice. I suppose we just have to pray for open eyes and hearts. Just keep moving on with what you know you're supposed to do. Be the invitation for them to come into something greater."

"You're right. I like that term, 'invitation.' That reminds me of something my friend Bill said. 'The gospel is not an ultimatum; it's an invitation.' I have to remind myself to operate in that place of invitation and kindness. The nitpickers make me feel like giving an ultimatum."

David smiled. "Maybe we should ask God to fix these situations, kinda like He did with the church sign issue several years before you arrived. We had months of meetings that the board spent arguing over whether or not we were getting a new church sign. Half of us knew we needed to replace the eyesore, but the other half felt it was a waste of money. Finally, one day, while we were sitting in the Sunday school room, debating over that stupid sign, we heard a crash." David chuckled at the memory. "An old fellow lost control of his pickup truck and drove right through the thing."

Dean laughed. "Are you serious? That's hilarious!"

David continued, "It's called providence. Apparently, God wanted us to have a new sign. I'll never forget that old guy driving the truck. His name was Henry. I've called him Saint Henry ever since he helped deliver us from that eyesore."

Dean was inspired. "If only God would show up that tangibly to deal with Beatrice and Eleanor's complaints." He looked at the ceiling. "C'mon, Lord. Help me out."

Lucy trotted to the counter with their chicken dinners in hand. "Here you go. I'll refill your teas. Can I get you anything else?"

David was famished and ready to dive in. "Thanks, Lucy! I think we're good."

David turned toward Dean, "You know, you could make the church more exciting for yourself if you'd go over there and invite Mike and Curt for the Christmas services." He nudged playfully.

Dean took a look at the two dirty men as they crammed strawberry shortcake into their mouths. Dean smiled. "I'll do it, but I have to confess, every time they've come to a service, Beatrice and Miss Eleanor cringe. I think I'd find too much pleasure in inviting them for all the wrong reasons."

David laughed. "I'm sure God will forgive you."

"Maybe," Dean replied. "Hm. What about Dick? I wonder what would get his mind off the platform and pulpit?" he joked.

David patted Dean on the back. "Probably just a big dose of love, brother."

THE WINDOWS OF HOLLY

Dean puckered his lips. "Or a big dose of something. My grandfather would say some people just need a good kick. Sometimes I wish I could live by that."

David grinned. "He sounds like an interesting fellow."

Dean smiled as he remembered his grandfather. "He was a funny man, for sure, and very compassionate when it came down to it. He'd say people needed a kick, but he'd turn right around and hug them. Grandpa was always making people laugh."

David asked, "What would your grandfather say about Dick Walker?"

Dean thought about the man's track record of being an overbearing know-it-all. A smile crept across his face. "Grandpa might say that if you gave Dick an enema, you could bury him in a shoebox."

David spewed tea from his mouth. He sputtered as he reached for a napkin. "Oh my!" He giggled while trying to maintain some element of dignity. "That's hilarious!"

Dean added, "But Grandpa would've embraced Dick and taken him out for coffee. He'd find out what made him tick and tell him to pursue his dreams. That's what I loved about Grandpa. He always looked for what lingered beneath the surface, you know? It's like he had a magical power to awaken the walking dead. God, I miss that man."

David smiled. "Not everyone has the privilege of knowing family members that leave a positive mark on their lives. You're blessed to know such a man. He'd be proud of you, Dean."

"You think so?" Dean asked.

"Absolutely. You're a good man," David assured him.

They sat in silence for a couple of minutes, content to eat and listen to the chatter around them. Pastor Dean found himself aware of a minor argument between spouses over Christmas plans. David was lost in thoughts about his own grandparents and the few memories he carried of them. *Life truly is a vapor. Here today, gone tomorrow.* He cleared his throat. "It's crazy how quickly life goes by, isn't it?"

Dean agreed. "Definitely."

David expounded. "When you're young, you think you'll live forever. I wish I'd learned sooner to value people and not take them for granted. It used to feel like everyone would be around forever. It seems as we get older and experience losses, we wake up to the reality of a short existence on this earth, you know?"

"I know what you mean," Dean agreed.

David continued, "One thing I've been thinking about lately is how we treat the younger generation. Sadly, some of the old folks just complain about the younger ones. I mean, not all of them complain, but many do. It's like there's a huge generational gap that shouldn't exist."

Dean acknowledged his concern. "You're not kidding. I hear a lot of derogatory comments about millennials. It breaks my heart."

David continued sharing his thoughts on the subject. "We need to build a bridge and bring people together. The younger generation needs the wisdom and life experiences of the older generation. The older generation needs to learn what the younger generation is learning, and we need to value them because they are the future of this world. We only live a short time, so we're limited in how far we can go, at least time wise. But young people are our access into the future; through them we go further than we can go ourselves."

"Absolutely," Dean concurred.

David thought about his grandparents. "I wish I'd valued my grandparents more. I was too wrapped up in building my own life. I never stopped to ask them questions that I wish I could ask now. It's like I had a time machine right in front of me and didn't even realize it. By the time I considered that my grandparents were a

THE WINDOWS OF HOLLY

time machine into another era, it was too late. I totally missed the opportunity to ask them about the time period they lived in."

Dean raised his eyebrows. "Wow. I never thought of the time machine thing, but you're right. They're our only access to a past we can never know."

David continued, "We should do something in our church to help bring the generations together. What do you think of that?"

"I love the idea. Come up with a plan and we can revisit that." Dean thought for a moment. A grin snuck across his face. "Can you imagine connecting Beatrice and Miss Eleanor with the youth?"

The thought caused David to chuckle. "We can have some fun with this. It'd do them good to realize millennials may be the ones changing their diapers or doing their surgeries down the road."

David shifted his attention. "Now, how about inviting Mike and Curt to church?"

Dean turned to get a good look at the two men who were playing a round of dominoes. "Sure. I'll go talk with them." He grinned as he dreamed about the ramifications. "Oh, Beatrice. The look on her face will be priceless. Father, forgive me for taunting the little grump."

Chapter Nineteen

YLAN AND LYNETTE SLEPT in each other's arms, wrapped in a soft, down blanket. Asa slept soundly in a portable crib at the foot of their bed. Lynette's eyes twitched in rapid eye movement as she descended into another realm. Images of herself traveled through the recesses of her mind. Like foggy, old video clips, she watched her emotionless face in a mirror as she examined it for blemishes. Small, bloody cuts and bruises spotted her skin. Her eyes were clouded and gray.

The sight of her ghostly visage caused her to back away from the full-length mirror, revealing the strapless, pale green wedding dress she wore. From the waist down, a beautiful, white overlay flowed toward her feet. She grasped a section of the white material in her fingers. As she touched it, the white fabric morphed into cobwebs that attached to her hand, climbing up her arms and across her chest. Terror struck her heart. She tried calling out Dylan's name, but her voice barely cracked with a whisper as she struggled to get air.

Owen's hardened face appeared before her, eyes piercing her soul with rejection and disgust. She felt her body slipping downward through stained, mauve carpet as she reached upward for help. Owen watched as her body sank and she cried out, "Help me." Her cobweb-encased hands trembled and her voice shook

THE WINDOWS OF HOLLY

with weakness and desperation. "Dylan." Owen knelt before her, placing a small, round mirror in front of her face. She caught sight of her clouded, colorless eyes staring back at her with fear and desolation. "Help me see," she pleaded through tears.

A voice echoed to her right, "Lynette, see in Me." She turned her face toward the sound. Bright, searing light penetrated her eyes. It traveled into her body, causing her to vibrate uncontrollably. The voice spoke again, "The eye is the lamp of your body. When your eye is clear, your whole body is full of light. But when it is bad, your body is full of darkness. Do you want to see again?"

"Yes," she cried.

The sound of waterfalls enveloped her being. Warmth moved across her eyes. She began to weep, overwhelmed by the love filling her soul. "Choose My sight, Lynette."

"I choose Your sight," she responded.

Her body was lifted into the light, shaking with elation and joy. She listened as Christ spoke. "Forgive and you will be forgiven."

"Yes, I forgive." Visions of faces of those she resented and judged flashed before her. "I release them all," she promised with trembling lips. Suddenly, her own face suspended vividly before her eyes. She knew she had to forgive herself along with the others who caused her pain. *If I don't forgive myself, I'll die.* As she looked at herself, compassion and gratitude filled her heart. "Father, I release myself from my judgment. Thank you for forgiving me." In that instant, a flash of light burst out from her.

"Now you see," Christ echoed.

Dylan was awakened by Lynette's convulsing body. "Lynnie?" He sat up quickly, touching her arm. "Lynnie?"

"I can see," she whispered, eyes still closed. "I can see." A tear escaped from her eye and rolled down her cheek.

Dylan thought she was having a seizure until she spoke those words. He placed his hand on her arm, watching her face as she reacted to the dream in her mind.

MARSHALL CITY

Kat Richland sat up in bed abruptly, breathless and heart pounding. She panted, trying to regain her composure after a nightmare about her husband, Preston, being with Fay. Preston woke up to the sound of Kat's breathing. "Babe, what's going on? What's wrong?" Preston placed his hand on her back. "Kat, answer me."

She burst into tears, "Why?" Her body shook with sobs. "Why is it so hard? I just want to get through one night, one day, without a thought about the past!" Tears soaked the sheets that lay across her lap.

Preston's heart sank, knowing it was about what he had done. He wanted to comfort her, but he believed his words would be useless. Still, he had to say something. "I'm so sorry, Kat. I'm so sorry. I wish I could go back and do that part of my life over again. I wish I'd never done that." He moved closer to her, embracing her as she wept. When Kat struggled with memories of his affair, he never knew if he should hold her or give her space to grieve. Kat reassured him multiple times that she always needed his presence in those moments. The affair left her heart feeling lonely and abandoned. When pain arose, she liked knowing he was with her.

"I'm sorry too," she cried.

Preston cringed when she'd blame herself for his actions. "Kat, you have nothing to be sorry for."

"Yes, I do. If I was a better wife, that never would have happened," she sobbed.

"No, Kat. I've told you a million times, that's not true. You didn't do anything wrong. It wasn't about you."

THE WINDOWS OF HOLLY

She slammed her fist into the mattress. "That can't be true! I wasn't enough for you. If I was enough, you wouldn't have felt the need to be with another woman."

Her anger caused him to flinch, but he remained by her side. "Kat." Preston shifted onto his knees, facing her. He lifted her chin gently, peering into her tear-drenched eyes. "You are more than enough."

His words were salve to her broken heart. "You are more than enough. You always have been, and you'll always be more than enough."

She wrapped her arms around his neck. "You are more than enough too," she whispered through tears. "Can we please never go through this again? I want to grow old with you. Just me and you forever." She squeezed her eyes closed tightly. "That's what I always wanted it to be: just me and you."

"That's what I want too," he replied. "Just us."

She spoke with frustrated determination. "I need to be fixed so we can move on and do life. I feel like I'm broken. I'm all jacked up inside."

Preston held her. "You are perfect," he declared with compassion.

They settled back into the bed, reclining on the pillows. "It was a horrible dream, Preston. The images, the pictures. It's too much to bear."

He tried his best to make her feel better. "Kat, maybe the things you're dreaming didn't actually happen. The way it's painted in your mind probably looks different than reality."

She interrupted, "But the fact is that it did happen! You had sex with her. Nothing can change that fact."

Her words pierced his heart. *What can I say?*

She shook her head. "And I used to teach the women at church that anything is possible with God, that anything can be erased and redeemed. Now I can't even believe it for myself." She wiped her face with a tissue. "I'm such a hypocrite."

"No you're not," he reassured. "I hurt you terribly, and you're not a hypocrite for hurting."

She vented her doubts. "I keep thinking about the party at Dylan and Lynette's. I really want to be there to support them. God knows, they've got a lot more baggage to carry than we do, but I'm struggling with the thought of going to Holly, you know? That's where you spent time with Fay."

He wished she wouldn't remind him of that fact.

"Some days I feel strong, but then there are days when I feel weak and I don't know if I can handle any reminders. That party is only three days away, and I'm trying to psyche myself up for it. That's probably why the nightmare happened. I've been so focused on not succumbing to the junk."

Preston listened with understanding. *Dang it. Why did I screw up so many things?* He really wanted to be there for Dylan. Dylan was a bright spot in Preston's darkness, and he was key to his awakening. "I understand, Kat. If you don't want to go, we don't have to."

She insisted, "I want to go. I just hope I can handle being in Holly. When I was a teenager, my aunt used to drive me through there on our way to visit her fiancé. We'd stop at Annie's Café for pie. It's been a long time since I've gotten to do that. It'd be nice to stop there on our way to the party, but I know you ate there with Fay. That ruins the whole experience for me." She leaned back against the pillows and sighed.

A shadow crossed Preston's face. "Would you please stop saying her name? I don't like hearing it."

While part of Kat wanted to tell him he had no right to demand anything, she knew that was wrong. She directed the sails of her heart to flow in peace and allow him to be repentant, freed from his past choices. "Okay, I'll do my best, but only if you'll take me to Annie's for pie before we go to the Vanbergs. I feel like I need to stuff my face full of sugar."

Oh God. Help me. Preston would rather not go to the place where he publicly lived in a delusion, but for Kat, he would do it. Preston was good at compartmentalizing, yet shame still threatened his heart when reminded of his stupidity. He knew that people who frequented the café would still remember him as a two-timing, worthless jerk. *Maybe it'd be good for them to see me with my wife.* He hoped people would be forgiving of his past impropriety.

Kat interrupted his thoughts. "So will you take me for pie?"

He smiled. "For you, yes."

She looked at the ceiling and exhaled, closing her wet eyes. "All right. I've got three days to pull it together for this party. God help me."

Miss Lilly's Floral Shop on Main

Old Mary Elliott shuffled her way into Miss Lilly's Floral Shop. Though she was in her early nineties, she carried herself with independence and grace, always dressed in elegance. Living in the heart of Holly made it possible for her to frequent the local businesses as much as she pleased, but these days, she usually stayed in her home to paint canvasses and pray for those in her community. The mission that moved her out of her comfortable living room on this particular morning was a mission of love for Dylan and Lynette.

The bell dinged as she entered the floral shop. "Hello, Miss Lilly," Mary smiled.

"Why, hello there, Mary!" Lilly trotted around the counter, greeting Mary with a hug. "It's good to see you out and about. What brings you in today?" Lilly's brown, bobbed hair blended right in with her chocolate-colored apron that donned the words, "All I want for Christmas is chocolate." Her eyes clearly shone the light of a thankful heart.

Mary answered, "I suppose you've heard about the Christmas party at the Vanbergs?"

Lilly replied, "I sure have! How exciting."

Mary smiled. "I'd like you to help me make it extra special. I'd like to order floral bouquets to be delivered about an hour prior to the party. I have five hundred dollars to spend."

"Wow!" Lilly placed her hand over her heart, touched by the gesture. "Mary, that's a beautiful idea, but I can't allow you to spend that much! How about we make a deal?"

Mary shook her head, "No, no. I appreciate that, but I want to be a blessing to your business as well. Besides, I have plenty of money sitting in my account and it doesn't do any good unless I use it. This is what I'd like to do for them. Those two have been through a mess over the last five years, and I want to help brighten up this special day for them. How many bouquets can we do for that amount of money?"

Lilly was thankful for Mary's generosity. "Well, Mary," she said, smiling, "I believe we can do twenty to twenty-five beautiful arrangements. It'll be gorgeous!" Lilly's eyes moistened. "I really want to thank you for your business, Mary. My daughter's family is going through a financial fiasco right now, and both of her kids desperately need a pair of glasses. I told her I'd cover the cost. Your purchase makes that possible."

Mary was pleased. "I'm so glad I can be a part of that." She beamed as she browsed at the plants and flowers. "Oh, I love roses. We need lots of roses. Red ones for Christmas." She smiled brightly. "If you throw in some greenery with them, that'll blend right in with the decorations. How about some poinsettias?"

"I have a good supply of those. The churches in town didn't

THE WINDOWS OF HOLLY

order as many this year. Budgets are down, according to them, so yes! I have lots of poinsettias we can use."

"Excellent." Mary looked toward the back wall. "What else would you recommend?"

Lilly walked across the shop. "We can't forget mistletoe and this red amaryllis. And what if I throw in some of these white-tipped pine cones? That would be beautiful. Oh, and the Star of Bethlehem would be beautiful with its white bloom! I can create some lovely baskets with these."

Mary clapped her hands together. "Yes, yes! How lovely."

Lilly cupped a flower with her hands. "Did you know that poinsettias represent purity and the Star of Bethlehem symbolizes purity, hope, and happiness? How appropriate for the situation." She pulled on another sprig of greenery. "I'll have fun with this. Speaking of fun, I heard Lynette has a baby?"

"She does. Baby's first Christmas, and that old bag of a husband abandoned them."

Lilly shook her head. "How sad. How could anyone do such a thing? I'm personally very happy to hear that she and Dylan are sticking together. What a gracious man he is."

"A saint!" Mary pointed heavenward.

Lilly walked toward a large shelving unit filled with gifts. "Let's do something special to acknowledge the baby. What is the baby's name?"

"Asa," Mary replied. "Sweetest little thing."

Lilly lifted a large, brown bear from the shelf. It wore a red-and-white shirt that said "Baby's First Christmas." Gold and silver thread highlighted the letters. "I've had this guy up here for a few months, but we haven't had any takers. Let's throw him in the mix along with a special ornament. Mr. Sanders has some ornaments on display that he's able to personalize with that new machine he bought."

252

Mary glowed with pleasure. Joy radiated from her wrinkled eyes. "I'll run right over there to check on that. Thank you very much for making this extra special. Oh, their house will look and smell heavenly!"

Lilly stepped behind the counter to make notes. "I'm honored to be part of this. Life can get pretty dull around here sometimes. It's nice to do something especially meaningful."

Mary assured her, "Every day of your life is meaningful, no matter where you spend it. You might feel alone in this little shop, but you have no idea how many lives you've touched with the flowers you send out. You're the one behind the scenes who's actually creating beauty. That's a gift. What you do matters and it makes a difference."

Her words warmed Lilly's soul. "Thank you so much for saying that. I needed to hear it."

Mary continued, "Oh, I'm not just saying something. It's more than that. It's the truth. Holly is lucky to have you here, adding beauty to people's lives."

Lilly's smile widened. "Thank you."

Mary handed her a check for five hundred dollars. "Will you be there for the party?"

Lilly wobbled her head in thought. "I'd love to be there, but I have quite a crowd arriving that evening for Christmas. Bob's brothers and sister are coming, along with their children."

Mary's eyes widened. "Where are you putting everyone?"

"Here, there, and everywhere in between Holly and Marshall City." Lilly chuckled. "It'll be a wild one for sure. It's a good thing Bob built the addition on the back of the house. We'll have plenty of room to set up tables for Christmas dinner."

Mary patted her arm. "Well, you enjoy your Christmas, and we'll be thinking of you at the party. With all those pretty flowers, you'll be the talk of the town. Well, dear. I'd better be going now."

THE WINDOWS OF HOLLY

She turned to walk away but remembered something. "Oh, and Lilly! Be sure to keep this purchase anonymous. I don't want them to know who sent the flowers."

Lilly smiled. "It's our secret."

Emma's phone rang in the kitchen. "Oh of course," she exclaimed. "You always ring when I'm sitting on the toilet!" *Oh shoot. I always leave the phone in the other room.* "When will you learn, you goofy, old woman?" She cleaned herself up quickly and jumped to her feet, pulling down her blue muumuu. *No time to wash these hands.* "I'm coming," she hollered at the ringing phone. Her fuzzy kitten slippers scooted across the wood floors, dragging toilet paper along. She picked up the phone, breathless. "Hello?"

Beverly's cheerful voice exclaimed, "Hey there! What are you up to?"

Emma tried catching her breath. "What am I up to, you ask? I was working on one of the most captivating parts of my daily life."

"Oh yeah? What's that? Your love life?"

Emma huffed down the phone. "I was using the crapper, Bev. It's about the most exciting thing going on over here."

Beverly howled. "Too much information, Emma! Have mercy on your friend. Now I've got all kinds of images dancing in my head, and sadly, it's not sugar plums and fairies."

Emma grinned. "You asked. So what are you calling for?"

Beverly repeated, "What am I calling for? I'm calling because I wanted to let you know that Rose agreed to bring two meat lasagnas, two vegetable lasagnas, a platter of her amazing breadsticks, and enough salad for an army."

Emma was thrilled. "Wonderful! What a woman. Do you mean she's donating all of that food or what?"

"She's donating all of it," Beverly exclaimed. "She's unable to stay for the party, but she'll deliver the food and stay for a few minutes. I didn't have to do a bit of convincing, Emma. She's been following the Vanberg saga from a distance, and she said she's been rooting for a reconciliation between Dylan and Lynette all of these years. Apparently, Owen has been in her restaurant with a couple of different women over the last couple of years."

Emma gasped. "Oh my gosh. Well, I shouldn't be surprised." She shook her head. "That nasty man."

"Yeah, you're telling me," Beverly replied. "It's God's grace that Owen left her. She and little Asa are in a much better place. Now we get to celebrate."

Emma quipped, "We should tell everyone we're celebrating Lynette's prison release. Being married to that man was punishment enough for her actions."

Beverly agreed. "Yep. I've known several men and women that put themselves into prison while looking for greener pastures. That's why I quit lookin' and decided to feast on what I had." She laughed hysterically.

Emma wondered, "And what exactly did you have?"

Beverly giggled, "Oh, lots of chocolate chip pancakes, donuts and cookies. Can't you tell? If someone yelled 'fire,' they'd have to roll me out of the building. This toosh bears the imprint of my love for snacking, you know?"

"Oh, Bev. You're not a fatty. I always wanted your figure," Emma admitted.

Beverly was pleasantly surprised. "Well, Emma Gray! That's the nicest thing you've ever said to me."

"Now, don't let it get to your head, but I always wonder why you're still single. You're lots of fun and not too bad of a looker."

Beverly laughed. "Not too bad of a looker? That's not much of a compliment, but I'll take it. I was hoping I'd have a boyfriend

THE WINDOWS OF HOLLY

this Christmas, but there's not a great supply of men in Holly. That's all right though. The positive side is that I don't have someone belching and farting around my house. It's not a bad deal, really." She began to sing, "'Count your blessings, name them one by one! Count your blessings, see what God has done!' How does that verse go? Oh, I remember." She continued entertaining Emma with her singing. "When you look at others with their men and gold, think that Christ has promised you peace untold. Count your blessings if you don't have a guy, your reward is a smell-free home on high!"

Emma shook her head, grinning from ear to ear. "And there's another reason why I wonder why you're single. If only the men out there knew what they were missing."

Beverly chimed in, "They probably don't notice me because I don't wear dresses as bright as yours. Let me borrow one of your muumuus and a microphone. I can sing and dance in the park and maybe some poor, lost soul will realize what he's been missing."

Emma played along. "I'll rent you one of my muumuus for twenty-five bucks. I can use the money to get the squirrel feeder I saw on television."

Beverly snorted. "Great idea, Emma. You can catch yourself a squirrel and I'll catch myself a man. We make a great team, don't we?"

Emma laughed. "We sure do." Emma glanced down at the floor as she giggled. "Oh geez Louise!"

Her sudden change in tone startled Beverly. "What's wrong?"

"Oh," Emma replied, "I've got toilet paper stuck on my slippers!"

Beverly laughed. "You regularly adorn yourself with toilet paper. That's nothing new. You came into the café bearing practically a whole roll of Charmin last year. And don't you remember the time you had Kleenex stuck to your nose? The waitress had to point it out."

Emma remembered. "Yeah, yeah. And why didn't you point it out to me? Isn't that what friends are for?"

"I wanted to see how long you'd wear it. Besides, it's a mark of maturity. Young people wear nose rings. Old people walk around with pieces of tissue stuck to their noses."

Emma disagreed. "That's not true, Bev. I've never seen anyone with tissue stuck to their nose."

Beverly joked, "Then you haven't lived long enough. Stick around for awhile."

"My goodness!" Emma declared. "How did this conversation digress so quickly? Back to the lasagna! Let's stay on track."

Beverly cherished moments of banter and laughter with Emma. She was thankful for her friend and partner in crime. "All right then. I think we should call Marcy and Lucy to meet us at the café and go over the plans. We only have three days to tie up any loose ends."

Emma agreed. "Sounds good. Let's do that."

"Cool. Keep me posted on the time and I'll be there," Beverly commanded.

"Yes, ma'am. See you later, Miss Sassy Pants." Emma hung up the phone.

Jamie, Lynette's sister, stared at the large, wooden clock on her wall. She was lost deep in thought, pondering the awkwardness that awaited her in Holly. She made very few visits to Holly, and each visit had been during a significant event. Her first trip to Holly was to attend the wedding of Lynette and Dylan. The second and third visits were for Christmas candlelight services at Dylan and Lynette's church, Hope Fellowship.

Jamie's last visit to Holly was to attend the wedding of Lynette and Owen. Emotions were running high that day as she battled

THE WINDOWS OF HOLLY

disappointment over the fact that her highly regarded, "do-it-all-right" sister's marriage to a perfect pastor had ended. She remembered driving down Owen's long driveway onto his ranch, wondering why her sister was choosing a totally different life.

Jamie questioned Lynette about her choices prior to the wedding day, but Lynette assured her that "you wouldn't understand unless you've walked in my shoes." Jamie retreated, believing her sister certainly must know what she was doing. *Who am I to judge? Happiness is the goal, right? Apparently this God thing doesn't work, so she might as well do what makes her happy.* Jamie swallowed her doubts and leapt into fully supporting Lynette's decision, figuring she would do whatever she wanted, despite how Jamie felt. *Who am I to stop her?*

As Jamie recalled her own actions on the wedding day, her stomach turned. After all these years, she still held a secret that tormented her heart. Lynette's marriage to Owen marked more than the beginning of Lynette's heartbreak, but also her own. After the ceremony and reception on that June day, Owen's friend, Will, approached her with words that warmed her soul and body. "The bride and groom shouldn't be the only ones having fun tonight. You're far too beautiful to spend the night alone," he whispered in her ear. Disillusionment with the loss of her sister's previous marriage of perfection caused her to let her guard down. *What am I holding onto anyway? Self-righteous beliefs and formulas that are absolutely powerless? What's the point of doing things right when everything will go wrong anyway?*

Will was an expert in identifying vulnerability in women. He and Owen shared that capability. They knew, from their own brokenness, how to see a wounded heart in need of companionship and reassurance. Owen had good intentions for the most part, but Will resigned himself to momentary pleasures frequently, and he was unwilling to dedicate himself to the healing of a heart. Will found more satisfaction in taking advantage of the weak.

While Owen and Lynette cut into their wedding cake, Will wedged himself between Jamie and another onlooker. He placed his hand gently on her lower back, leaning his mouth over her ear so she could feel his breath on her cheek. "Do you wanna join me for a drink after this is all over?"

Will's appearance was rugged and weatherworn, but he carried an element of manly charm that enticed her. The touch of an older man captivated her. The feeling of his hand on her back made her body tingle. "Yes," she answered without thinking. Her lack of caution both frightened and intrigued her; the mystery erased all wisdom and discernment. *Oh my God.* His closeness intoxicated her. *Jamie, get a hold of yourself. You don't know anything about this man.*

The rest of the reception was a foggy memory from that point. Sensations awakened, arresting her thoughts for the duration of the day. Will drove her to his beloved barn that evening. "There's nothing like a summer day in the hay," he told her. Jamie surrendered herself to his will.

Several weeks after the wedding, Mother Nature's failure to show up threw her into a panic. Will ignored her phone calls and desperate, pleading voicemails. Ashamed to tell Lynette what she'd done, and absolutely terrified of what her parents would think, she resorted to calling her closest friend, Savannah. "Oh, Jamie," Savannah lamented. "You don't have a college degree, not to mention you only make minimum wage and don't even get a full forty hours a week at your job. It's obvious this guy isn't going to help. The best thing you can do is end this pregnancy."

"I don't know, Savannah," Jamie replied. "I don't know if I can do that."

Savannah insisted, "What choice do you have? I mean, look at the situation. There's no way out of this. You need to salvage your

THE WINDOWS OF HOLLY

life; it's about to be hijacked by a baby. Once you have a baby, there's no turning back. You're talking eighteen years of slave labor to take care of a kid."

Jamie was plagued with nausea and guilt. "I'd rather not have an abortion."

Savannah couldn't think of a better option. "Well, if you don't abort, there's adoption, but that means your whole family will know about it."

Jamie considered the seemingly endless sobbing of her mother who was devastated by Lynette's divorce and remarriage. The look of pain and disappointment on her dad's face was something she couldn't bear, and she certainly didn't want to be part of increasing their pain. She resigned herself to Savannah's advice. "You're right. There's no better way out."

"Trust me," Savannah assured her, "You'll get through the procedure just fine. A few of my friends have been through it and they said it was simple. Nothing to it. And I'm here for you."

"Thanks, Savannah."

Four years later, here she sat in her bedroom on a cold December morning forcing the painful memories to remain locked behind her eyes. *Don't cry, Jamie! Pull it together.* No one warned her about the turmoil her body would inevitably present to her mind as special dates rolled around. Even when she was oblivious to the calendar, her body remembered, and it forced her to recall the loss. Every March greeted her with grief. *I would have been celebrating my baby's birthday this month. Was it a boy or girl? What would he or she look like?*

Now she would have to be in Holly for Dylan and Lynette's Christmas party. She dreaded entering the town that reminded her of that June day in Will's barn. She sighed. "God, help me." She always shuddered when she dared to ask for His help, but she knew there was nowhere else to look for mercy and relief from her

260

terrible secret.

Jamie looked at the wooden clock once more, taking note of the time. Ugh. Lynette would be expecting her call. Jamie had agreed to bring her made-from-scratch pumpkin spice cookies to the party and help Lynette clean the house before the party. She loved her sister, but it was painful seeing her. *What if she sees right through me?* Jamie feared that Lynette would never be able to forgive her for aborting a baby when Lynette fought so hard to conceive and deliver one. *She'd think I was a monster. She'd freak out if she knew I slept with Owen's friend, not to mention on her wedding day. How could she ever look at me the same way?*

Jamie often struggled with anger toward Will, wondering how he could put her in that situation and abandon her. *It makes sense now. Owen abandoned my sister and her baby. Will and Owen are exactly alike.* She cringed at the thought of them. Her anger toward Will increased since hearing that he beat up her sister. Jamie wanted him to pay severely, but Lynette assured her that jail time was enough. She also warned that if someone tried to retaliate, it could escalate the situation and ultimately put Asa in harm's way. It took all the self-control she could muster to not plot revenge. Many nights, she couldn't sleep due to thoughts of vengeance that steamrolled their way through her mind.

Jamie was counting down the days, nearly holding her breath. Three more days until the party. *God, please help me not to lose it when I drive into Holly. I'm so sorry for every stupid decision I ever made, and I'm sorry for letting go of what I knew to be true.* In her spirit, words echoed, "You are my daughter. Go and find your peace."

Chapter Twenty

ECEMBER 22, 5 P.M.
The Vanberg's front porch was dressed in twinkling lights, reflecting on silvery snowflake decorations that hung along the roof's edge. Seven o'clock was fast approaching. Everyone worked quickly to finish preparations. It seemed as if Beverly brought her entire Christmas decoration collection to dress up the Christmas House to enhance the spirit of the moment. A large, rosy-cheeked Santa Claus sat in the porch swing, swaying in the cool breeze. Mr. Sanders placed his Star of Bethlehem on their rooftop, and he adorned the weeping willow with icicle lights. Marcy set up a hot cocoa stand on the front porch beneath a sign that declared:

Welcome to the North Pole.
Grab some cocoa to warm your soul.
Come inside. Share your smile.
We hope that you will stay awhile.

Marcy hoped the message would serve as a good reminder to keep things on the positive. She wanted smiles, not naysayers and critics casting their negative comments around the Vanberg home. She and David spread the word that this night was to be a night of

THE WINDOWS OF HOLLY

hope and encouragement for every person in attendance, and that, yes, Dylan and Lynette were in fact reconciled and to be celebrated.

A beautiful green garland wove its way between the spindles of the porch railing. Red poinsettias graced each end of the garland. An archway of lights framed the door, highlighting a wreath of holly. The living room was an invitation into the heart of Christmas. Three Christmas trees, graduating in size, enveloped the room in a cheery embrace. The fireplace glowed with a small fire, thanks to David. Above it hung three stockings bearing the names Dylan, Lynette, and Asa.

In the kitchen, Jamie and Lynette placed final touches on the gingerbread men, beautifully covered with Jamie's homemade icing and artistic skill. Lynette sincerely appreciated her sister's contribution. "Jamie, thank you so much for coming over to help. I'm really glad you're here."

Jamie smiled. "Thanks, sis. I'm glad to be here too. It's so nice to be back in this house. It holds good memories for me, especially now that you and Dylan are back together." She removed another tray of cookies from the oven.

Lynette was still feeling a bit insecure about what her family and friends would think of her running to her ex-husband so quickly. She wondered if they'd misjudge her intentions or the driving force behind her return to Dylan. She figured some people would think she was taking advantage of Dylan's kindness, but that was the furthest thing from the truth. "Jamie, did you suspect that I was still in love with Dylan over the years?"

"Yes."

Lynette was slightly surprised. "How did you know?"

Jamie turned to look at her. "Sis, I knew by the look on your face the day you married Owen."

"Really?" Lynette was stunned. "Then why didn't you stop

264

me?"

Jamie shrugged. "You seemed to know what you wanted and I figured you must've had good reasons for leaving Dylan. I just wanted you to be happy."

Lynette sighed. "I didn't have a good reason. It was just stupidity." Her chin quivered. "And I need to apologize to you. I slacked off on staying in touch with you when I got wrapped up with Owen. I really regret that."

Jamie wiped her hands on a dish towel. "Oh, sis." She approached Lynette, wrapping her arms around her. "It wasn't just on your part. It was me too. I felt like I needed to separate myself from the whole thing."

Asa's whimper came through the baby monitor. Lynette held her sister for a few seconds as she listened to his little voice. "I'd better go feed him. Would you join me? I could use some sisterly conversation."

Sure." Jamie was delighted by the idea. "I'll turn off the oven and I'll be right there."

As Lynette walked down the hallway, she couldn't help but wonder why Jamie felt the need to separate herself from her after the wedding. *I must've been such a huge disappointment to her. After all, who would be crazy enough to leave a man like Dylan? And especially for someone like Owen? Ugh. Disgusting.* She stepped into the master bedroom to retrieve Asa from his crib. "Hey, mister man. You woke up!" She smiled. "How are you, little buddy?" She lifted him into her arms and snuggled her nose into his neck. "Mommy loves you."

Jamie entered the room, watching her sister caress her baby boy. The bond that she witnessed pierced her heart. *I would've been a mom too.* Lynette reclined in the rocking chair near the window. "Whew. The party hasn't even started and I'm already tired. I need a second wind before this gig begins." She pointed to

265

THE WINDOWS OF HOLLY

a chair. "Grab that chair in the corner and sit by me." Jamie did as she commanded.

Jamie offered, "Would you like me to make some coffee or tea?"

"No thanks. I'm trying to limit my caffeine intake for now since I'm breastfeeding. You know me. I typically live on caffeine, so it's a bit of a challenge." Lynette lifted her shirt and positioned herself for feeding. "All right, Asa. Don't take too long. Mommy has to get dressed for the party." She smiled adoringly at her little boy.

Jamie observed the connection. Seeing her sister in the role of mother was something she used to dream about. Long ago, she dreamed of being an aunt. Now she found it to be painful. Jamie feared getting too close to her nephew, afraid that his tiny frame would uncork the flood of sadness that she worked hard to keep bottled up inside.

After experiencing an unwanted pregnancy and the abortion, something inside her had turned off. Babies made her sad and uncomfortable, even angry. She wasn't sure why she was angry, except that anger was a coping mechanism she'd used since childhood to control her pain. *It's better than crying,* she'd tell herself.

Lynette noticed the look on Jamie's face: deep, withdrawn into another world. "Jamie?"

"Yeah," she replied.

"Earlier you said you felt the need to separate yourself from me after the wedding. I was curious to know the reason why. I know you must have been angry with me for leaving Dylan. Rightfully so. I wouldn't blame you if you felt that way. I know I really let you down. Why did you feel you needed to separate yourself from me?"

Jamie's eyes were set on her sister, but her question wasn't registering with her brain. She stared at the image of her sister holding a baby.

"Jamie?" Lynette questioned. "Are you okay?"

Emotionless, Jamie was staring right into her. She tried to shake off the mysterious obstacle that was keeping her from answering her sister's question. *Say something, Jamie! Speak. What's wrong with you?* She felt as if brain signals crawled slowly to deliver the message to her mouth. She bobbled her head, trying to awaken her speech. "I'm sorry. What was your question?"

Lynette repeated herself, knowing that something wasn't right with her sister. "Why did you feel the need to separate yourself from me after the wedding?"

It was a question that Jamie never had the chance to answer for herself. She'd become a master at stuffing her feelings. She learned to force her secrets into a locked box that seemed to grow into a prison chamber as each year passed. *How do I answer that question? Why did I need to separate myself?* Memories flipped through her mind of Will touching her. She remembered how she played along and surrendered herself to a man she didn't even know. She recalled the moment she found out she was pregnant and how she thought perhaps he would marry her and it would all turn out to be a blessing. The sadness of rejection and loss, the pain of being abandoned, crept up on her unexpectedly. Her lips began to quiver. Her chin shuddered.

Lynette watched her sister's expression collapse into pain and regret. "Oh, Jamie. What's wrong, dear?" Lynette wanted to jump up and comfort her sister, but Asa was latched on tightly. "Jamie, what's going on?" Lynette started to scoot herself out of the chair, but Jamie spoke up.

"No, no. It's okay. Stay right there," she demanded. "It's fine." Her mouth quivered. "I guess there are things I've suppressed, and I don't know. Just give me a second." Jamie took a deep breath

THE WINDOWS OF HOLLY

and exhaled. "Oh, Lynnie." She shook her head, squinting her eyes in an attempt to keep tears inside. "I did something awful. It's absolutely horrible." Jamie leaned forward, covering her eyes with her hands.

Lynette stood while feeding Asa and pulled the rocking chair in front of Jamie. She sat back down, leaning forward to be close to her sister. "Sweetheart, it's okay. Whatever it is, you can tell me."

Jamie shook her head. "I don't see how you could ever forgive me. It's horrible."

Lynette spoke calmly. "Jamie, look at me."

Jamie kept her eyes covered.

Again, Lynette gently encouraged her. "Jamie, look at me."

Jamie mopped her tears, lips pressed tightly together to prevent sobs from escaping. She looked at her sister with a pained expression. "Oh, Lynnie." Getting the words out was difficult. Several years of being the keeper of sorrowful secrets was proving to be too much. She wondered if her chest might explode.

"Jamie," Lynette said tenderly, "you're sitting in front of someone who lied, cheated, and broke the heart of an amazing man. I destroyed my marriage and stepped into a life with a liar. I destroyed trust and caused pain for my church, family, and friends. So whatever it is, believe me, I can handle it. I have no judgment toward you at all, I promise."

Her words filled Jamie with the hope that she could finally come clean and release the secrets that tormented her. She caught her breath and closed her eyes. "Okay. Give me a minute." Jamie tried to calm herself. *How do I say it? What do I say?* She knew she had to start somewhere. "The day you married Owen, I did something terrible."

Lynette thought to herself, *You and me both.*

Jamie continued, "Owen's friend, Will." She swallowed hard.

268

"He came onto me at the wedding and I..."

"Did he rape you?" Lynette interrupted, breathing hard.

Jamie shook her head. "No. He asked me if I wanted to go to his barn. I knew what I was doing and I didn't care at the time. I went..." she hesitated, "and we had sex."

Lynette's stomach turned. *That horrible bastard.*

"The worst part is that I found out..." Her breath escaped her for a moment as sobs robbed her of her ability to speak. "I was pregnant."

Lynette's heart sank. *Dear God, I want to kill that man.* She worked hard to stay calm, as she'd promised Jamie that she could handle anything. "And? It's okay. Tell me the rest."

Jamie wiped her tears. "I called and called him. For days, I tried getting him to answer but he wouldn't. I left messages, and I'd get nothing. I was so scared and ashamed, I couldn't bear to tell Mom and Dad. Or you. Mom and Dad were so upset about you and Dylan and the whole Owen thing. I just couldn't bear to tell them."

Lynette nodded, appearing strong. "I understand." *Oh my God. What have I done? I've hurt so many people.* Lynette was overwhelmed by the consequences of her selfish decisions. Self-hatred flashed through her body, but she reminded herself that to entertain self-hatred would be to deny all that Christ had spoken to her. *But how can I not hate myself?*

Jamie tried to speak the hardest part. "Lynette, I, I . . ."

"Go ahead, Jamie. Let it out," she encouraged.

Jamie took a deep breath. "I decided the only way out was abortion."

Lynette's heart shattered into a thousand pieces. *I'm responsible for my sister's abortion. I caused the death of my niece or nephew. I took away my parent's first grandchild. Oh my God. But it was Will's child.* The thought was repulsive. All of it. She

THE WINDOWS OF HOLLY

felt responsible for the whole thing. *Had I not married Owen, Jamie never would have been there.* She felt like a bigger monster than she'd ever imagined. Anger, guilt, and shame came crashing in on her, causing her insides to shake, but she kept it hidden from Jamie.

Jamie poured out her heart. "I hate myself for what I've done," she cried.

Lynette was determined to bear her self-punishment. "Jamie, do not hate yourself. It was a moment of weakness. You were in a bad situation and you saw no way out. Don't hate yourself for doing what you did." *Let me hate myself for you. I'll carry both of our punishments.*

Jamie was relieved by her sister's words. "You don't hate me?"

"Absolutely not! I love you, Jamie." With that declaration, Lynette melted into a puddle of tears. "I love you so much, and I'm so sorry you went through this."

Before Lynette could begin speaking blame over herself, Jamie saw it coming. "Lynette, don't you dare blame yourself for my actions. One of the reasons I was afraid to tell you was because I didn't want you to blame yourself for anything. I'm a grown woman. It was my choice every step of the way."

Lynette battled emotions that threatened to consume her heart. "I know, but if I hadn't left Dylan, if I hadn't married Owen, you never would have met Will." The regret stung.

Jamie wanted to assure her sister that she was blameless. "That doesn't matter. I would have met someone along the way and probably would have made the same dumb decisions. You're not responsible." Jamie watched as Lynette's tears fell on little Asa's cheek. The vision dug at her soul. "I'm responsible for what I did," Jamie declared, chin shaking. "And I cry over my baby." A flood of tears released like a waterfall. The sisters leaned in together, forehead to forehead, as Asa continued eating peacefully. "I love you, Lynnie. You and I've been through some stuff, but we're going to make it together."

"I know," Lynette accepted.

Jamie knew the party would be starting soon. *We've gotta pull it together before everyone shows up.* Jamie was determined to fix the situation. "Look where you are now, sis. This is how it should be. You and Dylan. Your baby and me, here together in this moment. I know we'll be okay. As hard as it is, maybe this is the start of our Christmas miracle."

Lynette whimpered, "Yes."

Dylan stood near the partially opened doorway, leaning on his crutches.

In the middle of the sisters' conversation, he started to enter the room to get dressed for the party. He overheard Jamie's confession and listened as the sisters conversed. His eyes were moist with tears. *This is a heck of a way to kick off the Christmas party.* He tried to quietly back away from the door, but the bottom of his crutches bumped the door, alerting Lynette and Jamie to his presence.

Lynette looked up. "Dylan?"

Not wanting to invade their privacy by entering the room, he spoke through the crack in the door. "Hey, I wanted to get dressed for the party, but I'll come back in awhile."

She replied, "Can you give us about ten minutes, babe?"

"Sure. No problem." He wobbled his way back into the living room.

Jamie looked at her watch. "Oh my gosh. We need to get dressed. Look at us. We're a mess." She wiped her tears away. "Good thing I wore waterproof mascara."

Lynette quipped, "Well, that's good for you. But look at me!" She sat up in the chair, pointing to her face. "I'm sure my cheeks look like a plowed field in a rainstorm."

THE WINDOWS OF HOLLY

Jamie grinned. "Yep, I'd say that's pretty accurate."

They embraced. Lynette patted Jamie's back. "You and I still have a lot to talk about. Can you stay here through Christmas?"

Jamie sighed. "I'd like to, but I only planned for one night."

Lynette was quick to offer a solution. "That's not a problem. We'll take a drive to Marshall City and do some shopping. I'd like to buy you some new clothes. I haven't done that in years. Besides, you and Mom and Dad are coming for Christmas anyway. You might as well stay here."

Jamie was touched by her kindness. "Are you sure?"

"Of course I'm sure." Lynette took her hand. "I want to help you work through this, and I have a lot to figure out myself. I need my sister right now."

"I know. Me too."

7:00 P.M.

The people of Holly never arrived late. In a small town, there wasn't much to offer, so when a special event took place, everyone raced to be the first in attendance, not wanting to miss a single second. Marcy and Lucy stood on the front porch, poised to greet arrivals and start them off with peppermint hot chocolate. The speakers on the front porch called worshippers and the curious passersby with "O' Come All Ye Faithful."

Lucy called out happily to the young men on bicycles, "Hey, guys! Would you like to join us for a Christmas party? We need help eating all the food."

The young men looked at each other and shrugged. "Maybe after awhile," one of them replied. "Thanks."

Jackson, David, Pastor Dean, and his wife, Grace, chatted with Dylan in the living room. Dylan never asked questions about Hope Fellowship since leaving five years ago, but his curiosity prompted him to inquire. "Pastor Dean, how's the church doing?" Dean

272

filled him in on the details of day-to-day life, the positives, and the negatives. When he mentioned the name Beatrice, Dylan couldn't help but chuckle. "Oh, Beatrice. I feel ya." At that moment, Beatrice walked through the living room door carrying a pan of homemade quiche. Dylan's eyes met hers. "Oh, Beatrice! How are you?" He shifted nervously on the sofa. *Speak of the devil!*

She eyed him, casting a partial smile his way. "I'm quite well, young man. I suppose I'm better than you. I can walk without crutches," she joked. Her eyes analyzed the living room. "Look at all of those flowers!"

Dylan smiled. "Aren't they beautiful? Miss Lilly made all the arrangements. It was an anonymous gift."

Being a treasurer, Beatrice couldn't look at anything without adding up the dollars in her head. "My Lord! There must be a thousand dollars worth of flowers in here." She shook her head. "Someone must have some money to burn. Do you know how many communion cups and paper towels that would buy?" The men stared at her, wide-eyed.

"Yeah. It'd buy a lot, but communion cups and paper towels aren't as pretty to look at, and they sure don't smell as nice." Dylan winked. "Isn't it nice to have people in the world who aren't afraid of going overboard when it comes to cheering people up and putting God's handiwork on display?"

Beatrice shook her head with disapproval as she shuffled into the kitchen with her tray. David and Dylan looked at each, snickering at her obsession with discontentment. Dylan shook his head, "Lord, bless her little Grinch heart."

David agreed. "Amen. A thousand times, amen."

Preston and Kat entered the house. Dylan was delighted by the sight of them. "Hey, guys!" He stood up, leaning on his crutches.

Preston beamed, "Dude! You don't have to get up. Sit down."

"No way," Dylan declared. "I didn't know if you'd be coming

or not. It's so good to see you.

Kat embraced Dylan. "It's so good to see you too! Thanks for the invitation. It's nice to have a night out." She lifted her arm to hand him a gift bag. "Here's a little something for you and Lynette." She patted his arm. "You might need this later."

Dylan eyed the gift bag, noting the bottle of wine inside. "Thank you, Kat. I'm sure you're right." He leaned toward her ear to whisper, "We'll probably need it by the time this party ends, especially if certain people show up." They laughed.

Kat grinned. "That's exactly what I thought. A little wine is good for the stomach, right?"

"True," said Dylan. If anyone has a problem with that, I'll give them chapter and verse."

David added, "And you can remind them of Jesus's first miracle, water to wine."

Dylan interjected, "And the church has been trying to change it back for the last two thousand years." They howled with laughter.

Mike toddled his way through the door and Curt followed. The two men wore blue jeans, white dress shirts with red vests, complete with red bowties. Dylan caught sight of them as they entered. "Holy cow. Would you look at that?" Dylan remembered the first time he ever saw Mike. The man wore a black trench coat and black baseball cap with the letters NRA as he entered Hope Fellowship on a particular Christmas Eve. Mike caused Dylan great alarm, unnerving him so much that as Dylan led the congregation in a round of "Joy to the World," he accidentally sang "let hens their songs employ" instead of "let men their songs employ." Lynette laughed over that blunder for months.

Tonight, Mike and Curt were shaven, clean as a whistle, and smiling from ear to ear. Dylan stared in astonishment. "Wow! You two look sharp."

Mike saluted Dylan with a "Thank you, sir."

Curt stood smiling, wide-eyed and gazing around the room. "Man, what a place! Look at all of them flowers, Mike. Have you ever seen so many?"

Mike shook his head. "I sure haven't. It looks like Miss Lilly moved her entire shop in here."

"Almost," said Dylan. "It was an anonymous gift from someone." He motioned toward the couch and the kitchen. "Feel free to make yourself at home, gentlemen. There's food in the kitchen."

Pastor Dean approached the festive pair. "Mike and Curt, I'm so pleased that you came. I love the matching vests. Nice touch."

Curt grinned with pleasure. "Thank you for inviting us, pastor."

Dean responded, "Dylan and Lynette are really the ones to thank. They were kind enough to open their home to all of us hooligans."

Mary Elliott stood in the doorway, watching the activity in the room with an immense, glowing smile on her face. She put her hands together as if to say a prayer. "Oh, Father. What a glorious sight." Her red, velvet dress complimented her fingernail polish, displaying timeless elegance. She surveyed the floral arrangements and the placement of Christmas decorations. "Oh, how lovely!"

Lynette entered the living room from the kitchen. She saw Mary standing alone with a huge smile on her face. "Mary!" Lynette ran to greet her with a hug. "Thank you for helping the ladies make plans. Everything is so beautiful, and there's more than enough food."

Mary held Lynette's hands as she looked into her eyes. "Young lady, it's my pleasure. This is like a dream come true."

Lynette's eyes radiated gratitude. After learning what her sister, Jamie, went through, the thanksgiving in her heart for good friends and second chances greatly increased. This evening was a precious

THE WINDOWS OF HOLLY

gift she would always cherish. "More than you realize. I'm blessed to be here. And Mary, I want to thank you for being here for Dylan when I wasn't." A look of momentary pain flashed across her face.

Mary spoke gently, "Sweetheart. We all do things we regret. I'm just glad you're here now." Mary motioned toward Dylan. "That young man over there absolutely loves you. He always has. Every painting in this house speaks of that love."

Her words drew tears to Lynette's already tender eyes. "I know." She bit her lip to discourage the flow of emotions from erupting. "I love him too."

Mary smiled. "I always knew you'd come back."

Lynette guided Mary to the kitchen. "Can I get you some tea or coffee?"

"That sounds delightful, dear."

Arnold, Burt, and Elsie made their way up the porch steps. Arnold was happy to find the hot cocoa stand. "Oh good! This is how you kick off a Christmas party."

"Can I pour you some hot cocoa?" Marcy asked.

Arnold gave an instant, "Yes. Yes, ma'am. And if you happen to have some rum or whiskey to add to it, please do. I might need it, depending on who's here."

Marcy grinned as she tilted her head like a parent trying to explain something to a child. "Arnold, there's no alcohol here tonight. We don't like to torment anyone who might be addicted, you know?"

He was disappointed but understood. "I can respect that."

Elsie piped up, "I don't need anything but the chocolate. Many a trial hath chocolate seen me through."

Marcy countered, "Tonight will be fun! You don't have to worry about trying to get through the evening. C'mon. How about instead of expecting others to entertain you, you go be the entertainment?"

276

Arnold interjected, "With Beverly and Miss Emma here, we should have plenty of entertainment. I just thought a swig of whiskey would help me muddle through the boring conversations."

Marcy looked him in the eye. "Consider what you have to bring to the conversation, Arnold. If it's boring, you might have yourself to blame for that."

"Ouch," Arnold exclaimed. "You're a bit brutal this evening."

Marcy smiled. "I'm not trying to be rude. I'm just saying you have lots of interesting things to share. I'm trying to encourage you to make the conversation fun. That's all."

"I'll remember that piece of advice," said Elsie.

Marcy helped them out by offering her personal experience. "When I find myself without much to say, I usually ask, 'What's your story?' I've found that to be enlightening. I've learned things about people that I never would have guessed. It's fun. You should try it."

Burt was amused by the interaction of his friends. "Thanks, Marcy. And thanks for setting Arnold straight. He needed it," he said with a wink.

7 : 1 5 P . M .

Dylan raised his voice, calling his guests together in the living room. "Hello, everybody! Can I have your attention? Let's all gather around." People shuffled into place, some carrying appetizer plates and drinks while muttering the end of their conversations. Dylan whistled. The room fell silent. "I want to say thank you for being here. This is a very special moment for me and Lynette. Most of you remember the Christmas gatherings we held here many years ago. We have so many wonderful memories of those times and have always felt it was a privilege to open our home to the church, our family, friends, and community." He

THE WINDOWS OF HOLLY

paused, aware of people's questions about their situation. *What are they thinking?*

Dylan cleared his throat and continued, "It seems that life takes us in different directions; sometimes it takes us in directions we never would've expected. Those diversions can turn out to be blessings even when they feel like a curse. I mean, I feel like God takes curses and turns them into blessings for us because He's good. At least, that's what I'm learning." He glanced at the clock on the wall as he willed himself to be unaware of the awkwardness. "With the passing of time, I feel like I'm beginning to understand the power of grace and God's mercy."

Dylan paused as he scanned the faces of those in the room. His closest friends surrounded him, with about a dozen people from Hope Fellowship, a handful of local business owners, and random characters he had befriended at Annie's Café. "This turnout tonight," he swallowed back his tears, "is a picture of the mercy and grace of God. This is one of the most beautiful pictures I've seen."

He looked down momentarily, grasping for the right way to address some of the questions he knew lingered in their minds. No matter how many times he'd rehearsed his speech for this moment, words failed him and nothing seemed adequate. He thought about not addressing the rumors about him and Lynette, but it wasn't Dylan's nature to let people wonder. Besides, he had hoped their reconciliation would be celebrated.

Dylan continued, "I'll tell you why this is one of the most beautiful pictures I've seen. All of your faces, your presence here, is a gift. You all know that Lynette and I went through great difficulty and we made decisions along the way that we never expected to make. I realize there are a lot of questions, but what I can tell you is that circumstances, both good and bad, have brought us back together. This Christmas, the gift we received was

278

reconciliation, and that's why we decided to open our home at the suggestion of Miss Emma Gray. When I say our home, that's because Lynette and I bought this home together and it has always been our home." He stopped, noting encouraging smiles around the room. Thank God.

Dylan swallowed. "We wanted to invite you to come and celebrate with us in the coming of our Savior, the One who came to walk this earth in the midst of our sorrows and troubles, our violence and loss. He walked among us exhibiting love, kindness, mercy, and the healing of all who were oppressed. Tonight, He lives within us and is still expressing Himself through us."

Dylan paused for a moment as he regarded each person as an expression of God. "I can tell you that Lynette and I have experienced supernatural visitations with God that brought healing and reconciliation to our hearts. I believe He wants to bring those same gifts to every person who desires it. There's something very special about Holly. Our little town contains many treasures in its people, and we count it a privilege to be a part of your lives." Dylan's eyes moistened as he worked to maintain his composure.

Miss Emma helped him along by interjecting, "And we are honored to be a part of your life, Dylan."

"Amen," Beverly agreed.

"Yes!" Pastor Dean exclaimed as he began to clap.

A round of applause broke out. "We love you, Dylan," someone shouted. "Yes, we love you, Dylan and Lynette," said another. Dylan motioned for the applause to conclude.

"Thank you, everyone." He placed his hands over his heart. "That means the world to us." Overwhelmed with the attention, he decided to shift everyone's gaze in another direction. "Now, let's move on to the fun stuff! You've probably noticed the incredible floral arrangements. They were an anonymous gift from someone, so if you're the anonymous one, thank you very much for adding

THE WINDOWS OF HOLLY

to the beauty of the evening. Thank you to Miss Lilly for creating the arrangements. They're stunning! Rose Reynolds was kind to donate her amazing lasagna and fixings for tonight. The ladies all worked hard to make a smorgasbord of fantastic dishes and desserts, so we'd like to pray and invite everyone to dive in. Pastor Dean, would you lead us in prayer?"

"Certainly," Dean agreed. He thanked God for the night, the Vanbergs, and the ministry of reconciliation.

8:00 P.M.

Conversations ensued as people mingled and indulged themselves. Emma, Beverly, Curt, and Mike gathered in front of the big Christmas tree, sitting in folding chairs. As Beverly shoved a mini cupcake in her mouth, Mike nudged Curt with his elbow. He spoke with a whisper, "Check her out, Curt. A woman with a mouth like that would be perfect for you." Curt wrinkled his nose and shook his head.

Emma continued her story about her daughter, Kathleen's work. "And on New Year's Eve, she's opening the fundraiser event for the African-American arts museum in her city. They sold two thousand tickets! I'm so proud of her."

Beverly nodded as she licked her lips. "She's an amazing woman."

Mike muttered, "African-American arts?"

Emma shifted in her chair. "Yes."

He rolled his eyes. "I don't understand why they need their own arts museum. Just mix up all the art by everybody. Isn't that racist to need your own museum? I mean, what about white people's art? We don't need our own white museum."

Emma and Beverly stared at him in shock. Beverly swallowed her food quickly so she could speak. "Mike. Are you not aware of what black folks have been through in our country? This was a

280

white man's world. In some ways, it still is."

Mike huffed, "White man's world? As far as I can see, most of us are barely getting by. I can't even afford health insurance right now. I don't see how it's a white man's world."

Emma explained. "You can't see it because you're white. You don't know what it's like to be treated like you don't belong somewhere. Your family never had to suffer under oppression. Can you imagine having separate water fountains, bathrooms, and seats, all because others think you're inferior? Were you ever treated like a dog?"

"No, ma'am," he responded thoughtfully.

Emma continued, "Generations of African Americans experienced terrible oppression. Why not have their own art museum where they can freely express and celebrate their culture? I don't see that as a racist idea in any way."

Emma wiped her mouth with a napkin. "I'm proud of my daughter for doing something significant. I believe that laying down our own agendas to honor others is one of the most powerful things a person can do. And why shouldn't we, as white people, take the time to do something empowering for the descendants of those who paid a very heavy price?"

Curt piped up, "Miss Emma, I've never heard you sound so smart before."

Beverly was desperate to steer the conversation out of a potential disaster. She wasn't sure how, but Curt's comment to Emma sparked an automatic retort. "Well, Curt. I haven't heard you sound smart ever."

Mike chimed in, "Beverly, that's because you haven't listened to Curt enough. You two need to go out on a date. Then you can see how smart he is."

"Date?" Beverly hollered with eyes wide open. Everything within her was repulsed by the suggestion, but she was tender

THE WINDOWS OF HOLLY

enough to not completely crush the man. "Curt just isn't my type. No offense, Curt."

He was embarrassed to be on display in such a vulnerable state. Curt would have been delighted had Beverly said yes to a date with him. The disappointment on his face pressed Beverly to action. "Well, not only that, but I'd drive this man crazy! You don't know how terrifying things can get with women my age. There are things that makeup remover and soap reveal that would cause a man to run, let me tell you! Have you heard of Spanx? Gentlemen, you thought Victoria had a secret? Oh no. Every woman has a real secret that no man knows until he's gone beyond the point of no return. We've got all kinds of secrets! Tape, creams, cover-ups, techniques, and magical pantyhose. We're the masters of extensions too. Eyelashes, hair, and, well, we can extend just about anything we want! I'm just letting you know you'd better find out what lies beneath. I'm doing Curt a favor by saying no to a date. Spare the man, Mike! Spare the man!"

Emma chuckled, "Now don't go giving away our secret weapons, Beverly."

Mike mumbled, "Sounds like a heck of a lot of work to me. I'm glad we don't have to mess with that."

Emma replied, "It is a lot of work. You men have no idea how much time, energy, and money women spend to make you happy. And we women just accept you men as you are. If I had a dollar for every time I've seen an attractive woman with a nose-hair-bearing, caterpillar-eyebrowed man, I'd be a rich woman."

Beverly chimed in, "Not to mention hair growing out of their ears! Yet the wife is supposed to be all plucked and picture perfect." Several of the men in the room reached up to check their ears for hair. "Can you imagine a man dating a woman who's got hair coming out of her ears and nose? No! That's unacceptable. But for men, no one seems to care."

Emma added, "And we bear the gas pains too. When I was married, I made an effort to keep the toots inside. I'd be writhing with stomach pain while ole hubby just lived in total freedom." She made a flatulent sound. "Rip! There it'd go, several times a day! Women are just expected to accept such behavior."

Curt threw in, "You should be glad for that. I heard a news report that said farts are actually healthy for you to breathe. It can fight cancer cells."

Everyone laughed. Emma snorted, "Curt, you actually believe that? I'm sure the person who made that up was a male scientist with an agenda. He probably got tired of his wife telling him to stop cuttin' the cheese, so he gathered his fellow scientists and fabricated a study about the health benefits of farting! I can see it now: a group of men snickering as they wrote it all out." She shook her head.

Several people overheard the ridiculous conversation. Beatrice was appalled. She approached Marcy who was across the room. "That's absolutely appalling!"

"What is?" Marcy asked.

Beatrice answered, shaking her head. "That little circus of people in there speaking of inappropriate things. Emma and Curt have used the f-word several times!"

Marcy's eyes stretched wide with horror. "What? You've got to be kidding? Who, exactly?"

Beatrice pointed to the group of offenders. "Them!"

Marcy's look of surprise turned to an amused confusion. "I don't understand, Bea. I'm quite positive that none of them use that kind of language. The f-word?"

Beatrice nodded. "Yes! On and on they went about undignified things."

"Like what, Miss Bea?" Marcy inquired.

Beatrice scrunched her nose up. "Just imagine people at a

Christmas party talking about bodily sounds. Gas and such. It's appalling."

Marcy realized the 'f-word' was not the word she supposed it was. "Oh!" She laughed. "You meant fart?"

Beatrice threw her hand over her mouth in shock. "Marcy! You shouldn't say that. You're an elder's wife!"

Marcy could see that Bea clearly believed the word to be inappropriate, so she nodded and patted her arm. Marcy innocently philosophized about the phenomenon. "It's all right, Bea. I think the good Lord will forgive. I mean, after all, He made us to pass gas. Why did He make it sound funny if He didn't want us to laugh about it? It's such an odd thing to do, right?"

Beatrice stared at her, unable to respond. Her gaze made Marcy uncomfortable, as if she were a child being reprimanded. Marcy quickly found a way of escape from the harsh stare. "I should probably be tending to the dishes right about now. Would you like to pass out song sheets, Bea? We should start singing in about ten minutes." *Hopefully that will get her mind off of the f-word! My goodness, she's uptight.* Marcy giggled under her breath.

Beatrice agreed to help. "Sure. Where are the song sheets?"

"Follow me," Marcy commanded. "They should be in the green folder in my bag." She lifted the bag from the floor. "Aha. Here you go. As you pass them out, would you let everyone know we'll be starting in about ten minutes? Thanks, Bea." Marcy smiled as she headed back toward the kitchen.

Upon returning to the sink, Marcy burst into laughter.

Lucy and Lynette were curious. "What's so funny?"

Marcy howled. "Oh my goodness. It's hilarious!" Laughter consumed her. "Poor Miss Bea. She was so offended because Emma and Curt were using the f-word repeatedly."

Lucy looked confused. "What?"

Lynette shared the confusion as well. "There's no way! Miss

Emma wouldn't say that."

Marcy continued laughing, holding her belly. "Yes. They were talking about farts. Poor Bea was so offended."

The ladies laughed with her. "Oh my goodness."

Lucy held her pregnant belly as she giggled. "That's the cutest thing I've ever heard. I love her innocence."

Marcy tried to compose herself. "Innocence? Or flat out pretentiousness?"

Lucy chuckled. "Whatever it is, I find it to be amusing."

Marcy made note of the time. "Okay, girls. Let's gather up the dishes and stack them here. I told Bea to let everyone know we'll start singing in about ten minutes."

"Excellent!" Lucy smiled.

Chapter Twenty-One

THE PARTY CONTINUES
DECEMBER 22, 8:45 P.M.

Dylan and Lynette's living room was filled with family, friends and acquaintances. After an evening of both serious and lighthearted conversations, they gathered to sing carols, sipping hot chocolate, coffee, and tea in between songs. A few chose only to listen. Others participated.

Lynette sat next to Dylan on the loveseat, holding Asa in her arms. Jamie sat cross-legged in front of the fireplace, enjoying intermittent conversation with a handsome man who introduced himself as "the new neighbor, Dimitry." He became fast friends with Pastor Dean during their twenty-minute conversation, and he promised to visit Hope Fellowship. Jamie enjoyed his warm personality.

The perimeter of the living room was lined with people, some standing and some sitting. Dylan and Lynette's eyes filled with tears multiple times throughout the time of singing as they regarded each face, lit with the joy of the season.

Burt skillfully played the piano, leading the group through an

THE WINDOWS OF HOLLY

array of Christmas carols. When he sat down on the piano bench that evening, many people gasped with surprise. "Burt plays the piano?" The people of Holly knew Burt as the man behind the counter at Annie's Café, as well as his knack for carpentry. It wasn't until tonight that they had learned about his two-year adventure of playing with a jazz band while living with his brother in New York City. What made the revelation more incredible was that Burt was self-taught—a natural musician.

His brother, Paul, had invited him to do local gigs during his time in New York. Burt enjoyed the jazz bars and classy restaurants, but it didn't take him long to realize that big city life was not for him. Burt was happier with a slower pace of life, and he preferred simplicity. Playing piano was normally something he did privately for his own pleasure.

Everyone easily slipped into the spirit of the night, especially as they broke into "O Holy Night." Dylan explained before the song began, "This one is my favorite. Pay close attention to the lyrics as we sing. The words are powerful."

Miss Eleanor shifted in her chair and leaned close to Beatrice's ear. "There he goes again with that power talk. All evening long, I've heard him saying those words like supernatural, mystical, and powerful. Every time I turn around, it seems he's telling somebody about these weird experiences he's having."

Beatrice replied with a whisper, "Sounds like witchcraft to me."

Pastor Dean overheard their whispers as he stood next to them. Dean moved close to them and spoke in a hushed tone, "Sounds like God to me." He grinned. *I'm sure I'll pay for that one later.* He was glad he had said it.

Burt moved with emotion as he pressed the piano keys. Dylan closed his eyes as they began singing.

"O Holy Night! The stars are brightly shining,
It is the night of our dear Savior's birth.
Long lay the world in sin and error pining.
Till He appeared and the soul felt its worth."

A tear streamed down Dylan's cheek as he absorbed the worth he had found in his Savior. When Lynette left him, he struggled with worthlessness. He had hated himself for not being enough. It was during that season of inadequacy that his Savior appeared and his soul felt its worth.

"A thrill of hope the weary world rejoices,
For yonder breaks a new and glorious morn."

Dylan remembered when hope first visited him. He dared to dream of reconciliation with Lynette. Now he was getting a second chance to have her as his wife. *God, let it be glorious. Please.*

"Fall on your knees! Oh, hear the angel voices!
O night divine, the night when Christ was born."

Lynette looked down at Asa's perfect, little face. She considered her unholy, chaotic circumstances and wondered how Mary must have felt. *I'm no Mary. Mary's circumstances were holy, but others thought it was unholy and scandalous. Here I am, unholy, a scandal, but through the power of her Son, perhaps my circumstances can be made into something holy. Please, God.*

"Truly He taught us to love one another."

Kat looked at her husband as he sang the words. *How*

miraculous that I can love the one who caused me so much pain. I don't understand it, but I feel love for him more deeply. She pondered love's ironic way.

"His law is love and His gospel is peace."

The phrase pierced Beatrice's hardened heart. Being a lover of law, striving to abide by law, the lyrics arrested her attention. *His law is love.* She'd never given it a thought. Bea often saw love as weakness, an overlooking of wrongs that would only encourage others to do as they pleased. She wondered if she had missed something all of these years.

"Chains he shall break, for the slave is our brother.
And in his name all oppression shall cease."

The slave is our brother. Mike flashed back to his brief conversation with Emma. The comment he had made about her daughter's passion for the African American arts museum stung his own heart. Mike recalled a moment from childhood. "Don't you go sharing your lunch with that black kid anymore," his dad had told him. Mike told his dad that Richie was his only friend, so he felt he should share his lunch with him. But his dad corrected him angrily, "I work hard to keep your mouths fed. When your mom packs a lunch, it's for you and you alone. If that kid's family can't afford to feed him, it's their own problem, not mine. I work hard. They don't!"

His dad used that experience to instill thoughts in Mike's mind that caused him to devalue other races. There was a time when he believed his dad and he saw other races as less than his own. Mike recalled when he was bullied multiple times by Harvey on the playground. Richie was always the one to come to his defense.

Mike had known Richie to be the kindest soul in his school. *Why did I turn my back on him?* He wished he could go back in time to embrace his "brother" Richie.

"Christ is the Lord
O praise His name forever
His power and glory
Evermore proclaim
His power and His glory
Evermore proclaim."

As the song came to a close, Dylan opened his eyes. He scanned the room, studying the faces of people he used to lead when he served as a pastor. Others, he barely knew. He lovingly observed a few faithful friends who had gently walked with him through the darkest night of his soul. Dylan noticed that hardened faces had softened by the end of the song.

He shifted his gaze to the left. *Nick!* Nick Brown stood near the front door, tucked into the corner inconspicuously. Burt moved into the next chorus. "Let's wrap it up with Joy to the World." Dylan stood slowly, steadying himself on his crutches as the proclamation of Christ's birth was sung. He locked eyes with Nick, smiling as he approached him. Nick returned the smile.

Dylan embraced the young man. "Hey. It's good to see you."

Good to see you too," Nick replied.

Dylan rested his hand on his shoulder. "I wasn't sure you'd come."

"I wasn't sure I would either. Mom almost came with me, but she's not ready yet. She's embarrassed about Dad, you know? She's afraid she'll have to explain things to people."

Dylan understood. "I totally get that." He motioned toward the kitchen. "You kinda missed the big dinner, but we still have lots of

THE WINDOWS OF HOLLY

food in there. Let's check it out." Dylan escorted him to the kitchen.

Nick felt ashamed as he watched Dylan struggle to move himself with crutches. He knew Dylan was trying to push through the discomfort. "This is why I almost didn't come," Nick blurted out.

"What is?" Dylan asked.

Nick took a deep breath. "I'm sorry I did this to you," he sighed. "It's the dumbest thing I've ever done in my life."

Dylan made light of it, hoping to soothe the young man's guilt. "Oh, this is nothing. It'll heal. Besides, I'm the one that got myself into this condition. I shouldn't have been snooping around your garage." Nick was aware that Dylan was going out of his way to ease his mind.

Nick questioned, "What if you had died? What if you were paralyzed? That would've been my fault."

Dylan stopped to face him. "That could've happened, but Nick, you're gonna have to let go of the what-ifs and just thank God for sparing you and me that tragedy. Consider it a chance to make some better choices in the midst of your pain. It's not always easy to do, but I believe in you. You can do it."

Nick smiled, "Thanks, Dylan."

Dylan encouraged him, "Each day, you get to choose how you'll write your story. Don't let the pain push you to the wrong choice. Let it press you into a good place, a powerful place, where you can make a difference in the lives of other people who are hurting the way that you hurt. There are people out there like your dad that you're going to be able to help if you don't let bitterness rule your heart, I promise you that." Dylan patted Nick's shoulder. "Plus, your mom has suffered a lot. She needs her son, you know?"

Nick was well aware of that fact. "I know. I want to make life better for her."

"You will," Dylan spoke with confidence. He knew he could say more, but he figured a Christmas party wasn't the best place for diving into such conversation. "What can I get for you? We have tea, coffee, Coke, and Eleanor's punch." He chuckled. "I'm not sure what she puts in that stuff, but I could have sworn I tasted mothballs and perfume, so I'd advise you not to go there." He crinkled his nose.

Nick grinned. "Coke sounds good. I'll get it." Nick jumped ahead of Dylan to serve himself.

Dylan wondered, "Do you and your mom have plans for Christmas?"

"Yeah," Nick replied. "We're driving to Marshall City to see my cousins. She said something about staying at my grandpa's house."

"Good." Dylan was relieved they had someplace to go. "Any word from your dad?"

Nick rolled his eyes. "Yeah. He's spending Christmas with his boyfriend." Nick stuck out his tongue and inserted his finger into his mouth. "Gag. I don't understand it at all." He shook his head.

Dylan was sad for him. "I'm sorry, man. Your dad's in a fight for his life that we can't understand. We don't know what it's like to walk in his shoes, he has so many demons to battle. People do all kinds of things when they're looking for peace. Sometimes we choose things that bring more chaos instead of peace. It's ironic. I know Pastor Dean is praying for your dad. I do too. We can reach out as much as possible and offer help. We just need him to be willing to receive it."

Nick sipped his Coke. "I know. That's the problem. He won't return phone calls or let anyone try to talk to him."

Dylan assured him, "He can come to that place in a split second, Nick. That's my hope and prayer, that he'll have a sudden

THE WINDOWS OF HOLLY

moment of awakening. Addiction is a powerful thing, but it's not more powerful than love. Miracles can happen."

Nick muttered, "And some miracles don't happen at all."

"True," Dylan acknowledged, "but what good is it to not believe at all? What if the only hope your dad has is for us to believe for him?"

Nick raised his eyebrows. "Well, then I guess we'd better believe, if that's the case."

Dylan continued, "Never give up, no matter how bad things look. Anything is possible."

Nick needed that spark of life. "Thanks, Dylan. On another note, I wanted to ask you about something. I'd like to help out around here while you recover. If you have any projects I can work on—mowing, cleaning, or anything—will you let me know? I'm not talking about for pay. I want to help you and Lynette. That's the least I can do."

Dylan was pleased. "Sure, man. That'd be greatly appreciated. I'll keep you posted on that."

A burst of corporate laughter arose from the living room, prompting Dylan and Nick to join the party. As they entered the room, they saw Mike sitting on the floor atop a broken folding chair and Beatrice mopping red punch off her face. Thankfully, Mike and Bea were both laughing.

Curt stretched his hand out for Mike, howling, "Can you lift your carcass off the chair?"

Mike was laughing so hard, he couldn't catch his breath long enough to make an ascent.

Curt picked at him, "You got lead in your butt, Mike? Man, you're heavy." He kept pulling on Mike's arm. "Miss Emma, it appears Mike's got one too many of your biscuits in his belly. He's heavy as a dinosaur."

Beatrice giggled as she watched the comical duo. Mike rolled

294

over on his side, propping himself up on his knees. As he bent over, the back of his shirt lifted up, revealing his crack. Beatrice threw her hand over her mouth, trying to hide her giggles.

Curt piped up once more, "Mike! There are ladies present. You can't have the moon coming out like that. You're one inch away from a felony!"

Mike reached down to correct the problem as he belly-laughed with tears rolling down his cheeks.

Curt took advantage of the attention. "Put away your pooter, Mike. No one wants to see that."

When Mike finally made his way to his feet and composed himself, he apologized to Beatrice. "I'm sorry about that, ma'am. I didn't mean for my cup of punch to go in your face. It was just plain outta my control. Everything went flailing."

Bea shook her head. "It was an accident. I'll survive."

Mike tried to be as considerate as possible. "I suppose you've got some super-powered stain remover for your dress?"

She smiled. "Of course I do. I've been on this earth long enough to know the importance of keeping stain remover in my arsenal."

Dean elbowed David to get his attention. "Can you believe it? Just look at Beatrice. Who'd have thought after all these years of trying to make that woman crack a smile, it'd be Mike and Curt that would make it happen?"

David was delighted with the sight. "I guess you can call that a Christmas miracle. Better write this one in the books."

Dean snickered. "Now if we could figure out how to keep that smile on her face at church. . . ."

David suggesting jokingly, "I suppose we could hire Mike."

Dean's face beamed red with hilarity. "Wouldn't that be entertaining?"

David agreed. "It'd be more than entertaining." He snickered as

THE WINDOWS OF HOLLY

he envisioned what life could be like with a Mike on staff. "I've always thought churches needed staff comedians. I mean, isn't it ironic how we talk about worshipping such an amazing, miracle-working, awesome God, yet people sit there looking like sour grapes? It's no wonder people don't want to be in church."

Dean shook his head, grinning.

"I mean, really! We need to laugh more and stop taking ourselves so seriously. If we could have more gatherings like this," David waved his hand across the room, "it'd do us a lot of good."

Across the room, Dylan turned to Nick, smiling. "Aren't you glad you came? You got here just in time to witness the highlight of the evening."

Nick had a huge grin on his face.

Beverly leaned into Emma, snickering. "I could've done without seeing Mike's crack, but that was hilarious."

Emma agreed. "It sure was, but the best part is watching prim-and-proper Beatrice try to control her laughter. This will either lighten her up or she'll go home and repent for being amused." She peered to her left. "Take a look at Eleanor. She looks a bit disgruntled."

Beverly eyed Eleanor. "What is she staring at?"

Emma glanced over. "Hm. She's looking toward that young man, Nick." She leaned closer to Beverly, speaking quietly, "He's the one that was throwing rocks at Dylan's place, you know?"

"Yeah," Beverly smiled. "But look at him now. Here he is in Dylan's home." Her eyes were filled with light. "That's our Dylan. Kind and forgiving."

Emma suggested, "Let's go talk to Eleanor."

Beverly jumped up from her chair quickly as Emma slowly lifted her body to a standing position. "Giddyup, Emma! The horse is waiting for you to get your rear in the saddle."

Emma wiggled her head in a sassy way. "I know, I know. That

296

horse needs to be patient. These legs take a little longer to get moving these days. I might need a winch to hoist me outta this chair. We've been sitting so long, the chair and I have become one." She huffed as she struggled to stand. "Too many cookies, I suppose."

Beverly gave her a hand. "You can do it. Don't let those gingerbread men hold you down."

The duo made their way over to Eleanor. She kept her gaze on Nick, watching as he chatted with Dylan. Beverly interrupted her scrutinizing glare. "Eleanor, you're lookin' a bit tense. We thought we'd pop over to see how you're doing."

Beverly's abrupt nosiness earned a look of disapproval from the serious woman, but Eleanor didn't mind sharing her thoughts anyway. "I just can't believe Dylan let that young man in his house. I've seen him speeding through town in that ridiculous sports car, totally ignoring the speed limit signs. He scared the daylights out of me when I was carrying my groceries across the parking lot. I nearly dropped my bag! And what's that ungodly thing he's always got pulled over his head?"

Beverly answered her question. "A hoodie, Eleanor. It's a hoodie. They're quite comfortable."

Eleanor continued, "Well, whatever it is, it looks ridiculous. He goes around looking like a criminal."

Beverly grinned. "Maybe that's what the young people think of you when you wear your scarf on your head," she quipped.

Emma intervened before Beverly went too far. "Now, now. Eleanor, don't take that personally. Beverly teases everybody," she assured her.

Eleanor's tightened lips showed her discontent as she glared at Beverly. "All of these years of churchgoing and this is the kind of behavior you've learned?" Her condescension was thick.

Beverly smiled, holding her humorous demeanor intact,

THE WINDOWS OF HOLLY

slurring, "Oh, Eleanor. I suppose if I were there every week like you, I'd be as kind as you are."

Eleanor's displeasure radiated from her face. "You have to be the rudest woman I've ever met!"

Beverly smiled. "Oh, do I have to? I'd rather not be a rude, pucker-lipped sourpuss such as yourself, my lady."

Eleanor and Emma both gasped at her rudeness. Emma noticed the change in Beverly's speech. It dawned on her that Beverly had digressed after her fifth cup of punch. "Dylan!" Emma hollered alarmingly. "Dylan! Lynette!"

Lynette hurried to her side. "What's wrong, Miss Emma?"

Emma pointed her finger at Beverly's cup. "Someone has spiked the punch!"

Her voice echoed throughout the room. Everyone turned to look at her in stunned silence. Emma continued, "Beverly's had five or six cups of punch and now she's acting like a hooligan."

Beverly stared at her punch, grinning. "Nah. It's just punch. I don't smell any alcohol."

Eleanor piped up, "It's probably that young man!" She pointed at Nick. "Only he'd do something like that."

Dylan raised his eyebrows. "Nick just got here a bit ago and he's been with me the whole time. He wouldn't do a thing like that. Emma, how do you know the punch is spiked?"

Beverly howled. "Shiver me timbers! Someone's gone overboard!"

Emma flicked her hand toward Beverly. "That's how I know. Just look at her. She's soused."

Several people snickered quietly as Dylan tried to solve the mystery. He couldn't help but grin a bit at Beverly's nutty behavior. "All right. Who else had punch during the last half of the evening? I know it was fine before that, because I drank it."

A few hands went up in the air. Pastor Dean, Mike, Curt, and

298

Beatrice. Dylan acknowledged them with a nod. "Okay. This could explain Mike's falling out of the chair." *Not to mention Beatrice's laughter!*

Pastor Dean giggled. "I'm feeling pretty good. I was thinking it's the Holy Spirit."

Eleanor spoke up, "Pastor Dean! How inappropriate! You shouldn't joke about drunkenness in relation to the Holy Spirit."

Dean replied gently, "It's okay, Miss Eleanor. I assure you I'm not being disrespectful. Acts chapter two, ma'am. It's biblical."

Mike and Curt snickered like a couple of schoolkids. Dylan looked at them. "Feeling a bit tipsy, gentlemen?"

"Nah. That was the chair's fault. It broke," Mike answered with a snicker.

Curt revealed the truth. "Well, Mike, that was cuz you were bouncing up and down on it, acting like you were riding on your motorcycle. Remember?"

Beatrice's face glowed bright red as she worked to hold in her laughter.

"Look at that," said Emma. "Miss Bea's tipsy too."

Lynette tried to hide her enjoyment over the situation. "Oh my gosh. Who would have spiked the punch?"

Eleanor prided herself on being appalled. "I never!" She shook her head. "I've never been to such a party. And of all people!"

Lynette explained. "Eleanor, you know we've never had any drinking in our home. We're careful about that for the sake of people who struggle with addiction." Lynette's eyes searched the room. "I can't imagine who would have done this."

Eleanor pointed at Nick once more." It has to be him!" Then she jabbed her finger at Jamie, Lynette's sister. "Or it's her!"

Dylan declared, "Listen, everyone! There will be no finger-pointing. We've had a beautiful night, and we're not going to ruin it with such a minor thing."

THE WINDOWS OF HOLLY

Eleanor was not pleased. "You're saying that drunkenness is a minor thing? And Pastor Dean just laughs about it, saying it could be the Holy Spirit? Young man, if this is how things are, I'll be finding myself a new church!"

Dylan spoke gently. "No one is making light of anything. I'm just not into accusation. I'd like us to stay focused on enjoying each other and what brought us together tonight. And to be honest, I'm glad for all the laughs! We all needed that. We're here to celebrate Christmas. So speaking of the birthday boy, let us not forget that Jesus's first miracle was turning water into wine, at a wedding in which all the wine had already been consumed. I think it's safe to say that no big sin has been committed tonight."

Old Mary Elliott stood from her seat, looking dignified in her elegant, red, velvet dress. "Pardon me, but I have something to say." She straightened her necklace and cleared her throat as the room became quiet.

All eyes were on Mary. "I was the one who added a bit of spirit to the punch." The room echoed with gasps and sounds of amusement. Mary continued, "I've been attending gatherings with you people off and on throughout the years. I've seen the highs and the lows. I've listened to your stories, and I'm smart enough to know when people peacock their way around each other, trying to impress one another. I'd like to remind you that I'm in my nineties. I don't know if this will be my last Christmas or not, but I felt I'd give myself the gift of seeing your walls come down. So thank you for participating, and Merry Christmas to me!" She sat down with a smile on her face.

Several people began laughing. Even Eleanor dropped her condemnation for a few seconds to admire Mary's daring spirit. "Mary, I suppose you're old enough to get away with it." She shook her head.

Dylan made his way near Eleanor. He whispered, "Miss

300

Eleanor. Would you please consider apologizing to Nick and Jamie? Nick has been through a lot, and he's worked really hard to do right. Jamie too. Accusations can do a lot of damage, you know?"

Eleanor pursed her lips. "I suppose I could, but I still don't like those little snowflakes. It's because of these millennials who live off of their parents and run around town, not contributing to society, that we have a lot of problems."

Dylan's jaw tightened. *My gosh. Such ignorance.* He tried not to judge the bitter woman, but rather enlighten her. "It sounds to me as if you've been given a lot of misinformation. I'm not a fan of using names and labels, but for the sake of the conversation and understanding, I will.

Millennials are some of the most powerful people of our time. Many of them have already surpassed where we were at their age. Most of them are passionate about taking the progress of the past generations and building on it, not destroying it. I know many hardworking people in that age bracket. We should be careful not to judge them, but to lift them up and empower them. Besides, they may be the ones changing your diapers someday."

The very thought shocked her. Dylan continued, "They will be the ones giving you medication and coming up with cures that you may need in the future. You might want to consider that."

Eleanor wasn't a fan of being told what to do or how to think, but she figured she should at least consider Dylan's words. She was not fully ready to relent however. "Maybe some of them are like you say, but I've never seen such a lazy generation in all of my life."

"Oh yeah?" Dylan questioned. "And what generation raised them? And who raised the generation that raised them?"

Eleanor was silent.

Dylan continued, "Perhaps instead of pointing fingers at the younger generation, we should look at ourselves."

Eleanor sighed in reluctant surrender, rolling her eyes. "Fine."

Dylan reminded her, "And one last thing, ma'am. Snowflakes are beautiful and unique in design. I'm not so sure that God would like us using one of His most awesome pieces of work as a derogatory term." Dylan patted her back, prompting her, "Thank you for apologizing to Nick and Jamie." He left her to do what needed to be done.

Most everyone was gathered around Mary Elliott, conversing and laughing with appreciation for the woman's uncharacteristic actions.

Beverly thanked her. "Well, Mary, you make a great powder monkey. You keep the storm brewing, and you're not one for battening down the hatches. I hope that ole scallywag doesn't give Pastor Dean the heave-ho after this party."

Mary appeared puzzled, but delighted. She shook her head. "Beverly, what in the world are you talking about?"

Emma explained. "Oh, she's been reading a lot of pirate books lately. Apparently, your special punch brings out the pirate talk in her." Emma rolled her eyes.

Mary nodded, smiling. "Oh, I see."

Beverly went on, "I remember someone saying you were like a combination of aristocratic granny meets Wild West granny. After tonight, I know what they meant!"

Mary giggled. "I guess they were right."

Jackson and Lucy sat in a corner with Preston and Kat. Lucy was happy to see evidence of Preston's love for his wife. She recalled the day when she unapologetically reprimanded him at Annie's Café, where he had dined with his mistress, Fay. Lucy marveled over the miracle of transformation in his personality and demeanor. *This is the real him.* She knew the man he used to be was selfish and confused, but somehow, the hardness of heart was obliterated.

Lucy smiled at Kat. "You'll have to give me some childrearing tips, because I have no idea what I'm doing. I'm reading lots of parenting books, but I know that's not enough."

Preston agreed. "Kat is an amazing mom. You'll definitely want to learn from her."

Kat shook her head with a slight smile. "I don't know about that. I'm usually just winging it."

Lucy interjected, "Then teach me how to wing it!"

A talk about parenting ensued between Lucy and Kat while Jackson and Preston discussed the latest goings-on in the farm community regarding new technological advances and financing options. Jackson offered his help. "If you need anything written up for the paper, contact me. I'd be glad to help. Farmers are close to my heart. My uncle's family nearly lost their farm to the death tax after his dad was killed in a farming accident several years ago. I want to see these family farms succeed and stay in production. I believe what you're talking about would help keep these smaller farms from dying."

Preston agreed. "Thanks, man. Yeah, since I've gotten into this, I've realized how farmers have been pushed aside in some areas. We get so used to convenience, especially in the cities, and we forget about where the food is coming from. Financially, we should be making it easier for farmers. Everyone's gotta eat, right?"

"Definitely," said Jackson.

The evening wrapped up beautifully with hugs and well-wishes for the holidays. Jamie and Marcy finished cleaning the kitchen after they convinced pregnant Lucy to stop working and get some rest. Dylan and Jackson spoke of the traditional Christmas Eve edition of the *Holly Herald* that would be released for the community. It was a tradition started by the founder of the paper, who fully believed that Christmas Eve was the perfect time to reach residents with stories and poems of hope. He knew many people would spend the holidays alone, and it was his mission to be their friend via writing.

He liked to remind his staff, "Emily Dickinson said that 'hope is the thing with feathers that perches in the soul and sings the tunes without the words, and never stops at all.'" The quote, handwritten by the founder, still remained on yellowed paper on the wall of the newspaper office. The staff kept it there as a reminder that their true mission was more than dispensing news; it was about bringing hope.

Dylan informed Jackson, "I'll have a brief paragraph on the front page. The poetry and stories submitted by residents will follow after that. Let's put the ads on the last page. Did you have anything else to submit?"

Jackson wiggled his head in thought. "Nope. I think we've got it all. Thanks, man. I know it's been a crazy month for you. I'm not sure how you've managed to keep up with everything. I'm impressed."

Dylan didn't hesitate in his response. "Thanks to you, man. You and Lucy are lifesavers." He looked around the room, now quiet, with trees elegantly lit and decorated. "Ah. We did it. The party turned out great, even with the little hiccups."

Jackson asked, "Do you think Eleanor and Beatrice will stick with Pastor Dean after the 'appalling, inappropriate' escapades? Poor old ladies. They were really out of their element."

Dylan grinned at the remembrance of Mary's daring stunt. "Are you kidding? We just gave them a year's worth of things to talk about. They need to stick around the church so they'll have a place to gossip." They laughed. "Who else would they tell? The postman?"

Jackson shrugged. "You've got a good point."

CHRISTMAS EVE
The *Holly Herald* Christmas Eve Edition

INSIDE THE WINDOWS OF HOLLY
By Nick Brown

Are you seeking the perfect gift this Christmas? This year, I discovered the difference between gifts that we seek and gifts that seek us. I was presented with a very unexpected gift that I never dreamed of receiving. You see, I failed to realize how lucky I am to live in Holly and to be a part of this community. In fact, the challenges I've endured in my own life caused me to see everyone through a hazy, dark filter of disillusionment. I allowed disappointment to turn to anger. I allowed anger and bitterness to move me to a place of being an accuser. I needed someone to blame for my pain. What I didn't realize is that, ultimately, I allowed my disappointment to steal my sight.

This Christmas, I received my sight through an act of kindness and forgiveness. Somebody that I accused of being a hypocrite turned out to be the one who was living in truth. He was the one who accepted me instead of casting me aside when I deserved punishment.

When we are hurting, it's easy to make other people our enemies. When we are sad, it's easy to blame others for our sadness. In creating enemies in our minds, I believe we rob ourselves of the gift of knowing each other's story and really seeing what's inside.

Two days ago, I visited the Vanberg home, which some of you refer to as the Christmas House. As I watched the interaction of those inside, something happened in my heart that truly began with the mercy of Mr. Vanberg. Darkness lifted off me, and for

THE WINDOWS OF HOLLY

the first time in many years, I smiled without trying. In that moment, I knew I received a valuable, priceless gift. It's a treasure that's difficult to describe. When I caused trouble for a good man, he paid me back with love, acceptance, and understanding. My eyes were opened to who he truly is, and I can't thank him enough for inviting me into his home.

The Christmas House has long been a representation of the town of Holly, and I believe that's what it is today. As you can see in the pictures on the next page, what I saw through the windows of Holly was acceptance, laughter, sincerity, and unity despite differences.

To everyone who gathered within the walls of the Vanberg home and allowed me a vantage point from which to see what is possible, thank you for showing me what really exists within the windows of Holly. You have given me my sight, and for that, I am forever grateful.

Merry Christmas,

From Nick Brown

FOUR MONTHS LATER...
THE WEDDING DAY

The fourth day of May greeted residents of Holly with the warmth of spring. A light breeze whispered through town, moving colorful blooms and leaves in peaceful rhythm. People awakened, aware of the newness that even nature seemed to indicate was alive and well.

Those who loved Dylan and Lynette shared mutual happiness over the event of the day: the wedding of the former pastor and his ex-wife. Though the couple decided to keep their ceremony private among their own family members, along with Jackson, Lucy, David, and Marcy, they made sure to send cards of acknowledgement to all who supported their remarriage. They asked that each person join them in spirit at eleven o'clock in the morning as they recommitted their lives to each other.

Lynette was more comfortable with a small group of people at their side, and Dylan concurred. The decision not to have a large celebration was a difficult one, but they felt the need for a quiet, intimate ceremony. Dylan invited his best friend, Jackson, and his advocate, David, to stand in as groomsmen. Lynette asked Lucy and Marcy to be her bridesmaids.

Lynette spent the night at Marcy's home in order to keep her groom from seeing her before the wedding. Lynette's parents retrieved Asa the day before, committing to keep him until their return from the honeymoon in Napa Valley. It was Lynette's first time to be without the baby. She slept deeply and peacefully throughout the night.

Upon waking, it took her a moment to remember where she was as she felt the urge to check on her child. "Oh yeah," she whispered as she remembered what day it was. A smile crossed her face. She stretched her arms above her head, palms wide open, ready to receive what the day had to offer. Newness: a chance to start over and do things right. Today was her opportunity to be the wife she wished she'd always been.

She breathed in the smell of freshly-toasted bread. *Aw, sweet Marcy.* Lynette was eternally grateful for Marcy's hospitality and kindness. She had no idea that when she and Dylan stepped into pastoring Hope Fellowship over a decade ago, that Marcy would become like a mother to her in both her darkest and most wonderful times of life. *What a gift.*

Dylan stood in front of his bathroom mirror after a fresh shave, studying his face for signs of renewed youth. He figured he was pretty lucky to have exited a few distressing years with only a couple of wrinkle lines. "Not bad, Dylan. Not great, but not bad," he encouraged himself. He rubbed his stomach in an attempt to

THE WINDOWS OF HOLLY

find the ripples of his abdominal muscles, but they were slightly fainter these days. He was still attractive and in good shape, but the mark of sleek-cut perfection was showing less than its former glory. He was thankful he'd started rounds of sit-ups and push-ups in the last three weeks. *Better late than never.*

Dylan and Lynette had chosen Analee Hill, about forty miles outside of Holly, for their wedding. Some referred to Analee Hill as a "thin place" or a "hole in the heavens." Leo Harvey Hughes, a wealthy man from Nebraska, had purchased the property for his ailing wife, Lacey, who loved mountains, castles, and cathedrals. He spent five years building a smaller-scale version of one of her favorite cathedrals. The intricate, towering piece of art stood at the highest point of Analee.

The cathedral reminded Dylan of the bridal painting he had created shortly after Lynette left him. The couple came to the realization that his painting was prophetic in nature, pointing to her return and their remarriage. The cathedral on the hill was perfectly fitting for the occasion. Their plan was simple: the ceremony would take place and then they would celebrate with a catered lunch in the garden before departing to catch an evening flight.

THE CEREMONY

Eleven o'clock arrived. Dylan stood at the altar donning a slim-fit, black tuxedo. He faced the doors with a smile as he waited to see his bride. David and Jackson stood to his left, beaming. Dylan and Lynette's parents waited expectantly on the front row. Her sister, Jamie, radiated joy as she held her nephew, Asa.

Outside, Marcy and Lucy assisted Lynette up the stairs of the cathedral. The sun highlighted her blonde hair, reflecting light like a halo that matched the glow of her smile. The floral vine hairpiece was delicately woven through her hair, laced with crystals and white pearls. Layers of white tulle cascaded weightlessly in the breeze behind her, creating a magical sight.

As Dylan waited for the doors to open, he took note of the beams of light breaking through the stained glass above the doorway. Luminous shafts of light intertwined as they shot through colored glass, meeting in the center of the aisle. The room's appearance of old, traditional things mixed with newer elements, in a perfect complement to Dylan and Lynette's plans for the wedding: a mix of nostalgia with unique originality. The blend was timeless.

The wedding coordinators opened the large, wooden doors as Canon in D began to play over the sound system. Lynette remained out of sight as Marcy began walking down the aisle with bouquet in hand. Lucy followed as the doors closed behind her. Once the two women took their positions at the front, the music shifted. Dylan and Lynette chose an unusual processional song, but they believed it to be a perfect match for the cry of their hearts. The words about staying together and being each other's love echoed across the vast room, drawing tears to everyone's eyes.

Lynette clutched the bouquet of pink and white roses tightly. Her smile radiated indescribable joy as her eyes sparkled through tears. She walked slowly, being conscious of every step, cherishing the journey. She chose to walk herself down the aisle just like the bride in Dylan's painting. She knew she wasn't alone and that her Father in Heaven had carried her right back to where she was supposed to be: with the love of her life. Her dad understood the significance for her and had assured her, "Honey, I walked you down the aisle the first time. Now I get the privilege of watching you. I get to see the look on your face, and that makes me happy."

The song continued as she floated down the aisle:

THE WINDOWS OF HOLLY

I have always meant what I promised
Even though I fell along the way
And I know now for sure
In the days we are still given
We'll walk in fields of love
We'll walk in fields of love

She and Dylan locked eyes during the entirety of her walk toward him. By the time she arrived by his side, the couple's cheeks were soaked with tears. Dylan stood in awe of her beauty that was accentuated by flashing specks of light coming from her veil as rays of sunlight met diamonds.

Before the music ended, Dylan reached for her hands, drawing her closer.

The minister began, "Today, we are gathered for a glorious reunion, a reconnecting of a beautiful and powerful relationship." He extended his hand toward the illuminated stained-glass windows. "I would say the heavens have set a majestic stage for this special moment. Just as the light breaks into this structure, there's a light that breaks into our own darkness. That light, Christ, is powerful enough to shine from darkness—that very thing which is contrary to light. He is strong enough to illuminate the blackest holes of our souls. John 1:5 tells us that light shines in the darkness.

"King David said, 'If I ascend into Heaven, You are there. If I make my bed in Hell, behold, You are there.' David realized that God would meet him anywhere and go to any depth and any extreme to be with him. This is the faithful light of the world who willingly and passionately breaks into the darkness of our lives to set us free. He comes to us, whether we are on the right path or the wrong path. He comes to us, whether we are in a good place or an ugly place. He is not afraid of our darkness. He is not afraid of our decisions. He is strong and sure, and filled with endless love and a mercy that endures forever. That's who your Father is."

The minister stepped closer to Dylan and Lynette. "And that is what brings us together today. You see, light broke forth in the darkness. Dylan and Lynette have found each other again, realizing that love never failed and it never will. Love never died. For them, love has always remained. I have the privilege of being a part of a beautiful mending, so it's my honor to rejoin these two together in marriage." The minister motioned toward the couple. "Dylan, you may begin the reading of your vows."

Dylan reached into his pocket to retrieve the vows he had written to Lynette. He cleared his throat. "My precious Lynette." Her name on his lips caused his voice to crack, overcome by emotion. He took a deep breath to compose himself. "Since the day I first met you, I knew I loved you. I know now, more than ever, that you are truly and forever my soul mate, my best friend, and the only woman I want to spend my life with. Both being together and being apart has taught me more than I've ever known about the nature of love. I am more sure now of the love that I have for you. It is eternal and never ending. It is my greatest desire and honor to be your husband, to love you unconditionally, and to encourage you in your dreams and passions.

I will walk with you through the highs and lows, in sickness and in health, in times of struggle and in times of prosperity. I commit to care for our son, Asa, as well as the children we'll have in the future. I promise to continue exploring the depth of my love for you, and I commit to set intimacy with you as preeminent above all else. Lynette, you will always be my first priority. I give myself to you, fully and forever. I love you." The feelings of his heart welled up in his eyes.

Tears streamed down Lynette's cheeks as she stared into the eyes of the man she loved. The minister encouraged her, "Lynette, you may read your vows to Dylan." She dabbed her eyes and cheeks with a tissue. She took a deep breath as she smiled. Lucy handed her the folded paper containing her vows. Her hands trembled as she unfolded it.

Lynette began, "My dearest Dylan, I stand in awe of you. I will never forget the moment you embraced me after five long years of being apart," she read, her voice quivering. "Your unending kindness, compassion, and relentless forgiveness is a gift that I will never take for granted. Dylan, you are precious to me beyond description, a priceless gift.

"When I took an interest in art, it took me awhile to see that the most exquisite canvas of beauty was right before me all along. It's an honor to behold you, Dylan Vanberg.

"As I stand before you today, I'm gripped by the wonder of who you are. It is my privilege to give myself to you completely, and I willingly open every facet of my being to you, to love you, to cherish you, and honor you for the rest of my life. I promise to listen to your heart, your thoughts, and dreams. I commit to consciously make a daily decision to be in tune with your spirit throughout our journey together. Dylan, I promise to be faithful to you as long as I live. I give myself to you fully and forever. All of me loves all of you." She smiled sweetly. "Completely."

The minister instructed, "Dylan and Lynette have requested that their family and friends encircle them as we pray together for their union. It's the wish of the bride and groom that God, their heavenly Father, be acknowledged for their restoration. With Him, all things are possible." Everyone surrounded the couple in prayer, speaking blessings over their new chapter of life.

As the prayers ended, Dylan and Lynette smiled, staring deeply into each other's eyes. Absolute satisfaction engulfed their hearts. The minister beamed as he continued the ceremony. "As a symbol of the love you have professed for one another, you've chosen to exchange rings. These rings are made of precious metals, purified by fire. This never-ending circle of purity speaks of your love for one another, tested, tried, and found to be strong and eternal." He motioned for the rings. "Dylan, place the ring on Lynette's left hand and repeat after me."

Dylan gently held Lynette's hand as he pushed the ring onto her finger. He spoke with passion, "Lynette, with this ring, set me as a seal upon your heart, as a seal upon your arm, for love is as strong as death. Take this ring as a reminder that many waters cannot quench love."

In return, Lynette placed a ring on Dylan's finger. "Dylan, with this ring, set me as a seal upon your heart, as a seal upon your arm, for love is as strong as death. Take this ring as a reminder that many waters cannot quench love."

The minister addressed the witnesses, "Throughout this ceremony, Dylan and Lynette have vowed, in our presence, to be loyal and loving toward each other. They have established the existence of the bond between them with words spoken and with the giving and receiving of rings. Therefore, it is with great pleasure that I pronounce them husband and wife. Dylan, you may kiss your bride."

Dylan looked delighted as he placed his right hand on the back of Lynette's head, pulling her in for a kiss while caressing her cheek with the other hand. They closed their eyes as they melted into each other. In that moment, it seemed no one else was in the room, just the two of them, locked in a lingering kiss.

Their parents and friends fought back tears as they joyfully applauded the couple. Dylan and Lynette embraced as they giggled with pleasure. The minister interjected, "Ladies and gentlemen, I am extremely pleased to introduce to you Mr. and Mrs. Dylan Vanberg!" Everyone broke into applause once more.

Dylan and Lynette exited the cathedral arm-in-arm to the

THE WINDOWS OF HOLLY

happy melody of "Ode to Joy." Their loved ones followed. A gentle breeze greeted them like a kiss of assurance. A coordinator directed their family and friends to the English garden for hors d'oeuvres. The photographer guided Dylan and Lynette to the bottom of the cathedral steps where they would begin taking photos.

Dylan kindly turned to the photographer and asked, "Excuse me, but would you mind if I have one minute alone with my wife? I just want to take in the moment before we continue."

The woman understood. "Absolutely. I'm in no hurry." She stepped away but kept herself within range of capturing the moment. "This will be perfect," she whispered to herself.

Dylan turned to Lynette, smiling. He took her face in his hands. "This. This is the beginning of a brand-new chapter. Me and you, forever."

She smiled happily.

He leaned in, pressing his lips into hers, eyes closed tightly. She responded with passion, surrendering herself to his touch. They felt as if they were the only two people in the world, wholly enveloped in the profound purity of love.

Epilogue

O N A HOT JULY EVENING, Dylan and Lynette carried trays of finger sandwiches and cookies to the front porch, arranging them neatly on the blue-and-white gingham tablecloth. Lynette's long, blonde hair was pulled tightly into a ponytail wrapped with navy blue ribbon. Her white and navy-blue sundress flowed gently over her body. Rosy pink lipstick blended with her summer-kissed cheeks. "Oops," she giggled as she knocked a chocolate chip cookie onto the porch. "I guess I'll be eating that one."

Dylan shook his head. "Nah, that's mine!" He picked it up and took a large bite. "Mmmm. So good," he mumbled with a goofy smile.

Lynette shook her head, grinning. "You're such a kid sometimes."

Dylan swallowed. "At least I don't require diapers." He winked.

"Thank God," she said with a laugh.

He loved making her smile. "But wouldn't I look adorable in a onesie?"

She shook her head, smirking. "Uh, no. That would be weird, I think." Her wedding ring glistened in the light of the sunset as she arranged the cookies in an artistic fashion. "What do you think?

THE WINDOWS OF HOLLY

Does this look good?"

Dylan admired her handiwork. "Cookies always look good."

She grinned, slightly amused. "No, I mean the way they're laid out. I wanted it to look nice."

His eyes smiled. "It looks great. I'll go get the lemonade and tea. Where do you want me to put them?"

She pointed to a white end table positioned next to the swing. "They should both fit on there."

He stood behind Lynette, wrapping his arms around her. He moved his hand to her waist, rubbing his hand across her belly button. "How's our little one doing in there?"

She smiled. "He or she must be doing well because I've been terribly nauseated. The doctor tells me that's a good sign, but I think she just says that to make me feel better."

Dylan's joy was tangible. The twinkle in his eyes spoke of the fullness of his heart. "I can't wait to tell them tonight. Jackson and Lucy are going to freak! It's so cool; our kids will get to grow up together."

Lynette agreed. "I'm excited about that."

Dylan entered the house, whistling as he fetched the tea and lemonade. Lynette plumped up the pillows on the porch swing, ready to welcome her friends. She was thankful for the shade of the weeping willow. The tree had always been the perfect companion for evening sunsets on the porch, casting its shadow for their comfort. *Thank you, Father.* Gratitude was Lynette's constant friend.

The reality of the mystical ways of grace awakened her heart and soul to a new awareness, and she found that words of thanksgiving escaped her lips in the most unusual places. Whether in the grocery store, the shower, while cleaning house, and even while making love to her husband, thank you was whispered frequently. It came naturally, without a thought. Gratitude became a euphoric way of living for Lynette.

Dylan pushed the screen door open with his foot and made his way to the end table with drinks in tow. "I think that's everything." He sat the items down and reached for his wife. "Come, my lady. Let's have a seat." He held her hand, drawing her to the porch swing. "Gosh, you're beautiful."

She nestled her head into his shoulder, smiling. "Thank you." Many times, she didn't feel worthy of the compliment, but Dylan had taught her to receive his admiration. It troubled him deeply when she'd reject his sincere words. She fought to allow herself to accept his applause. "And you, sir, are absolutely handsome. You're the kindest person I know."

"Hey, you guys!" Lucy's voice echoed as she and Jackson crossed the street, pushing a stroller with a pink and white cover. Lucy continued calling out to them, "Look at those awesome lovebirds. Whew-whee! Making Holly look good." Her red lips framed a radiant smile. Jackson grinned from ear to ear, entertained by his wife's vibrant personality.

Dylan called back, "Look who's talking!"

Jackson and Lucy lifted the stroller onto the porch. Lynette stood to admire their baby girl. "Well, hello, sweetie. It's Aunt Lynnie." Lynette touched Madison's soft, brown hair. "You're such a pretty girl. Yes, you are."

Dylan observed, "My goodness. How do babies grow so quickly? Every time I see her, she's changed a bit." He smiled at her. "Hi, Maddie girl."

Lucy interjected, "Tell me about it. She changes on a daily basis. She's been cooing and smiling a lot lately. She's also starting to hold onto her little toys. It's so cute!"

Lynette acknowledged Lucy's excitement. "It's fun when they start doing new things, isn't it? Asa's crawling all over the place, and it's hard to keep up with him! Enjoy this stage while you can, because once she starts moving around, you'll be burning a million calories a day trying to keep her out of things."

"Speaking of Asa, where is the little guy?" Lucy wondered.

Lynette yawned. "We played hard today. He fell asleep about thirty minutes ago. I was trying to keep him awake, but I could tell he was on the verge of turning into a monster. I knew I needed to put him down for the evening before that happened."

Lucy was impressed. "Will he sleep through the night if he goes to bed this early?"

Lynette shook her head. "Probably not. It's highly likely I'll be up around three in the morning."

Poor you," Lucy sympathized. "But hey, if you're awake at that hour, you can always call Miss Emma. You know what she says about that hour?"

Lynette laughed. "Of course. Everyone in town knows it's Emma's witching hour in which the potty piddle parade takes place. It's nice to know I'm not the only one awake at that hour." She motioned toward the swing and the two rocking chairs. "Have a seat. We've got some sandwiches: chicken salad and ham and cheese. Would you like tea or lemonade?"

Jackson and Lucy responded in unison, "Tea, please."

Lynette giggled. "I don't know why I even asked. I should've known."

Jackson explained, "I was going to say lemonade, but after talking about Emma's nighttime bathroom habits, I want to stay away from yellow beverages."

Everyone laughed hysterically.

Lynette poured drinks while Dylan opened up with conversation that would lead into revealing their exciting news. "Jackson. Dude, I'm loving the podcast. It looks like we're getting a lot of good feedback, not just from locals, but from the cities. Lucy, that was a brilliant idea. You kicked off something that might be bigger than we expected."

Lucy smiled. "Thanks, Dylan. We're having fun with the concepts and dreaming a bit."

Jackson nodded. "You should see this woman's notebook. She's coming up with so many ideas, I can't keep up."

"Cool," Dylan replied. "Let's go over it next week and make it happen. With the expansion of the paper, combined with the podcast and the events we've been doing, we're going to stay pretty busy."

Lynette served their drinks and made herself comfortable in the rocking chair. "I've enjoyed working the events with you guys. It's so much fun." She smiled. "I say we drink to us." She raised her glass of tea. "To the coolest team in Holly." Everyone raised a glass in agreement.

"Hear, hear!" Lucy exclaimed before they drank.

Jackson considered all that had taken place over the last several months. "Lucy and I were talking about the number of innovative, creative ideas that are flourishing in Holly this year. I've never seen anything like it. We tried to pinpoint what played a role in shifting this community. I mean, it's like an awakening has happened. Lucy pointed out that things started popping up shortly after Christmas. She likes to think your Christmas party kinda kicked it off."

Lucy explained. "Seriously, guys. I believe it's totally connected. With your reconciliation and opening your home to everyone, I think it sparked hope and helped people to believe for the impossible. Your relationship is a perfect picture of anything being possible. The gathering at Christmas was pivotal for our town. Now we've got creative ideas like unusual businesses and services that are leaking over into Marshall City. When the people in the cities take notice, you know something special is happening." She smiled radiantly. "It's like a flood of innovation

THE WINDOWS OF HOLLY

has been released."

Dylan and Lynette looked at each other, moved by their enthusiasm. Dylan was humbled. "Wow. That's quite the observation. Well, if we got to play a part in that, that's pretty amazing. But you know what's even more amazing?" He looked at Lynette once more, reaching for her hand. "Do you want to tell them, babe?"

Her face was full of light. "Sure." She looked at Jackson and Lucy, smiling. She leaned in toward them, speaking softly. "Dylan and I are on our tenth week of pregnancy." She grinned from ear to ear.

"Oh my gosh!" Lucy jumped up from the swing. "This is the best news ever!" She threw her arms around Lynette.

Genuine joy flashed through Jackson. He stood to embrace his friend. "Man, I'm so excited for you." Jackson's eyes moistened with the happiness of seeing his best friend's life being restored.

Lynette put her finger over her lips. "We can't be too loud. This is just a secret for the four of us right now. Okay?"

Lucy nodded cheerfully. "Sure thing! We won't say a word."

Emma Gray watched through her window as the two couples shared celebratory hugs. She smiled to herself. "Well, would you look at that?" She picked up her telephone and dialed Beverly. "Hey Bev. I'd bet ya we'll be planning a baby shower before too long."

Beverly gasped. "Emma! What have you been up to? A baby at your age?"

Emma chuckled at her friend's sense of humor. "That's disgusting, Beverly!"

Beverly snickered. "Well, my guess is the Vanbergs."

Emma explained, "That's what I think is happening. I see them with the Sawyers across the street. They were all chatting on the porch. Jackson and Lucy suddenly hopped onto their feet and they all started hugging. Lucy, of course, was flapping her arms around like she always does when she's excited."

"Well, Emma. You might be right, but you could be wrong, so don't go flapping your jaws around town until they tell you themselves," Beverly advised.

Emma sighed. "Of course I won't! I just wanted to tell you, that's all. No one else."

"Awesome! Then it's our secret. By the way, do you wanna go with me to Nick's coffee shop? It opens tomorrow."

Emma didn't hesitate. "Absolutely!"

Beverly was eager to try something new. "They did a good little write-up about it in the *Herald.* Apparently, the young man is sort of a closet coffee guru. Who'd have thought?"

Emma wiggled her head. "I never would have guessed. I used to think that boy was just a plain mess, but he's turning out pretty good. He's worked hard, saved up money, and tried to bring something good to the community. What a kid."

Beverly spoke excitedly, "And, Emma, did you see that even Marshall City is writing about it? They wrote a piece about his signature drink, the 'Snowflake.' It's a light, sweet, creamy drink. I'm definitely going to try that one."

Emma joked, "That's perfect for you. You're a bit flaky, my friend."

Beverly countered, "Right back at you. I'll see you tomorrow."

On the Vanberg's porch, Lucy and Lynette conversed about pregnancy and future plans while Jackson and Dylan went inside to find the case of dominoes. Lucy was thrilled for her friend. "I'd say it's quite a miracle that Owen sent you that money from the sale of the ranch. Two hundred thousand is a good amount of money. I didn't think he'd be that generous."

Lynette agreed. "I was absolutely shocked. I didn't expect it at all, especially since he showed no signs of feeling guilty or wrong

THE WINDOWS OF HOLLY

about anything."

Lucy gave him the benefit of the doubt. "Well, you never know what's going on inside a person. They can do the dumbest, most horrible things, and yet there may be some goodness inside there somewhere."

Lynette shook her head. "Maybe. But Owen still doesn't acknowledge his son. That, I don't understand at all."

Lucy always tried to believe the best about a person. "Maybe that's his way of trying to do the right thing? Like, he's relinquishing his rights because he knows he wouldn't be the kind of father that Asa needs."

Lynette smiled. "You're a very nice human." She patted Lucy's shoulder. "By the way, don't tell Dylan, but I'm going to buy him a new car. Old Blue's been faithful, but I think with two babies, we're definitely going to need a newer, bigger vehicle. Would you be up to car shopping with me this week?"

Lucy's eyes lit up. "I'd love to!"

Dylan and Jackson returned to the front porch, dominoes in hand. Dylan pulled the card table close to the swing. "Will you ladies be joining us?"

"Absolutely," Lucy declared.

As the two couples played in the light of the setting sun, a man and woman drove through town, admiring the charming neighborhood. The woman remarked, "I love these homes! They're so quaint." Passing the Vanberg home, the sight of the smiling couples caught the woman's eye. "These homes carry a sort of magic about them, don't they? What stories have these porches heard? And look at those amazing windows. Think of what people have seen through these windows over the years."

Her husband replied, "Listen to you being all poetic." He smiled. "But that reminds me of something I read the other day, something Maya Angelou once said: 'There is no greater agony than bearing an untold story inside of you.' I suppose an old front porch is the perfect place to relieve oneself of that agony."

"True. As far as the porch goes, I think it's the best place to create stories that bring people hope." She regarded every detail as they drove past. "That's what home should be: a place of hope, and a setting for all that's possible." She looked at him. "And we all need home."

The man nodded. "Yes, we do."

If you enjoyed this book, please help Traci by posting a review for it on your favorite online bookstore sites. Thank you!

About the Author

Traci Vanderbush enjoys the simplicity of being married to her best friend and childhood sweetheart, Bill Vanderbush. She is mom to two amazing humans. Traci's passions are writing, dancing, exploring, and pursuing the Creator. She desires to bring hope to hearts of all ages through her writing. Certainly, every person has a dream deep inside, and Traci wants to see each person live his or her dream, no matter how big or small. A believer in redemption, she believes there is gold to be found in the most unlikely places.

WEBSITES
www.theporchesofholly.com
www.thewindowsofholly.com
www.tracivanderbush.com

FACEBOOK
facebook.com/tracivanderbushwrites

TWITTER
@tracivanderbush

INSTAGRAM
tracivanderbush

For excellent life-giving teachings by Traci's husband, Bill
Vanderbush, please visit www.billvanderbush.com.

OTHER BOOKS BY TRACI

THE PORCHES OF HOLLY (2015)

In the midst of long-held secrets, extramarital affairs, and addictions, a supernatural force visits the small community of Holly and awakens hearts that were once threatened by destruction. The trials of life chose their victims at random. Lies knew no boundaries. And neither did the grace of God. An unseen presence pursued the resurrection of the dead and the sight of the blind. Local pastor, Dylan Vanberg, battles his own torment as he comes to realize the power of grace while the town newspaper reporter, Jackson Sawyer, begins to understand the power of words. The porches of Holly...where old stories are repeated, babies are rocked, and kisses are given. Where life happens. What secrets do these porches hold and what stories will they tell?

VIGNETTE: GLIMPSES OF MYSTERIOUS LOVE (2014)

Raw, unstructured, free-flowing. Love is an indefinable mystery. This is one couple's attempt, after learning the art of falling in love with each other once again, to articulate the limitless depths of the human soul. Through various journal entries, thoughts and poetic expressions regarding love, mercy, grace, and sexuality, join them on this journey of glimpses into mysterious love.

SOUL REFORMATION: WHOLENESS FOR THE BODY (2017)

Soul Reformation is a simple, short prayer and meditation project inspired by the author's personal experience as she sought relief from pain that was triggered by the memory of a traumatic car accident. Whether you are suffering from physical or emotional trauma, Traci's hope is that you will find some relief and encouragement as she shares her prayer and declaration for healing. Throughout the book, words of truth are intertwined with photographs of places where Traci felt the presence of God. She invites you to come to that place.

THE MAGIC OF OUR FOREFATHERS: AWAKENING TO THE VALUE OF THE OLDER GENERATION (2014)

The Magic of Our Forefathers speaks of the hidden gifts of past generations and how they affect our lives and future generations. The author creatively unwraps the revelation of our ability to experience "time travel" through becoming aware of the value of our connection with the older generation. Through personal recollections and short stories, life lessons are revealed and hope-filled strength is given to the reader to overcome life's challenges. Basic principles regarding work ethic and walking through adversity are discussed as part of the journey.

MR. THOMAS AND THE COTTONWOOD TREE (2014)

After several recurring dreams about a tree where children would encounter God, Traci Vanderbush felt led to write a book for children that would release emotional healing, based on some of her personal experiences with the Father. Within the dreams, she kept hearing "Mr. Thomas and the Cottonwood Tree." She began researching cottonwoods and found that they exude a resin that some refer to as a "balm of Gilead." This confirmed to her that there would be healing within the story. Her husband, Bill Vanderbush, offered illustrations which they chose to keep simple and without color in order to allow children's' imaginations to paint a picture. Based in Austin, Texas, William and Traci continue their journey into discovering the immense goodness and grace of God, and His ability to bring healing and redemption into

the most impossible situations. As a wife and mother, Traci desires
to inspire others to hold to a hope that exists beyond our realm.

LIFE WITH LUMMOX (2015)

Lummox is a cuddly, bubbly, bouncy, happy, lovable character
that's full of fun and wonder. The hard part about being a Lummox
is that the world is filled with stuff to trip on, knock over, and
break. So to be a happy, hairy fellow means you smile with every
smiley smile you've got. The story of Lummox encourages
children to embrace and find treasure in the seemingly awkward
and eccentric. *Life with Lummox* is written by Traci Vanderbush
and delightfully illustrated by the love of her life, Bill Vanderbush.
The rhythm and rhyme combined with jolly pictures will bring
smiles and laughs to all who read. Perfect for reading to
preschoolers. Early elementary students would also enjoy reading
this delightful story. Adults of every age also find themselves
smiling over Lummox.

LUMMOX AND THE HAPPY CHRISTMAS (2015)

The cuddly, bubbly, bouncy Lummox returns in this special
Christmas adventure. Lummox encounters Santa and is given a
gift that reveals the power of the baby boy who grew up to change
the world. Join Lummox and his buddies as they celebrate the
season. Beautifully illustrated by Bill Vanderbush. For children
and adults of all ages!

WALKING WITH A SHEPHERD (2006)

Is it possible that pastors fight depression? Is it possible that a
large percentage of pastors' wives wish their husbands would
consider another profession? On the outside, most churches look
great, but on the inside, many churches are being ripped apart by
gossip, division, and suspicions. Often, this leaves the minister's
family wounded and struggling. In this book, you will discover

some secrets of joy and learn simple principles of action and forgiveness. If you are a pastor's wife facing any of these issues, Traci Vanderbush has lovingly prepared a book of practical principles based on her own experience as a pastor's wife.

ACKNOWLEDGMENTS

Special thanks to my husband, Bill Vanderbush, for his constant encouragement and empowerment to release the stories in my heart. Thank you, Bill, for prompting me to write and create. Over twenty-six years of marriage to you has taught me more about love, grace, and the power of union beyond what I could have imagined possible. The way that you live your life, and your passion for the world to know their Father, inspires me to create stories that reveal Him. Thank you for your constant, precious, unconditional love. You are a true man.

To my children, Britain and Sara, you infuse me with smiles and gratitude as you teach me along this journey of life. I am so thankful that I get to be your mom.

To all of my family members and friends who have told me to keep writing, thank you. There are too many to name and it seems impossible to accurately express my gratitude. Dad and Mom, thank you for giving me life and gifting me with a love for writing.

Sally Hanan, you are the queen of author support. Thank you for saving me from many tears throughout the process of writing this story.

Thank you to every person who read *The Porches of Holly* and enthusiastically asked, "When are you writing the second book?" Your love and support mean more to me than you could ever know. As I continue this journey of learning and growing in putting my creations and thoughts onto paper, I am thankful for those who have taken time to dive into them. You are a blessing.

Made in the USA
Columbia, SC
22 January 2019